Decade of the Dragon

Decade of the Dragon

a celebration of Welsh rugby
1969–1979

John Taylor

HODDER AND STOUGHTON
LONDON SYDNEY AUCKLAND TORONTO

British Library Cataloguing in Publication Data

Taylor, John
    Decade of the dragon.
    1. Welsh Rugby Union Football Team
    I. Title
    796.33'365'0924   GV945.6.W35

ISBN 0 340 25273 1

Contents

Foreword by Cliff Morgan — 9

Fifty-five miles by thirty — 13

1 Building on Aberavon sand, 1967 and 1968 — 21

2 The Cwmtwrch sound, 1969 — 27

3 A sobering experience, Wales in Australasia, 1969 — 45

4 Chico Hopkins' finest hour, 1970 — 58

5 Slam by a whisker, 1971 — 69

6 Cymru am Bloody Byth, the Lions in Australasia, 1971 — 85

7 O ye of little faith! 1972 — 96

8 Scarlets rule OK, 1972/73 — 108

9 Blind Irish referee, 1973/74 — 124

10 Lions World Champions, the Lions in South Africa, 1974 — 136

11 The Pontypool front row, 1974/75 — 144

12 Bennett, P., third choice, 1975/76 — 157

13 J.P.R., Scourge of the English, 1976/77 — 169

14 Tourists at bay, the Lions in New Zealand, 1977 — 180

15 A Triple Triple, 1978 — 187

16 A sizzling burst from six inches, 1979 — 198

17 A very serious nonsense — 214

Statistics — 219

Index — 241

I should like to thank Beverley Cheetham for coping with my handwriting and typing the book; Maggie Body at Hodders for keeping on nagging me and for compiling the index; and Chris Rhys for his invaluable help with research and for assembling the statistics.

J.T.

Illustrations

facing page

Maurice Richards' record four tries[1]   32
Clive Rowlands at Aberavon[2]   32
The Murphy incident[1]   33
First try for Wales[3]   33
An Edwards try disallowed[3]   48
The most memorable conversion since St Paul[4]   48
Finger-tip passing by John Dawes[3]   48
Barry John[3]   49
Dai Morris feeds Edwards[3]   64
Hymns before France[5]   64
A long look at Stade Colombes[5]   65
Gerry Lewis in control[5]   65
Wales v France, 1971[5]   80
Final Test, Auckland, 1971[6]   80
'We've really done it!'   81
Scourge of New Zealand golf courses   81
Relaxing at a *hangi*   81
A typical Edwards try[1]   96
John Bevan is over the line[3]   96
Delme Thomas's hour of triumph[7]   96
Llanelli 9 – Seland Newydd 3[7]   97
Last kick against the All Blacks 1972[3]   97
Arthur Lewis scores from an 'Arthur'[1]   112
A scoring pass from Gerald to Gareth[3]   112
Mike Roberts in the air[3]   113
Terry Cobner stays on his feet[3]   113
Cobner's debut try[1]   128
Mervyn Davies scores against England[3]   128
The Pontypool front row[1]   129
John D. Bevan and Steve Fenwick[3]   129

facing page

Gerald Davies beats the cover again[3]   144
J. J. Williams makes a spectacular dive[3]   144
Charlie Faulkner crosses the line[3]   145
Never too old to run[3]   145
The pack protect Edwards[1]   160
Mervyn Davies at the height of his powers[1]   160
Allan Martin beats Bastiat in the line out[3]   161
J.P.R. leaves the English in his wake[1]   161
A Phil Bennett side-step at Murrayfield[3]   176
Steve Fenwick about to score[1]   177
Graham Price makes a break[1]   177

following page

Geoff Wheel rips the ball free[3]   200
Paul Ringer scores against England[1]   200
A storming try for Derek Quinnell[3]   200
A quicksilver try from Dai Richards[1]   200
Terry Holmes and Gareth Davies[3]   200

CREDITS
1 Western Mail and Echo Ltd.
2 Radio Times Hulton Picture Library: Ieuan Davies
3 Colin Elsey, Colorsport
4 Jon, *Daily Mail*, London
5 *Sunday Times*
6 Wellington *Evening Post*
7 Alan T. Richards

FOREWORD

More often than not, a fly half would decline any invitation to pay a compliment to the work of any flank forward. Those, like me, who have suffered the indignity of their attentions over the years have a feeling that they were all born slightly off side anyway! So there.

Still I am so pleased to congratulate John Taylor on the writing of this book. It is a first class read and a fine addition to the bookshelves which, for the most part, have been lacking in the basic literature of rugby. It is pleasurable for those who care about the game to see more and more distinguished players going into print. It will take many years to bring rugby in line with golf and cricket in particular, but there are encouraging signs. This is one of them.

This book is full of staggering detail and analysis and vision and insight. It tells of a remarkable ten year period with a new and exciting approach to fitness and tactics; an era when coaching raised the standards and when we saw quite the best rugby that has been played anywhere in the world at any time. This decade brought a much needed face-lift to the game which became a thrilling spectator sport and made household names of the star players.

And yet, as the book clearly shows, rugby still managed to retain its singular quality as an amateur game played for enjoyment. As you thumb through the pages you will find how disappointments can deepen into despair and failure, and how 'Gin and Tonic has played a large part in the Welsh team preparations.' But read on – and you will find that success involves sweat and study and dedication and character. You will find the story behind the miserable Welsh tour of Australasia in 1969 – a 'sobering experience', according to John. Again the innermost secrets of the dressing room and the passion of Clive Rowlands;

why Barry John with his unique style and confidence was truly the 'King'.

I liked the story of Barry who, when asked by Chico Hopkins about the arrangements for the Lions' assembly before the tour of New Zealand replied, 'Well, you lot are going to Eastbourne for a week to get yourselves in shape but I'm off to the South of Spain for a break.' As John says, only a remarkable man like Barry John could get away with that.

The 1971 tour 'down under' gets the full treatment. This chapter was of particular interest to me as I had followed it with admiration from the touch line. I thought I had seen everything but John has given that experience a new dimension. Some of the stories that would only be known to the players are told here. We are privileged to share them. On the subject of stories in this book, my favourite is of the Irish prop forward, Phil O'Callaghan, when he came on the field as a replacement. As he packed down in a scrum, a box of matches and a packet of cigarettes fell from his pocket. He picked them up and gave them to the referee with the comment, 'Hold on to these until half time. I'm not too keen on oranges.'

What I like most about this book is that as you read you can actually hear John saying all these things. It is a very personal style – and style is what he played with for so many years. Rubbing shoulders with John Dawes, who had a burning desire to play the game with style, obviously had a profound effect on the author. Many years ago I recall reading what Judge Rowe Harding had to say about the excitement of rugby. 'For my part I would not exchange my aesthetic experiences in rugby for those of any painter because they are, after all, merely concerned with symbols. The rugby player during the course of a game is living life at its most intoxicating. There is movement, energy, strength, fear, intelligence, competition, everything.'

This book has most of these ingredients. It ends with a sobering and sane comment. 'At the end of the day we must remember that sport is a lot of nonsense – a very serious nonsense, but still a nonsense.' These are the words of Hugh McIlvanney, one of the best of all journalists. John Taylor is obviously a disciple.

CLIFF MORGAN

Decade of the Dragon

FIFTY-FIVE MILES BY THIRTY

One Thursday in January 1966 my whole life changed. It was then that I heard, completely out of the blue, that I had been selected for the Final Trial for the Welsh national team. It really was unexpected as I had only played a handful of games for the London Welsh XV and only on the Christmas tour had I made sure of a regular place in the team. I had, of course, had dreams of playing for my country but they had been no more than fantasies without any hopes of fulfilment. Now suddenly I was in the trial. True I had been selected for the Possibles, or the 'Impossibles' as the veteran internationals call them, but from that moment the dream at least had a chance of becoming reality.

It was a very strange feeling because there was also an added awareness of responsibility. If I was selected I would not just be playing for myself or even my team. I would be playing for a whole nation, all fanatically in love with the game of rugby. It was an awesome thought and one which was difficult to come to terms with initially because I was sadly lacking in background and pedigree for a potential international.

There are certain players who have been tipped for a Welsh cap almost from the day they began to play competitive rugby. Take J. P. R. Williams for example. He progressed through the Under 15 schoolboy side to the Under 19 team and his career moved logically to a full cap from there. I had been brought up in England away from the Welsh rugby arena and, although I had spent most summer holidays in the valleys, I had had to return to London before the season got underway. By the time I was picked for the trial I had begun to understand. Half a season at the London Welsh Club had brought home to me that the support was a little different to what I'd been used to, and the distress the supporters felt when we lost was every bit as great as the players'. It was nothing like the English clubs to which I had belonged until then.

That Christmas tour had also furthered my education. I had spent the whole Christmas holiday period in Wales and it had been totally dominated by rugby on and off the field. At that time London Welsh used to play Neath on Christmas Day, Llanelli on Boxing Day and Swansea the day after and I shall never forget the atmosphere at those three great clubs on my first playing trip. Again, the intensity of the support is the memory that lingers most.

I remember in particular a man and his son standing up against the end wall at the Gnoll. He was obviously a fanatic and anything Neath did was wonderful and anything London Welsh did was rubbish and even if they did something worthwhile it was the referee's fault. His method of support was to hurl abuse at the opposition and at the referee, and his son repeated everything word for word a second later in a high pitched squeak. He had one problem – every time he repeated a swear word he was cuffed around the ear. By the end of the match he was still faithfully echoing his father but he must have had a very sore head.

On the field, too, the atmosphere was totally different. Not only were the games harder in the physical sense, but they were much more competitive. It remained true throughout my playing career that playing against a Welsh club was always more difficult than a club from any other country because they wanted to win more, even if fielding a mediocre team. It was almost as if a player was aware of upholding a national heritage and also aware that a hundred others would like to be on the field instead of him.

When I returned to Swansea for the trial (after good wishes and taunts that it was only the second time I had crossed the Severn Bridge from London Welsh colleagues) I still felt very much the outsider. Players who had been heroes only months before were now opposition or even team mates. Most were in the Probables but Brian Thomas who had already gained fourteen caps had lost favour and was leading the pack for the Possibles. He took me aside and gave me a little pep talk which put back the confidence that, minutes before, had suddenly drained away. He was a tremendous help that day but I was to learn the other side of his character very quickly. London Welsh met Neath in a club match just a few weeks later. I tackled Brian and we ended up at the bottom of a maul. As play moved away and players peeled off, leaving us to get to our feet, he gave me an unceremonious and fairly painful thump and growled, 'You'll never be any bloody good, Englishman.' That day his loyalties were different.

Having emerged from the 'Impossibles' to win my first cap against Scotland in February 1967 I immediately came up against the resentment that goes hand in hand with the intensity of feeling about the game. We were playing in Edinburgh and arrived there on the Thursday before the game. Many of the members of the Welsh Rugby Union Committee were already there and one of them singled me out for attention straight away in the public lounge. He was from Abertillery and I had effectively taken Haydn Morgan's place, even though the selectors had not included him in the trial, obviously having already decided that his international career was at an end. This particular gentleman clearly did not agree and told me very forthrightly that I had no business to be in the side and would never hold a candle to Haydn. I must admit to taking a little malicious pleasure over the years as I asked him whether I was getting any better. His remarks were hardly a confidence booster before one's first international match, but it was all part of learning the strange mixture of loyalty, passion, jealousies and the incredible enthusiasm that makes Welsh rugby what it is.

That same weekend was also a revelation of the lengths that Welsh supporters will go to in order to see their side. To walk down Princes Street on the Saturday morning was like walking down St Mary Street with a mass of red and white scarves and rosettes proclaiming that there were more Welshmen in town than Scots. In those days Murrayfield was not 'all ticket' and you could pay at the turnstiles to gain entrance to the huge open bank, so they saved rest days and took part of their holidays so that they could spend the weekend before the international in Edinburgh. Those who could not arrange time off were the real heroes. Having left Cardiff by coach or train on Friday evening, they would leave at midnight on Saturday to return home in time for work on the Monday. Later when entrance to the games was by ticket only they would still travel in the hope of picking one up outside the ground. Some even forged friendships with the people living in the roads leading to the ground so that they could knock on the door and watch the television if they failed to find a method of entry.

It is difficult to define the difference between Welsh rugby support and that elsewhere. The French can match the enthusiasm of the Welsh and the exuberance with which they show it. The New Zealanders can equal the knowledge of the game and the South Africans can emulate or even beat the fanaticism attached to wanting their side to win, but in no other country is it quite such an integral part of the everyday life of the community.

Part of the reason must be the size of Wales. It is a particular joy to us that we can match the best in the world from such a tiny country. Although the whole of Wales shares the love of the game, ninety per cent of Welsh players come from the strip of land on the south coast bounded by Pontypool and Newport in the east and Llanelli in the west, with Ebbw Vale, Tredegar and Merthyr Tydfil forming the northern limit. The area is no more than fifty-five miles from east to west and only thirty miles at its widest point north to south but it contains a great concentration of rugby and all Wales's first class clubs which are the equivalent of area teams. Every tiny village will have its own club and will act as a feed to the likes of Llanelli, Swansea, Neath, Aberavon, Bridgend, Cardiff and Newport, the main towns at the mouths of the valleys. Though if the up valley town is big enough it, too, will have its own major team and Pontypool, Newbridge, Ebbw Vale, Pontypridd and Maesteg all have proud traditions of producing fine sides, again drawing from the smaller teams around. Only the biggest clubs run second teams, as the Welsh mentality seems to find it anathema to play for the reserves. A player would rather change clubs in the belief that he will be given a fairer chance and prove that he really is a better player than the man who has displaced him.

Club rugby is the heart of Welsh rugby. While most countries work through area representative teams towards the national team, in Wales these mean very little and it is from the clubs that a player wins national selection. Because of this the rugby is more consistently competitive throughout the season than in any other part of the United Kingdom. Some of the clubs will play against each other four times a year, even apart from cup clashes, which produces an intense rivalry. It is a very different situation to that in New Zealand for example. There a player will play for his club for half the season and then, if he is selected, he will play for his province. The province does not play against all the other provinces in one year and the vast distance from one end of the country to the other often means that North Auckland will only play against Southland every three or four years. Thus players do not know the play of their opponents well and many supporters will never travel to an away match.

In Wales everyone involved in the game, including the spectators, sees enough of all the players in contention for a national team place to be able to venture an opinion. They also know the place the player comes from not just as a dot on the map but as a town or village similar to their own. Because in this fifty-five mile stretch of Welsh geography the staple industries of coal and steel make for a bond that is something greater than just being a fellow countryman – it is the bond between people who have shared what has historically been a tough life. The overall result is an intimacy between all those involved which is to me the hallmark, above all others, of the game in Wales. Players are normally a part of the community for which they play and therefore the support on a Saturday is from work mates in the steelworks or the pit, and the player is their representative on the field, giving them an extra involvement. This is naturally extended to the whole of the national side on the day of an international match.

It shows itself in the way Welsh supporters approach their team. Apart from the incredible backing they provide at the match itself, after the game they have to be able to talk to somebody who actually played and to argue about what was good and bad. So as a player you may suddenly find yourself involved in a detailed breakdown of the match, even on the short walk between the ground and the Angel Hotel. And just to show you it's a real friend talking that analysis will always include some criticism of your own game or at least praise tempered with doubts. I well remember one match when the parting words on one of these discussions were, 'Well, John, you were great today. Mind you, I wouldn't have picked you 'cos I went for Tommy David.' With that remark my friendly critic was really proving to himself, me and anyone in earshot that he knew me well enough to talk straight from the shoulder.

This feeling of intimacy can have its drawbacks. If the team loses, then it does verge on a national disaster until the next match and criticism of players can become completely unjust. I was cornered once after we had lost to France in Paris and told categorically that the reason we had lost was because a number of us had been seen in one of the Montmartre bars at three o'clock on the morning of the match after a Friday night on the town. It was a friend ('and a bloke who I can believe') who saw us – it always is. The truth was totally different. Every night before a game the team, including the reserves and some of the selectors, go to the pictures or, in Paris, usually to the Folies Bergères or the Casino de Paris under the watchful eye of Gerry Lewis, the team physiotherapist, and return to the hotel by 10.30 for a hot drink and bed. There used to be a tradition of going backstage to be photographed with the lovely ladies of the chorus but that was stopped in about 1967 because some critics felt it might put the team off its game.

Rugby players during their career are certainly placed higher than film stars. I can say this with some authority as I once travelled with Hywel Bennett down to his parents' home in the Amman Valley after a match against the All Blacks. The following day a friend came up to us and, with a great grin on his face, told us that he knew we were in the village because someone had said to him 'Guess what! Phil Bennett and John Taylor were in the Rugby Club last night.' Thank goodness Hywel is not sensitive about his ego. If his pride was dented it was restored slightly when we went for lunch and the only other person in the bar, an old man enjoying his morning half of mild, listened to our accents for a moment and exclaimed, 'I don't go to the rugby or the pictures but you must be Mr Taylor and Mr Bennett.' Word had travelled from the rugby club to the next village and we had only been there about fifteen hours.

To live in such a community makes you even more of a public property who must discuss selectors' decisions, trends in the game, recent matches and, above all, reasons for Welsh failure. I once rang Derek Quinnell at home in Five Roads and dialled the wrong number. The phone was answered by another resident of the village. When I asked to speak to Derek, he not only informed me that I had the wrong number, but gave me the right one immediately and then advised me not to ring straight away because the car was not outside his house and therefore he was out. That could only happen in Wales.

Some players find it difficult to cope with the invasion of privacy, the duties such as speaking at dinners and other functions, the strain of being constantly on parade, but drawbacks aside, in Wales the player who makes it to the top is a privileged man. He will undoubtedly have better job prospects than his peers and will also enjoy the benefits of being a celebrity. Anything from suits to motor cars will be offered at trade prices and if he can stand the non-stop questions on the game, he will never have to buy a drink.

Because rugby is so important in Wales it follows that the most powerful man in the country is the Secretary of the Welsh Rugby Union, a post occupied by Bill Clement throughout the period covered by this book. The following story might be apocryphal but it illustrates the point. Bill plans an international day like a military operation. He has stewards deployed in every corner of the Arms Park and when Prince Charles came to watch the game against Ireland in 1969 he equipped them all with two-way radios. Each steward was told to inform *Mr* Clement the moment he spotted the car. Inevitably the royal party was late and Bill, doubly anxious that nothing should go wrong on his big day, was yelling at his men every two minutes to find out what had happened to his principal guest. When the car eventually arrived a triumphant official rushed up to it, yanked the back door open and, without so much as a bow, said to His Royal Highness, 'Hurry up, you're in dead trouble. Mr Clement's been waiting for you for the last half hour.'

The 1980/81 season sees the celebration of the centenary of the Welsh Rugby Union. This in itself is remarkable because it makes Wales the youngest of the four Home Unions. England was the first to pass a hundred years in 1971, followed by Scotland in 1972 and Ireland in 1974. In the light of the way that Wales has since adopted the game for itself it may at first seem strange that it took ten years from the formation of one organised governing body in England for the same thing to happen in the principality. But the answer probably lies in the very intimacy and compactness of those fifty-five Welsh miles. We just didn't need centralising so much. Perhaps it is a good thing that some time elapsed before the Union was formed, because there's another fact to consider. The miners and heavy industrial workers in the north of England found they could not afford to obey the code of amateurism laid down by the R.F.U., so they founded the Northern Union and professional Rugby League. The great acrimony and rift between the two codes has never been healed.

Wales almost went the same way but fortunately, after attempts by some clubs to follow suit, the union held together.

The result of this is that the game in Wales really is the game of all the people, from the professions to the blue-collar worker. It is the national game, and just as in Manchester or Liverpool and other soccer strongholds you find pictures of the local team everywhere in pubs, social clubs and dance halls, you find the local or national rugby team on display in Wales. The history of the game is preserved in the same way, so that you will find collections of jerseys and other memorabilia in all sorts of village halls or even non-rugby clubs if the particular local hero had an association with them.

Happily there is no class stigma in the Welsh game. During the season no matter where you go, whether it be Aberystwyth Univerisity's Senior Common Room, or Llanwern steelworks canteen, the Glamorgan County Club in Cardiff or the Clwb Bach in Burry Port, there will be people discussing rugby, with all the intensity of a pair of Mancunians in the week before United meet City in the Cup Final.

1

BUILDING ON ABERAVON SAND
1967 and 1968

Like all good fairy stories this one begins unhappily. Having won the Home International Championship in 1964, 1965 and 1966, by 1967 the Welsh team was ageing and stale. The 1966 Lions tour to New Zealand had been a disaster. The team left Britain with high hopes and came back thrashed and demoralised, and this probably killed off any remaining ambitions for the senior players. The Welsh selectors decided that it was time to bring in some new blood and during or before the new season great names such as Haydn Morgan, Alun Pask, Ken Jones and Dewi Bebb were all replaced.

Uncharacteristically the selectors became dreadfully uncertain and chopped and changed as the English selectors have done ever since, also without success. At scrum half, a key position where an understanding with the fly half is vital and must be built up over a number of games, they tried three players in four matches. Billy Hullin, then a member of the very successful Cardiff club, was given a first cap against Scotland with Barry John, his clubmate, outside him. Defeat cost them both their places and the veteran Alun Lewis was recalled for the match against Ireland. Another defeat and another change, the young and promising Gareth Edwards, still at Cardiff College of Education, was the surprise selection – there were no more changes at scrum half for many years to come.

Meanwhile, the same thing was happening at full back. Terry Price was still a relatively young player but had had a bad knee injury and never really recovered his fitness or his form after the Lions tour. He was picked against Scotland and then replaced by another veteran, Graeme Hodgson, for the Irish match. That did not work, so Price was recalled against France but another poor performance caused the selectors to pick Keith Jarrett, the young Newport centre still at Monmouth School, for the match against England. He was out of position, inexperienced and was played on the strength of some phenomenal place kicking in a few club matches. Most people thought it a gamble that was totally foolhardy but his debut against England is now legendary. He scored a record 19 points, including a try, to give Wales victory by 34–21, the only success of the 1966/67 season.

To add to Wales's problems two of the most experienced players, David Watkins who had replaced Barry John for the last three matches, and Terry Price, both still with plenty to offer Welsh rugby, went north, as if to say 'We're not going to do ourselves any favours hanging around down here.'

Many new players were introduced during that season. There were the future greats, Barry John, Gareth Edwards and Gerald Davies, and several others, among them Dai Morris, Delme Thomas and I who all played at least twenty-five times for Wales. Only Keith Jarrett really made his mark straight off and it is ironic to think that had the rest of us been English we would probably have been banished to the side lines, never to be heard of again. Thank goodness the Welsh selectors have basically stuck to the maxim that if a player is good enough on a Friday night, he's still good enough on a Sunday morning, unless something really drastic has happened to force them to change their opinion.

Basically, nothing drastic had happened. Matches had been lost narrowly and mainly through inexperience. It was no wonder. Barry, Gerald and I were all twenty-one and in our first season out of college while Keith Jarrett and Gareth Edwards were only nineteen.

There was also no coaching set up and my own experience shows what a ramshackle outfit we were. Having only just entered the first class arena, and having taken most of the first half of the season to establish myself in the London Welsh 1st XV, I had never met most of the players before the final trial in January 1967. On February 4th I was playing my first international. I can well remember meeting Alun Pask for the first time at the North British Hotel in Edinburgh and then, after one short practice, packing down beside him against Scotland. It was quite a thrill as he'd been a schoolboy hero of mine only three years before, but it was not likely to help us play well together.

This is not to say that there were no good Welsh sides before the days of coaching, but without coaching and a squad system it took much longer for the people involved to get to know one another and form the sort of understanding that leads to team-work. That 1967 team against Scotland was particularly inexperienced. Before the game the players totalled 102 caps between them and 76 of those were shared between Dewi Bebb (30), Brian Price (22), and Alun Pask (24). There were six new caps – Billy Raybould, Billy Hullin, Brian Rees, John O'Shea, Billy Mainwaring and myself. Gerald Davies, Barry John and Ken Braddock were winning their second caps and eight different clubs were represented. The pack alone was selected from seven different ones, with four of the forwards gaining first caps. Hardly the basis for being able to talk in terms of a team.

By the 1967/68 season quite a lot had changed. At the start of the season Wales had decided to appoint a National Coach and David Nash, that brilliant and very unlucky back-row forward who had his career ended prematurely by illness on the 1962 Lions tour to South Africa, was appointed. He was to be unlucky again. He had been appointed only for that season and, as with many new ventures, it was a toe in the water exercise because at the end of the year he was not re-elected and Clive Rowlands replaced him. It now seems very unfair, particularly as he had to cope with all the problems of setting up a new system, that he was not appointed for a three-year term as is now the accepted practice. Only over such a period can a coach develop his own particular coaching theories and methods. At the end of that time he must stand or fall by the success of the team, especially at international level when the coach only sees the players on about ten occasions.

David Nash was a quiet, shy man which probably made him ill-equipped to deal with some of the political infighting, but he immediately made his mark on the players and most were impressed by his knowledge of the game. Most, and I include myself, learned a great deal in that year and the first National Coach certainly made his contribution toward the successes of the next decade.

The 1967/68 season set the pattern which has remained largely unaltered ever since. Sunday sessions at Aberavon began that year and few international players since then will ever forget that dreadful feeling on a Sunday morning after a heavy game and a heavy night when they realised they had to report by 10.00 a.m. or risk the wrath of the selectors. For London Welsh players it was particularly traumatic. At that time it was a four-hour drive with no M4 from Maidenhead almost to Bristol and the 5.30 reveille at John Dawes's house in London (he was the only one with a car) was almost enough to persuade some of us to argue against the squad system in principle. Nobody did, we were all far too worried about keeping our places.

As it was, the season was not spectacularly more successful. It began with a sound beating by the All Blacks and the Welsh performance was remarkable only in that the captain, Norman Gale, scored his only points in twenty-five games for Wales. Late in the game, after several misses by the recognised kickers, Wales were awarded a penalty thirty-five yards out and in front of the posts. Norman, an occasional kicker at Llanelli, elected to kick it himself and, although it hardly 'soared' between the posts, it went over.

In the Home International Championship, Scotland were beaten 5–0 at Cardiff and Wales managed to draw 11–11 at Twickenham. Then followed an extraordinary game in Dublin because it included two drop goals that should never have been allowed. First Gareth Edwards took a snap shot and the ball curled wide of the left-hand upright. Gareth with his normal exuberant form of gamesmanship threw his arm in the air and cheered as soon as it left his boot and poor Mike Titcomb the referee, who was genuinely unsighted, fell for his con trick and gave the goal. He was grateful when a few minutes later Mike Gibson replied in kind. I, in fact, touched the ball which in those days invalidated the kick, but there was no way that it was not going to be given. Not only would he not allow me to have attention for two very sore fingers but got most upset when I shook my hand vigorously to draw his attention to the fact that I had touched the ball.

The crowd invasion that followed Gareth's non-goal was quite frightening and I think Welsh players as well as the Irish were almost relieved when Micky Doyle scored in the dying moments to give Ireland a 9–6 win. That was also, incidentally, John Dawes' first match as captain of Wales and the beginning of his re-emergence on to the international scene. He was dropped as captain for the next game, even though he retained his place, and it was not until his last two seasons that the world realised just how good a captain and player he really was.

France visited Cardiff for the final match of the season and won with something to spare to take the Championship. Thus Wales's record over the two seasons was played 10, won 2, drawn

1 and lost 7. It was hardly the basis for incredible optimism, but to take the record on face value is to ignore several of the developments that had taken place.

By this time all the new players had seven or eight games under their belts and that alone was important. International rugby is a completely different experience to club rugby and it takes players four or five matches to adjust to the different pace and atmosphere. One of the biggest differences is just in the size of the crowd. An average Welsh club gate is probably less than 5,000 but in international rugby you are pitched into an arena where there are between 50,000 and 70,000. Later on you learn to ignore it or even revel in it, but at first it can be intimidating.

At Cardiff the one thing you cannot do is ignore the crowd. In 1967 we played so badly against Ireland, my first match at the Arms Park (as it was then known), that the crowd was almost silent. Having watched matches there and marvelled at the volume of the singing and cheering, it was an eerie feeling. At that time the singing only began when the team were in the home straight and heading for victory and the silence was the ultimate reminder that you were letting down Wales. Against Ireland we lost 3–0, so there was not even a Welsh score to celebrate. However, the singers made up for it in Jarrett's debut game against England and have never stopped since. The singing now starts regardless of the state of the game and if the visitors score first there's 'Calon Lan' to lift the team, or these days 'Hymns and Arias', and it is the solemn tone of the singing that impresses the importance of the occasion on the player and causes the *hwyl*. The more honest visiting players admit to finding it intimidating, although one or two do say that it stimulates them too and increases their will to win.

Another reason to feel optimistic for the future was that the selectors had shown faith in the players and had stuck with them and because of the introduction of squad training the team was much more of a team than ever before. Players' strengths and weaknesses could be identified and the rest of the side knew what to expect. For example, Barry John had already made it very clear to me that such mundane things as tackling were beneath him, except in the most extreme situations and that was why God had invented wing forwards. He had also made it clear that he considered forwards in general were lesser beings to be tolerated because someone had to get the ball to him, but thereafter they should stay out of the way in case they messed things up.

The summer of 1968 provided further opportunity for developing the togetherness that was to prove so important to the success of the next decade. Eleven of the team were selected to tour with the British Lions in South Africa. Although the tour was not successful and we were thrashed in the Test series, it continued our rugby education and all the Welsh contingent came back much wiser and better players. Those who did not go with the Lions went to Argentina for a short tour under the leadership of John Dawes. Again it was not a particularly successful tour, but there is nothing like a tour for uniting a group of players into a squad. The only reputations made were off the field. John Lloyd has been known as Mr Greedy ever since because of his capacity for devouring two or even three giant Argentinian steaks at one sitting and Harry Bowcott, the assistant manager, won everyone's respect as a gin and tonic drinker. Many of the players tried to outlast him, but without success, and as they staggered into breakfast the following morning, holding aching heads, they were amazed to see him immaculately turned out, finishing his meal, having already been for a three-mile walk. Gin and tonic has played a large part in Welsh team preparation ever since.

There were also two new boys on that tour who were to become vital to the success of Wales over the next few years. One was a player just out of Millfield School, J. P. R. Williams, a surprise selection; the other was Clive Rowlands who took over as Welsh National Coach from David Nash. Sad as it was to see David Nash replaced, nobody can argue about the importance of the role played by D. C. T. (Top Cat) Rowlands in making Welsh rugby supreme once again. After the tour he was appointed for a three-year term and such was his success that he completed another three-year term before stepping down to allow John Dawes to take over.

Although there were still great problems in the composition of the Welsh team for the following season, things were slotting into place. Full back had been a problem position which was solved by the emergence of J. P. R. Williams. No. 8 was another. The selectors had even resorted to playing Dai Morris (a great flanker but too small to play No. 8 at international level) in that position at one stage, but before the start of the 1969 Home International Championship that problem had also been solved and the scene was set for the Decade of the Dragon.

2

THE CWMTWRCH SOUND
1969

For a Welsh nation starved of success 1969 was a tonic and then as if to prevent the team, or the supporters, getting any false ideas about just how good they were, the summer short tour to Australasia put the whole season back in perspective and reminded the rugby world in the northern hemisphere that the European Championship was very much the second division when it came to real world rugby supremacy.

The Welsh team of the season before had lacked the vital spark to make the chemistry work but during the first half of the new season two players emerged, coincidentally both from London Welsh, who were to have a telling effect on international rugby over the period of this book.

J. P. R. Williams joined the club having toured Argentina with the Welsh party in the summer of 1968. He had been in London a year studying medicine at St Mary's Hospital, but had preferred to play with the hospital side and his home club, Bridgend, until the 1968/69 season. John Dawes who had captained the Welsh touring party undoubtedly used his considerable powers of persuasion to convince John Williams (the J.P.R. came later) that if he had aspirations to a place in the Welsh team they were not likely to be furthered by playing for a hospital side.

I can remember his first game. I arrived at Richmond and saw John in the changing room. I had not met him and did not have a clue who he was. In fact I thought he was a schoolboy with his pudding-basin haircut, but when all the well-wishers left he was still there and I was thinking, 'Why doesn't he leave us now to get on with it,' and 'Who's brought him in here anyway?' I was completely amazed when he began to change, so I sidled up to John Dawes to ask what was going on. I was, after all, vice-captain and thought I had a right to know. I was duly introduced and with some scepticism (we had a very good full back in Gareth James) set about changing for the game.

Although J.P.R. did nothing in that first game that we would now consider spectacular by his standards, it was obvious from the moment he took the field that he was no schoolboy. London Welsh had become used to a running, attacking full back (even though the Australian dispensation of not being permitted to kick directly into touch from outside the 25 had only been introduced that season) and it was also obvious that he was made to fit into the team.

The other player to emerge was Mervyn Davies. His rise to prominence was more surprising and meteoric than J.P.R.'s. He had no real success at school and, although his father had been a fine Swansea forward and a 'Victory' international at the end of the war, even his schoolmaster felt that he was probably better off using his height to play basketball. However he had turned out a couple of times for Swansea before taking a teaching job in Guildford where he had for a while been content to play rugby with friends at the Old Guildfordians. At the start of the 1968/69 season he decided to try his hand at London Welsh, soon made the second team, and was playing quite well without setting the world alight. Meanwhile in the first team there was a definite problem in winning line out ball, particularly at the back. After a few weeks of the season this was discussed at selection and Glan Richards, one of the selectors, came up with one of those statements that will live with him for the rest of his life: 'Well, there's this big boy Mervyn Davies, he'll win you line out ball without doubt, but he won't do much else.'

On November 2nd he played his first game for London Welsh and on February 1st he played his first game for Wales. In the final trial he was perhaps lucky in that he was moved from the Possibles into the Probables to take over from Dennis Hughes, who had originally been selected but was forced to drop out through injury. It was one of the few trials at that time when the Probables won a resounding victory and therefore the team was selected en bloc. However, it was Wales who were really the lucky ones. They had been pushed into making a decision that might otherwise have taken much longer and Mervyn Davies immediately set out to show the world just how wrong Glan Richards' assessment of his talents could be.

The other really important factor that gave a new impetus to the 1969 Home International season from the Welsh point of view was the appointment of Clive Rowlands. In many ways that too was unlikely because the team was developing a running style of play and certainly from his playing days Clive had no pedigree to coach in that vein. He lived, and still does, in Upper Cwmtwrch where rugby is all about a big pack of forwards who win the ball and a scrum half who shunts them down the touchline until they are close enough to force themselves over the line. Three-quarters were strictly for snuffing out opposition attacks if they decided to get fancy and move the ball, and even the outside half was lucky to touch the ball more than half a dozen times each half. Clive recognised the absurdity of the situation himself. He summed it up one day with typical wit. 'What am I doing coaching a passing game when in our house the kids don't know the meaning of the word. They even say, "Kick me the sugar, Dad!"'

The reason for his appointment was his personality. I think the whole team believed that he had had to take some private lessons from Ray Williams, the National Coaching Organiser, who baffled us all with his theories and breakdown of the mechanics of the game. But it is no coincidence that 'Top Cat' Rowlands' international record remains unique – he played fourteen times for Wales and captained his country in every one of those games. It takes a special kind of man to win a first cap and the captaincy in the same game.

He soon established a rapport with the players based on a mixture of jokes, impassioned pleading and a fair amount of bullying. He was always a showman. As the team began to achieve success and his confidence grew, the showman in him came more to the fore. At that time, with the practice pitches behind Afan Lido newly laid and often waterlogged, much of the training was done on the beach and a fair crowd would often collect along the promenade to cast their own critical eyes over the preparations for the next match. It was hard enough running and scrummaging on sand all day, having played a hard game the day before, but Mr Rowlands became very unpopular when he insisted that we finish each session with some fitness training. His favourite instruction was to send us sprinting up the beach out of the wet and relatively hard sand, through the soft sand, and up the dozen or so steps to touch the sea wall and then sprint back. We would be accompanied all the way by his abuse and derision, much to the enjoyment of the spectators. Most of us believed it was all for their benefit rather than ours, but even if Clive was playing to the gallery nobody dared to tell him so.

That style of running practice sessions had far reaching effects. Whereas some of the other national teams lock themselves away behind closed doors, Welsh squad sessions have always been public affairs. They also changed the relationship between the players and selectors. Until then the Big Five had been very much a remote body to be feared, making judgements that could change your life, seemingly without reason at times, and totally unanswerable to anyone – except the nation at the end of the season. Because of the new approach to preparing the team they too were expected to attend sessions on a Sunday and became people rather than figureheads.

In 1969 the selectors were a very mixed bunch. There was Cliff Jones from Pontyclun, the legendary outside half from the 'thirties who had already been doing the job for ten years. Rees Stephens, who won thirty-two caps between 1947 and 1957, was still turning out for Neath Athletic and enjoyed nothing more than proving he was still harder than some of the youngsters in the squad. London Welsh were represented (the cynics claimed that as the reason for such a large representation in the team) by Harry Bowcott, known as 'His Majesty' because of his initials and cultured speech, who won the first of eight caps in 1929. The fourth was Jack Young the fiery little W.R.U. representative from Ogmore who had apparently been so critical of selectors during committee meetings that he decided to have a go himself. He caused great embarrassment to his nephew Jeff Young. Jeff was the hooker in the side and, even though it was total nonsense, any Welshmen who were not fans of his play convinced themselves that he was only there because of 'Uncle Jack'. Vernon Parfitt from Newport made up the Big Five. Like Jack Young, he lacked an international background, but he had served on the W.R.U. Coaching Committee for many years. A great deal of wrangling went on between them but, even if it was an unlikely combination, it worked.

Now that the squad system had been introduced the timetable for an international weekend took on a shape that has remained largely unaltered. If the game was to be played at Cardiff the team would meet for a practice session on the Thursday before and then the players would return home. Nobody actually believes that anyone is going to be able to concentrate on work on the Friday but International Board Regulations forbid meeting more than twenty-four hours before a home match presumably to show just how important amateurism is to the spirit of the game.

For an away match the team are allowed to meet forty-eight hours before the game and then stay together for the whole weekend. Thus for the first match of the 1969 season the team met on the Thursday, as it was against Scotland at Murrayfield. The mood of the party was even more anxious than usual at the start of a new international season. Everyone was conscious of the lack of recent success and players and selectors knew that heads must roll if results were not forthcoming.

Brian Price was the new captain and the selectors had also brought back Brian Thomas with him into the second row, plumping for experience and strength rather than the extra mobility of Max Wiltshire and Delme Thomas who had been the players in possession at the end of the previous season. There were also the new caps John Williams and Mervyn Davies, but apart from them the team was, if not exactly experienced, used to the arena of international rugby.

The Thursday practice session is always a difficult affair and this one was no exception. Having trained hard for the big day, nobody believes that anything more can be done, but the ritual run-out must take place with cameras and pressmen looking for interviews and pointers to pad out the previews that will appear on the Saturday. Players and coach know that nothing new can be attempted at this stage and unless there are doubts about the fitness of a player, everyone is loth to risk injury so close to the game. Even scrummaging practice is often bad tempered because the local pack, imported to provide opposition for the occasion, goes berserk and, determined to do well, undermines the confidence of the side by scrummaging harder than ever before. Keen young reserves have the same effect.

At least time goes by quickly on the field because the biggest problem from this point on is preventing the minutes from dragging. Eventually we arrived in Scotland and after the obligatory reception on the way from the airport to the hotel, booked in, as always, at the North British. Like the Angel, the North British is right in the centre of town, which has a plus and a minus side to it. On the one hand there is no peace from the fans who hang around the foyer, and would sleep there if they were not kicked out, but on the other hand their very presence helps in the build up to the game, Some teams prefer to stay a few miles out of town, but most of the Welsh players certainly prefer to be able to gauge the atmosphere of the place.

Mervyn Davies and I were both back row forwards and both from the same club. I was relatively experienced and it was his first cap, so naturally we were listed to share a room. From then on until the end of my international career we were always room mates and established a pattern of behaviour for international weekends. The players are always billeted in double rooms for international matches with only the captain being given the privilege of a single. Strangely enough I always found it took some of the tension out of trying to get to sleep the night before a game when there was someone else in exactly the same boat with me. Other players also built up similar partnerships. John Williams always shared with Gerald Davies, who won forty-six caps and still had to give pride of place to John – that must be the longest partnership ever. Gareth always shared with Barry John, Dai Morris with John Lloyd (the two quiet men of the side) and so it went on.

Mervyn was obviously particularly nervous and after the statutory visit to the cinema or theatre (it was either the Black & White Minstrels or the Stanley Baxter Show that year), we played cards for a while before retiring. Then the real problem, going to sleep, began. Most hotels overdo the central heating and double glazing and the North British is no exception. The hot-house atmosphere is normally countered by opening the windows, but that year a new store was being erected and pile driving operations continued all night. It was a simple choice – silence and stifling heat or a reasonable temperature and noise. It seemed hours before we drifted off and then no time at all before Gerry Lewis was knocking on the door.

Gerry is a living legend for the Welsh team and nobody can really imagine an international weekend without him. His most important function is team physiotherapist and there are very few players who do not owe one or two caps to him. He took over the job from his father in 1962 and has worked miracles with his massage and medication ever since. Apart from that he organises the weekend, doing everything from looking after the kit to ordering the theatre tickets.

But first thing in the morning, usually around nine o'clock, he is nothing short of a nuisance. However badly any player has

A youthful J.P.R. looks on as Maurice Richards runs round behind the posts on the way to his record four tries against England, 1969.

Clive Rowlands lays down the law on the sands at Aberavon. None of us believed he knew much about forward play but we did as we were told.

Brian Price horrified and Noel Murphy in agony — or in Hollywood?
Later, my first try for Wales, with a building site as the backdrop, Wales
v Ireland, 1969.

slept they all agree that for some reason they are asleep at the time Gerry calls. Sometimes Gerry deigns to knock but if he is really working well he has persuaded the hotel management to give him a pass key. Whatever happens, he will not go away, the door has to be opened and he is so cheerful it makes you sick. In five minutes everyone has had an enquiry into their health, a weather report, the latest on a player with a slight twinge, the routine programme for the day, the latest news, apart from the match, and the latest in his never ending supply of stories. Then with an 'O.K. J.T., O.K. Merv, have a good day', the whirlwind is on its way leaving two unhappily awake players realising that there is no chance of going back to sleep.

The first official preparation for the game is at 11.30 when the coach holds a team talk and in Edinburgh in 1969 it was something of an unknown quantity. Clive Rowlands had already set great store by such things as punctuality, but even then someone had been held up in the vast red and white crowds on Princes Street while buying presents for the family or hiring a D.J. for the banquet in the evening. He arrived just in time to avoid more than a caustic remark as Clive was anxious to launch into his own special brand of persuasiveness. At that time it was not perfected and the calls for togetherness and heartfelt (literally if we believed all he said about his ticker) appeals for the greatest effort ever for Wales were not as fluent as later. But by the time we left that tiny smoky hotel room, meant to take two not twenty-two, even the Chairman of the Selectors was mentally fully prepared for the match. Some of the lads were motivated to the point of punching walls and from that moment thoughts were of nothing else but the game.

Lunch followed immediately and the players began to prepare in their own special way. For John Lloyd and Delme Thomas, a substitute on this occasion, this meant the normal ideal meal of a big steak with all the trimmings and then somebody else's leftovers if possible. Delme would always accompany this with milk. Brian Thomas was perhaps the most eccentric always insisting on a bunch of grapes, while the rest of us alternated between fish, on the grounds that it was lighter than meat, and toast and honey, usually preferred by those who had been to physical education colleges and made pretence to some knowledge of diet and conversion of sugar and carbohydrate into energy. We never ever convinced Delme that his mixture was totally indigestible and would hamper his game – but then he was right. It worked for him and he always had just as much energy as the rest of us and never collapsed with stomach cramp.

Even the time between lunch and the game drags. Nobody can think of anything but the task in hand and the television offers some distraction with the soccer match previews and a build up to the game. Then at least, having been together for what seems like a lifetime, it is time to go. The coach is waiting and there is the excitement of a police escort, but by this time most players are immersed in their private thoughts so that even half-hearted attempts to raise our patriotic fervour by singing Welsh hymns are met with indifference. For me, and I believe for quite a number of other players, this is the time when the greatest self-doubt creeps in.

On arrival at the ground the activity ritual takes over and there is not much problem. First an inspection of the pitch and acknowledgement of the cheers from the thousands of standing customers who have arrived early to make sure of a good spot and then into the dressing room to find that Gerry Lewis already has a list a mile long of players requiring a rub down. He always managed to get through everyone, although it never seemed that he would, and you could always bet that Gareth Edwards would jump the queue. That always caused a strange tension. Everyone was longing to kick him off the rubbing table, but with the match so close, nobody wanted to upset anyone so every player accepted it, as Gareth knew they would. But then everyone else knew that Gareth was good enough to get away with it.

Fortunately no two players like to prepare in the same way, so the last rub down is not quite the problem it might be. By half an hour from kick-off some of the players are fully changed and some, like Phil Bennett, have not even begun to strip off. Again, this can in itself cause tension, but as the team became more of a team it was noticeable that everyone was conscious of the effect they were having on each other and moderated towards a happy medium. Gareth still jumped the queue.

Final team talks from captain and pack leader are seldom necessary at international level. The players are motivated and, especially since the introduction of the squad system, the preparation is thorough. Nevertheless they highlight one stage closer to the game and greater concentration. Then it is normally up to one of the physical education teachers to go through a warm up routine. After that photographs and a return to the dressing room to add the final touch of grease and put on the tie-ups. Then the call comes to take the field. Even here superstition takes over and those who like to go out last or second find that they have to give way to the more senior players who have the same superstition. The compromise is often to give way down the tunnel and come abreast as you hit the field. Eventually the anthems are over and the game is ready to begin.

The Scotland game in 1969 was quite special for Wales. It was the first game of our season but three weeks previously Scotland had travelled to Paris and had beaten France 6–3. Next to the Arms Park, France has to be the most difficult place for a visiting side to win and the previous season France had won her first Grand Slam. Therefore the Scottish confidence had to be running high and, with Wales desperately in need of success, it promised to be a memorable battle.

Unfortunately the game was a disappointment. The first half was tight, hard fought and unimaginative with neither side managing to establish a real advantage, although Price and Thomas had the better of the lines out against the giants, Stagg and McHarg. Keith Jarrett kicked two penalty goals having won his place back as a centre after being dropped for the last two matches of the previous season, and at the interval the game was still wide open. The second half was a different story with Wales scoring three times to run out easy winners by 17–3.

First Gareth Edwards eluded the cover from a set scrum and, using all his power, alternately went round players and knocked them out of the way to score the sort of try that was to become the hallmark of his play. At 9–0 Wales were certainly in the driving seat but by no means home and dry, when Scotland hammered two very big nails in their own coffin and the game was over.

Brian Price had developed a move with Stuart Watkins at Newport. Close to the opposition line when they expected a long throw to launch the back division on the open side, or when the opposition were throwing a short defensive ball, Brian would move up to number three in the line out and, using his enormous spring, would deflect the ball forward and back to his own blind side winger who would hopefully sprint around the front of the line out to score. On this occasion he worked exactly the same ploy with Maurice Richards and the Cardiff winger, always alert to a half chance, darted through to score. It was Richards' first try for Wales and it may have come from a crafty trick rather than a winger's classic dash, but the huge grin showing the gap where front teeth had once been proved that he had never been more pleased to score.

Wales then received another gift from Scotland. The Welsh pack were becoming increasingly dominant and when Scotland won the ball it became more and more ragged. Having been forced back into their own 25 they won just the sort of ball they did not want and by the time it was moved to Colin Telfer at fly half, Barry John was homing in fast. He not only charged down Telfer's kick but regained possession himself. With just one man to beat, a try was a certainty, Barry shimmied his hips and Blaikie was left clutching thin air. Desperate Scottish cover tried to get to him but could only make contact as he went over the line between the posts. Keith Jarrett converted and Wales had won by the comfortable margin of 17–3.

It was the biggest Welsh victory at Murrayfield since 1947. Brian Price was forced to admit that Scotland had contributed largely to their own downfall. 'We planned to make our own tries but it turned out that we scored mostly from Scottish mistakes,' he said. However, even if there were doubts about Wales's ability to create tries, it was still a tremendous tonic to begin the season with such an emphatic win.

Having played on February 1st Wales were not due to play again until March 8th against Ireland at Cardiff. Such a gap between matches would now be impossible but in 1969 it created a strange situation. With Wales about to play the second match in the Championship, Ireland were playing their last. What is more they had thrashed Scotland 16–0 at Murrayfield, had beaten England 17–15, and France 17–9 in Dublin, and were therefore going for the Triple Crown and the Grand Slam. And as Ireland had only won the Triple Crown four times ever, last in 1949, they were obviously very determined, all the more so because Wales had prevented them from pulling it off after they had beaten England and Scotland on no less than ten occasions. To have the Grand Slam in sight was even rarer as they had only ever won it once, in 1948.

Quite apart from the rugby and regardless of the result the day was bound to be a unique and special occasion. 1969 was the year of the investiture of the Prince of Wales, Prince Charles, and he had agreed to attend the match as part of the celebrations. It was also the year that the old North Stand had been demolished and the new one had not replaced it. Therefore the crowd was limited to 29,000 and ball boys had to go chasing into a wilderness of steel and iron to retrieve the ball each time it was kicked into touch on that side.

After being presented to the Prince (he had heard I was resident in London and offered me a lift back after the game, claiming his car was much too big for one) the game got under way and turned out to be both spectacular and controversial. It was that sort of day. The tension was evident at the very first line out. I was in my normal position at the back of the line next to Noel Murphy. Noel was and is a great competitor, but by that stage of his career he had lost much of his speed and was determined to make his presence felt. He gave notice of his intentions by landing a quick jab on my ear. Fortunately it did not land properly and caused no damage but it was no surprise at all when, after only five minutes, he received a right uppercut from Brian Price. I have no doubt that Price was provoked (and I was right beside the incident). There is also no question in my mind that Murphy made the most of the situation. Newspapers talked of Murphy falling as if 'pole-axed'. He did no such thing, as the photographs show. I have never seen anyone punched unconscious who has been able to lift his hands to his face as Murphy did. The blow was not hard and did not knock him out. Nevertheless it was a very irresponsible action and could have cost Wales the game as the referee was right on the spot and would have been perfectly justified in sending Price off. Fortunately he was not fooled by Murphy's overdramatisation of the situation and allowed Price to remain on the field. After the match Price, the captain and a vital ball winner for the team, apologised to his own men for his irresponsibility, fully realising the impossibility of the task facing his team had they been reduced to fourteen men so early in the match.

The whole incident added to the tension surrounding the game. Tom Kiernan at one stage threatened to take his team off the field and during the rest of the first half violence smouldered and flared up at intervals. There was one incident in which Ken Kennedy was punched genuinely unconscious in a set scrum and that was far more indefensible than the Price-Murphy affray. The hooker is absolutely defenceless and could not have given provocation with both arms stretched around his props' backs. At that stage the rugby was secondary and it looked like being a black day in the history of Welsh rugby. To make matters worse it was being witnessed first hand by the Prince of Wales.

While all this had been going on, Ireland had taken the lead with a penalty goal which Barry John had cancelled out with a drop goal and then Kiernan had put his side back into the lead with another penalty. Ireland were obviously still well in the hunt, even though their forwards were being outplayed. Price and Mervyn Davies were winning most of the lines out and the whole pack was quick to support the backs so that Wales had enjoyed the territorial advantage. Even so they looked like going into half time trailing Ireland until they delivered a sucker punch (a metaphorical one this time) which gave them an unusual try.

Wales were awarded a penalty just inside the Irish 25 and the Irish team immediately assumed that Keith Jarrett would kick for goal. Certainly that was his intention as he walked forward to collect the ball. Before he had signalled his intention to the referee, however, that wily old warhorse from Ebbw Vale, Denzil Williams, had noticed that all the Irish players had turned their backs. He immediately broke into a canter, a gallop would be exaggerating, and called to Jarrett to feed him from a tap. Jarrett, equally quick to assess the situation, obliged and gave Denzil the perfect pass, allowing him to trundle over in the left hand corner. It was Denzil's twenty-third cap and in winning it he became the most capped prop ever to play for Wales. He went on to win thirty-six caps for his country but this try against Ireland remained as his only score. To rub salt into the wound Jarrett converted from the touchline and immediately the whistle went for half time. The half had lasted forty-eight minutes because of all the stoppages and for the first time Ireland were behind 8–6.

Early in the second half Brian Thomas left the field with a nasty gash on his head, received at the bottom of a ruck. The look of defiance as he stood up and glared at the Irish pack, who he clearly thought had done it deliberately to exact retribution for what had gone before, plainly indicated that he intended to return. He did, triumphantly, ten minutes later with his head swathed in bandages to confirm his image as the iron man (the wound needed ten stitches). The roar with which he was greeted as he re-emerged from the tunnel almost demolished the partly-built new stand and showed just how gladiatorial the crowd felt about the game. His return also signalled the opening of the floodgates as Welsh superiority was at last turned into points.

Taking the lead seemed to take the tension out of the Welsh play. We had had the better of the first half but had been unable to turn it into points, now in the second half it was all Wales. Barry John made the first try. From a set scrum he took Edwards' pass and with that deceptive pace and almost wraith-like elusiveness that was to become his hallmark he drifted through on a classic outside brake to within ten yards of the line and then fed Stuart Watkins with a long pass to give the winger an unopposed run in.

Eight minutes later it was Gareth Edwards' chance to show his brilliance. Having received bad ball from a line out he was forced to chip back to the box. Somehow he also managed to get there before his opponent, and hacked on before picking up and finding Dai Morris in support twenty yards from the line. Dai seldom needed help from that distance and stormed in to score. Jarrett converted and Wales was out of reach at 16–6.

Next it was my turn. John Williams joined in a back movement which began in the Welsh half and sold a dummy to streak through and then link up with Stuart Watkins. The right wing, was stopped just short of the Irish line but got the ball down behind him and I was able to pick up and dive over. It was hardly the wonderful forty-yard run, breaking through tackles and sidestepping players, that one hopes will accompany one's first try in an international but, looking at the television recordings afterwards, my grin was every bit as big as Maurice Richards' had been in Scotland.

Jarrett again converted from the touchline with a superb kick but within five minutes I had cancelled out my score by giving the ball away to Mike Gibson in front of the Irish posts. It did not seem dangerous at first but Wales by this time were so committed to attack that he hacked the length of the pitch to score under our posts. Jarrett replied with a final penalty and Wales had won a memorable victory 24–11.

It was a great day. Not only had Wales set themselves up for an obvious chance of the Championship and Triple Crown, but several players had gained the confidence to play in international football as they did for their clubs. The tremendous talent of Mervyn Davies had given the back row the balance it needed and for the first time the critics accepted that we were worth our places. Gareth Edwards and Barry John also blossomed as a partnership as never before and Maurice Richards had played with great presence, threatening danger every time he got the ball.

The next match was in Paris and Wales had high hopes of victory. France had won the Grand Slam the season before but had then experienced the sort of disaster that only they could have. Success had been built around the Camberabero brothers at half back and the leadership of Christian Carrère. At the end of the 1968 season the Camberaberos had retired and on their tour to the Antipodes France lost three Tests against New Zealand and one against Australia. Worse was to follow, for they lost to England, Ireland and Scotland in 1969 before meeting Wales and Carrère had been axed. So last season's Grand Slam winners went into the game against Wales trying to avoid a whitewash.

It appeared unlikely at the end of the first half. Wales were leading 8–0 and seemed to have the match under control. Gareth Edwards had opened the scoring with the sort of solo try only he could score, using pace, swerve and strength to get past the opposition. He also set up the second try with a kick which Maurice Richards ran onto. Jarrett converted the second try. Immediately after half time the game changed drastically. A kick-off to the wrong side, a ploy we often used to try, went to the French and slick passing on the exposed Welsh flank gave Campaes a try which Villepreux converted. He then kicked a penalty and the scores were level. Even though Wales regained the initiative and went close on several occasions the points just would not come and the game ended up 8–8. The whole team was disappointed. We knew we had lost it, rather than France had gained the draw. However, there was still the chance of the Triple Crown and the Championship if England could be beaten.

The match did create one piece of history. Near the end Gerald Davies injured his elbow and had to leave the field. He was replaced by Phil Bennett of Llanelli who won his first cap and became the first Welsh substitute at the same time, as the 1968/69 season was the first time they were allowed in the northern hemisphere. In the few minutes that Phil was on the field he did not touch the ball.

For the first three games of the season Wales had kept the

same team but had to make changes for the game against England. Brian Price was forced to withdraw through injury and was replaced by Delme Thomas. Gareth Edwards became the youngest player ever to captain Wales. Gerald Davies was also missing. He had not recovered from the injury to his elbow and John Dawes was recalled to replace him.

The tension on the morning of the match was unbearable. Only Denzil Williams, John Dawes, Stuart Watkins and Brian Thomas had been a part of the last Welsh side to win the Triple Crown (in 1965 under Clive Rowlands), and the rest of us were desperate for success. It showed particularly in the team talk. Clive Rowlands always finished his rantings covered in sweat but this time the beads of perspiration were standing out on his forehead before he had begun. Everybody was there five minutes before 11.30 which was also unusual and Clive spent the first minute or so just pacing up and down before he launched into the now familiar routine.

Togetherness was essential so before the talking began we had to go through a series of simulated scrum feeds. Gareth would grab the ball and get us ready. 'Steady now, steady . . . Right! Coming in . . .' and on the 'Now' the whole team would yell. This would go on until the twenty or so voices sounded like one and Clive was satisfied that they could hear us in the Royal on St Mary Street.

Now it was time for Clive. 'Right, boys, you're not playing this one for yourselves or for me or for the selectors, you're playing for Wales . . . Is your ticker going? Mine's going like the bloody clappers. If yours isn't it bloody well should be. I know they're all thumping, I can hear them from here.'

By this time his voice is high pitched, sounding more Cwmtwrch than ever. Suddenly it's a scream.

'What are we going to do today, Delme?'

'Win,' answers Delme with plenty of feeling but not much volume. He's a quiet man.

'Say it as if you mean it!' screams Clive.

'Win!' shouts Delme.

'Louder!' screams Clive.

'Win!' shouts Delme.

'Louder!' screams Clive.

'Win!' yells Delme even louder than before.

'Great,' whispers Clive, his voice has gone by now. 'Really

great, now I know you're all on the right wave length. We've even got Delme shouting.'

On it goes, one moment at a crescendo and then complete silence. Everyone's looking at their shoes or the ceiling through a haze of cigarette smoke, but only looking Clive in the eye when being spoken to specifically. Suddenly it's back to the win theme.

'What are we going to do, Merv?'

'Win!' he yells to Clive's satisfaction.

'Keith?'

'Win!'

'Dawesy?'

'Win!'

'By God you've got to go some today and prove to that lot out there that they're wrong' – there had been some criticism of John's selection.

'Now come on, Denz, Jeff, Greedy. Come on boys, it all starts with you. If you're not firm the rest might as well go home. Fairbrother's been opening his mouth again. You make sure it's closed for good after today. Greedy, you can eat Powell. What are you going to do, Denz?'

'Win!'

'Jeff?'

'Win!'

'Greedy?'

'Eat 'em. EAT 'EM!'

It was said with such passion he meant it. The tension had become too great and to Barry John this was the final straw. He giggled, tried to suppress it, then gave up, and the whole room collapsed in laughter. Even Clive was forced to grin.

The beauty of the National Stadium in Cardiff is that it's right in the middle of town so there are no coach rides, just a stroll across the road to the dressing rooms via the sports shop in Quai Street to buy a new jock strap, my particular superstition for all internationals played at Cardiff since we had beaten England in 1967. Merv always bought some new clothes on the morning of the game, Clive Rowlands always wore the same suit.

Changing in 1969 was miserable. Not only had the North Stand been demolished, the changing rooms had gone too and were housed in temporary huts at the end of what is now Cardiff's pitch. Nevertheless despite the cramped conditions nothing could detract from the occasion. Brian Thomas had taken over as pack leader in the absence of Brian Price and just in case anyone had gone off the boil, gave a rousing talk. One part of it was unforgettable.

'Their scrum half is Trevor Wintle. I was at Cambridge with him. We used to call him Wanger Wintle. Now we're going to push their pack back so fast that we'll have his own players trampling on him. By the time he comes off the field I want him to look as if he's been sunbathing in the Bahamas with a string vest on.'

The game belonged to Maurice Richards. He scored four tries to equal the record for Wales held by Willie Llewellyn of Llwynypia who achieved the feat against England in 1899 and Reggie Gibbs of Cardiff who did it against France in 1908. It was to be Maurice's last game for Wales on home soil as he turned professional upon his return from the tour of Australasia.

The game was played to a pattern that was to become very much the trademark of the Welsh team over the next ten years. A hard fought and close first half with the scores fairly even would give way to a free scoring second period when the Welsh forwards had achieved domination and the brilliant Welsh backs were freed to run.

Bob Hiller, that ever-reliable goal kicker for England, opened the scoring with a penalty and then Maurice Richards scored the first of his tries. It came from a counter-attack, proving yet again how effective this can be in a tight game when the defences are unpierceable from set pieces. England attacked and Finlan grubber-kicked into the Welsh 25 where the ball was fielded by Stuart Watkins. Stuart, always ready to attack, ran instead of clearing to touch and then kicked upfield. The first to reach the ball was Plummer but Dai Morris and I hounded him (like good flankers should!) and won the loose ball. Gareth Edwards spun it away to Barry John and he threw a long pass to Richards who scored in the corner.

Any thoughts that Brian Price would be badly missed in the line out vanished as Delme Thomas quickly established his mastery in that area and generally the Welsh pack won plenty of ball, but at half time it was still 3–3.

Early in the second half Keith Jarrett kicked two penalty goals to give Wales confidence and then the backs really began to take advantage of the forward superiority and went on a scoring spree. Barry John scored the next try. Once again it came from a misdirected kick ahead. He caught it on the full and, with the English defence in disarray, he weaved through four or five defenders to score one of the great individual opportunist tries. Keith Jarrett converted and then Richards scored his second try. This time it was the result of good rucked ball on the English 25 and then quick passing leaving him with a clear run in.

Hiller made a token gesture by landing a penalty goal but John again demonstrated his superb all-round skill by pivoting on a sixpence and dropping a superb left-footed goal.

It was now 20–6 and although Hiller finished off the scoring with a consolation penalty the rest of the match belonged to Richards. His third try came from a set move where he took the ball running on an inside line and surprised the defence so comprehensively that he scored under the England posts. The fourth came from open play and when he received the ball on the 25 his blistering pace was just too much for the cover. Although he had support (albeit forwards struggling to keep in touch) he knew it was his day and made it by himself with defenders hanging on as he dragged them over the line. Jarrett converted both these tries to give himself a points total of 12 and England were hammered by 30–9, the second consecutive time that they had had 30 points scored against them on a visit to Cardiff.

In the light of the successes to come during the 'seventies a Triple Crown, while never won easily, might not seem a great feat, but to us, the players, it was the equivalent of the World Cup. We desperately needed success and even the most self-confident among us was beginning to doubt his ability. The draw against France did nothing to dampen our spirits, we felt that we had had the game in our control but allowed it to slip away. The main thought was always that throughout the season the forwards had won the battle up front and the backs had capitalised handsomely on the ball they had received. The second part of the equation might have been true, but the forwards were to get a rude awakening on the other side of the world.

3

A SOBERING EXPERIENCE
Wales in Australasia, 1969

In retrospect the itinerary of the tour was quite ridiculous but that was far from the players' thoughts as we set off from Heathrow. Confidence and morale were high and everyone believed it would be possible to avenge the 13–6 defeat in Wales in 1967 by Brian Lochore's all-conquering All Blacks. The touring party was managed by Handel Rogers from Llanelli who had forged close friendships with many of the New Zealand players when he acted as their Liaison Officer in Wales during the 1967 tour. His assistant and coach was, of course, Clive Rowlands.

There were only twenty-three players in the party because with a total of seven games it was felt that to take more would mean certain players not getting a game. All the matches were going to be tough and the 'first' team would have to be selected whenever possible. In addition to those who had played in the home internationals Norman Gale, the veteran Llanelli hooker, Barry Llewelyn of Newport, Dennis Hughes of Newbridge, Alan Skirving of Newport and 'Chico' Hopkins of Maesteg were selected.

The first ordeal the team had to face was the journey to New Zealand. Again, because it was a short tour the decision was taken to make the trip in one go. Thank goodness two years later when some of us returned with the Lions we had a couple of days' rest in Hong Kong. However, in 1969, there was no time for that and fifty-two hours after take-off from Heathrow, after having dropped in at Teheran, New Delhi, Singapore and Sydney, as well as various European capitals en route, we arrived in New Zealand. Even allowing for time difference there had been thirty-six hours of actual flying. Upon arrival we were not allowed to rest, but bundled into a little Fokker Friendship for the internal flight to New Plymouth, where the first game was to be against Taranaki four days later. The final flight through an electrical storm was probably the worst part of the journey and everyone was exhausted when we at last arrived. It was quite late in the evening but we were still not allowed to go to sleep. The whole of the town, or so it seemed, had turned out in the main street to greet us. Quite a few people were towing bulls around behind them and the focus of attention was on a giant mock bull on the back of a lorry. Taranaki is the main beef and dairy province of New Zealand and Ferdinand the bull has always been their mascot. Half an hour later, after stumbling through a few choruses of 'Calon Lan' and 'Sospan Fach', we were eventually allowed to sleep.

During the night there was a fairly severe earth tremor, chimney pots fell off houses and the odd window broke. Some of the locals ran into the street but it had little effect on the Welsh rugby team. Several remembered waking up but thought they were still on the aeroplane and assumed it was banking for the hundredth time. The next three days were a nightmare of trying to shake off jet lag and prepare for the match. Players would suddenly find themselves wide awake at four o'clock in the morning and dog tired at noon. Second year medical student, J. P. R. Williams, informed us that it was circadian disrhythmia and this was confirmed by Dr Alan Skirving. Nobody knew enough to argue and few cared – they just wished it would go away.

During the stay at Taranaki there was still time for fun. Two episodes stand out. The first was a mock battle on the local boating lake. Most of the party took out row boats for some gentle exercise and one thing led to another. Suffice to say that most people got wet and the main culprits, John Lloyd and Dai Morris, retreated to an island in the middle of the lake. They repelled all attempted landings but did lose their boat and were marooned for a short while. The local press photographers could not believe their luck.

The second involved the court. There is a court set up on every tour. It serves a useful purpose and is an opportunity for a private party, as outsiders are always strictly excluded. Court sessions are usually held on a Sunday when there are no other commitments and at the beginning of a tour a judge and prosecuting counsel are appointed. On this trip Brian Thomas was appointed judge. Contrary to the impression he might have given on the field Twm always did things in style and his new role gave him plenty of scope to play to the gallery. One of the maids at the hotel was a very big girl, she was also very tall, and he persuaded her to lend him a dress and various accoutrements. A wig, a very close shave and plenty of make-up completed the transformation from the iron man of Neath into a large but presentable woman. The whole session was conducted in a very serious manner with only the judge allowed to camp it up. Constant puckering of lipsticked mouth and side-long glances from mascaraed eyes threatened to cause an adjournment on several occasions, but instant heavy fines for laughter or even a smile retained order.

Through all this Gerald Davies was bringing charges against various players for not being dressed in the regulation uniform or being late for the coach to training. The fines went straight into the players' kitty, except in the case of Maurice Richards. He was found guilty of having a hair out of place (he was always neat and tidy) and was made to drink a bottle of beer, the only time I ever saw him drink.

Brian Thomas's female impersonation affected some players more than others. Jeff Young and Chico Hopkins, who had suffered heavily during the proceedings, wandered round for hours afterwards worried about their masculinity. 'Did you start to believe he was a woman? I did,' Chico kept saying and was only slightly mollified when Jeff agreed and admitted he had almost found him attractive at one stage and did that indicate latent homosexuality.

The selection for the match against Taranaki caused some controversy. It was well intentioned but wrong. With only three provincial matches on the whole tour the selectors decided that Taranaki was possibly the easiest match and therefore picked a side which was not the strongest. They did not want a repeat of the 1964 situation, when some members of the tour party to South Africa did not play at all. They were being too kind because the next game was the first of the two Test matches against New Zealand and it meant that several players, myself included, would be going into the Test match not having played a game on tour. In fact we had not played a really competitive game of rugby for almost two months, since the game against England on April 12th. In a typical first match of the tour the Welsh team on the field played poorly, still obviously affected by the journey, and only managed to draw 9–9 with the spirited

Taranaki side. But nobody was too worried, knowing that an extra few days would get the flight out of everyone's system.

The party moved down to South Island and Christchurch for the first international. It always seems to rain on days when British teams play at Lancaster Park, Christchurch and May 31st was no exception. The greyness of the day there was transferred to Wales the next day as the result became known. The All Blacks had hammered the European Champions 19–0. There were plenty of excuses that could be made but at the end of the day the whole of the Welsh party knew that nothing would have made any difference, the New Zealand forwards were simply too strong.

As expected, Wales had picked the Championship-winning side en bloc. Even though Gareth Edwards was suffering from a slightly pulled hamstring it was felt he should play. He last out the match but, especially as he was receiving ball constantly under pressure from the dominant All Blacks pack, it might have been better to play a fully fit Chico Hopkins. New Zealand won an enormous amount of possession from every phase of the game and Wales were immediately made aware of the difference in interpretation of the line out laws in New Zealand and Europe. Pat Murphy, the referee, allowed far more compression and blocking than was allowed at home, with the result that Price and Thomas found they were never allowed a free jump and Meads was often able to take the ball in splendid isolation without leaving the ground as his support forwards cleared the opposition out of the way.

Mr Murphy really became the Welsh bête noire when he constantly penalised attempts to do the same thing in retaliation. The problem was that the Welsh players, not used to being allowed to compress, had not practised it and therefore were rather clumsy at it. The game consequently became bad-tempered and this culminated in Jeff Young having his jaw fractured by a punch from Colin Meads in retaliation for jersey pulling. This put Jeff out of the match, where he was replaced by Norman Gale, and out of the tour. So Vic Perrins, the Newport hooker, was flown out to join the party.

My own memories of the game are of nothing but tackling. They seemed to have at least twenty forwards as wave upon wave bore down on us. It was a huge pack and once it was rolling forwards it was incredibly difficult to stop. Great players such as

Above: One that got away, Edwards diving through Hannaford and Neary, but the try disallowed. Below left: 'A large scotch for Mac and he'd like it in John Taylor's left boot.' Below right: Always an advocate of finger-tip passing, John Dawes shows what he means.

Despair on Fergus Slattery's face as he realises Barry John is not within his grasp after all.

Ken Gray, Colin Meads, Bruce McLeod, Brian Lochore and Ian Kirkpatrick were in their element. It was reflected in the scoring. There were four tries, one from winger Malcolm Dick and the rest by the forwards. Lochore scored one and the two front-row men, Gray and McLeod, scored the others. McCormick added two conversions and a penalty goal to complete the rout.

Keith Jarrett had had an off day with his goal-kicking, missing five attempts and some people tried to find an excuse there, but all the players on the field knew that there were none. The problem was how to combat the strength of the New Zealand forwards in the Second Test. As Clive Rowlands ruefully reflected afterwards, 'When we made mistakes we didn't lose six yards as we did at home, we lost eighty.'

The morning after, still counting our bruises, some of us went off to see an even more battered Young in hospital. His jaw had been wired up and someone asked him what had happened.

'Oh,' muttered Jeff through clenched teeth, 'it was my fault really. I'd been holding him down and he warned me that if I did it again he would thump me.'

'Did you say anything back?'

'Yes, I said bugger off! The trouble is I didn't say it very loudly.'

It was absolutely typical of Jeff. No matter what happened he could always see the funny side of the situation. He was a great morale lifter, particularly on tour.

The thrashing by New Zealand had been so comprehensive that the New Zealand critics began to tip Otago and Wellington, the opposition before the Second Test, to beat the Welsh team. They were the strongest of the New Zealand provinces at that time and Otago in particular had an impressive record against British touring teams. They had beaten the three previous Lions teams in 1966, 1959 and 1950 and from the moment we arrived in Dunedin we were bombarded with tales of the prowess of Otago rucking. Vic Cavanagh was God in that part of the world for the way he had coached this aspect of the game, and since the Second World War Otago sides were accepted as masters of the art. Whatever misgivings Wales might have had before the game, the team forgot them once the match got under way and, playing the sort of football that had made them European Champions, ran out convincing winners by 27–9. Another victory by 14–6 over Wellington increased the confidence in the Welsh camp and there appeared to be some hope for the Second Test in Auckland.

By this time, there was no question of jet lag or travel weariness. The team had had four matches to get acclimatised and there could be no excuses. Several changes were made after the First Test, some forced and some tactical. Stuart Watkins and Alan Skirving were both injured and so Gerald Davies was moved to the wing with John Dawes coming in at centre. At the time Gerald thought that it was strictly a temporary move, but having won eleven caps as a centre he was to go on to win another thirty-five on the wing.

In the forwards it was decided that we had to try to match the All Blacks for size. Thus Brian Thomas was moved up to prop, with Delme Thomas joining Brian Price in the second row. It was a selection that was difficult to understand because it had been tried without success against New Zealand in Wales in 1967. Prop is a totally different position to second row and requires a different build. Whilst a specialist prop can sometimes move back to second row to good effect if he is tall enough (as Denzil Williams often did for Ebbw Vale), a second-row player can rarely make a success of moving up to prop. In the back row I was injured and Dennis Hughes replaced me. It was his second cap, the first having been against New Zealand also in 1967. He had been playing extremely well and with his extra weight and height he could almost certainly have replaced either Dai Morris or myself in any case.

The game began well for Wales. After twenty-five minutes we were in the lead 6–3. The forwards were holding on gallantly, even though outplayed, but a great try from Maurice Richards and a penalty from Keith Jarrett gave us the lead. Richards' try was a typical effort. He had blistering acceleration and was very adept at stopping the opposition and then using his speed to go round them. He did just that. Receiving the ball on the left, he feinted to go inside to stop the cover which was tearing across to envelop him before he reached the corner, and then went away from it on an outside curving run that took him back to that same corner.

Unfortunately that was the high spot of the game for Wales. Their superiority began to tell and even our scrummaging began to fall apart. By the interval the All Blacks led 14–6 and worse was to come. They piled up 19 points in the second half and

Wales could only reply through a try and a penalty from Keith Jarrett and this time it was a 21-point difference between the teams, New Zealand winning 33–12.

For one man it was a very special day. Fergie McCormick the tough and very abrasive Canterbury full back kicked 24 points to create a new world record for international rugby.

Once again the Welsh team felt they had been treated harshly by the referee, Pat Murphy. His decisions were inconsistent and he constantly seemed to favour the All Blacks. By the end of the Second Test, all the Welsh players were convinced he was dishonest and a 'homer'. This feeling was so great that in 1971 when the Lions returned to New Zealand the management resisted all efforts by the New Zealand Rugby Football Union to have him appointed a referee for the Final Test.

Before New Zealand writers and players, Mr Reyburn and Mr McLean in particular, leap to their typewriters to cite this as another example of the Welsh being unable to accept defeat, let me put the record straight. Not one person on the tour believed that the referee cost Wales the Second Test match. New Zealand won because they were a vastly superior side and, contrary to the opinions expressed by the gentlemen named above, no member of the Welsh party made excuses. The team left New Zealand thoroughly humbled and very aware that the European Championship was strictly Division Two where world rugby was concerned.

Before the team left for Australia there was a day of relaxation that few of us will ever forget. It was organised by 'Snow' White who had propped for the All Blacks in the 'fifties. Earlier in the week, knowing from his own touring days the sort of thing that the players would like, he had borrowed an old sailing schooner and took us on a trip through the islands in Auckland Harbour. His sons had already sailed down to a remote little cove and had caught enough flounders to feed the whole party. These beautiful flat fish were cooked in butter on a tin plate over an open fire and there has never been a more delicious meal. It was washed down with beer and there were rock oysters to be prised from their stones for dessert.

Unfortunately the day almost ended in disaster. The schooner was too big to get close to the shore and the party had been ferried ashore in the dinghy. When it was time to return everyone was feeling playful and a few boulders were thrown to splash the occupants of the dinghy on the first trip back to the boat. To avoid getting wet Chico Hopkins over-reacted and tipped everyone in the drink. Naturally, those of us still on shore fell about laughing. However, our laughter turned to apprehension when the second load neared the schooner. Those who had been soaked, determined for revenge, dived back into the water and capsized the dinghy yet again. There was only one hope, to stick close to the Manager and make sure you were in the same load. Handel's pleadings that he was an old man and needed his official blazer to speak at a function that night only just worked. Fortunately, there were plenty of blankets on board but there were a few watches and cameras that never worked as well again.

On the last day there were no boat trips just a *hangi* at Snow's rugby club. The hospitality was magnificent with gallons of wine donated by one of the local vineyards we had visited to wash down the *hangi* – the Maori equivalent of a barbecue with the food cooked in sacks buried under red hot stones and left for several hours. Most of that Welsh team still have their footprints on the ceiling of the North Shore R.F.C. club house.

Next day it was off to Australia and a rainy Sydney. The team now had to lift itself after the humiliating defeats in New Zealand or the unthinkable could happen – with Australia winning as well. Having been continuously under the spotlight in New Zealand, it was a change to be training on a public park and to walk around unrecognised in Sydney. But the important thing was the match and Clive Rowlands had everyone training flat out. It had been raining all week and on the day of the match it bucketed down. We were to play on the Sydney Cricket Ground and to our amazement learned that, unlike at St Helens, the famous cricket square was smack in the middle of the rugby pitch. To make matters worse it already had water visible on the surface as it would not drain through the marl, or whatever preparation the groundsman used. Still it was our job to win the rugby match, not worry about the damage to the sacred turf. By the end of the match we had taken all the grass off the square, but such is their weather in the spring that we were assured that it would be in perfect condition for the start of the cricket season.

The selection committee had abandoned their policy of trying to make the pack bigger and the Triple Crown-winning pack was selected. But in the backs there was one change. The experiment of playing Gerald Davies on the wing had been one of the few successes of the Auckland Test and he was retained with John Dawes and Keith Jarrett in the centre.

The game began disastrously for Wales. After twenty-three minutes Australia were leading 11–0 with a try from the centre, Smith, and the conversion and two penalty goals from full back, McGill. Then Wales pulled themselves back into the game. Keith Jarrett kicked a penalty and then Gareth Edwards raced away from a scrum in typical fashion to find Dai Morris, 'Shadow' to his team mates, right on his shoulder to take the scoring pass. It was then that the experiment of playing Gerald Davies on the wing really paid off. He scored a beautiful try after being put away by an orthodox passing movement from a set piece, beating the remaining cover devastatingly with a side-step at full speed. Jarrett converted to bring the scores level and then kicked a huge penalty from fifty yards to put Wales into the lead for the first time. Then Gerald again, revelling in the extra space that playing on the wing allowed him, beat all but the final cover and put me in for a simple try. Jarrett again converted and it appeared that we had broken the back of the Australian resistance. It was not to be. Suddenly Australia were awarded a spate of penalties and had several attempts at goal. The kicks failed but the penalties did, however, give them a foothold in Welsh territory and, with the Welsh players feeling aggrieved at so many decisions going against them, eventually five minutes from the end Australia scored a try. It could have saved the match for them.

Mr Ferguson, the referee, was definitely a 'homer' in the eyes of the Welsh boys. He had given more penalties against Wales than Australia and when they were penalised the Aussies seemed to get them for technical offences in kickable positions, especially once Wales had taken the lead. He finally became an out and out villain to us when he awarded McGill a try after the Wallaby full back seemed to all of us to have been tackled well short of the line by Maurice Richards and then wriggled over. Ferguson ruled that his momentum had taken him across the line and Maurice Richards was so upset he looked as if he would tear the referee apart. Fortunately he only remonstrated with him, but so vehement was his protest that Mr Ferguson awarded a penalty on half way to Australia to restart the game instead of the normal kick-off. McGill had converted his own try from the touchline but fortunately Skinner could not kick the penalty from the centre spot. It could have been a try worth 8 points but Wales hung on to win 19–16.

In Britain there is never a referee from the host country but everywhere else it is the norm. The Welsh party left New Zealand and Australia branded as whingers by the natives, but firm in their belief that the sooner neutral referees were introduced the better it would be for the game. Even if a referee doesn't cheat it is ridiculous to put him in a situation where he can be accused of doing so.

If Australia and New Zealand had been hard work it was all made worthwhile by the final week of the tour in Fiji. It may not be paradise but most of the 1969 team would have settled for it. As soon as we arrived the Fijians welcomed us with such enthusiasm that we knew our stay would be something special. We had the smartest coach on the island put at our disposal and the children would chase after it whenever it passed their homes or schools. The hotel was magnificent. Called the Esa Lai, which means Welcome, it was built in the shape of a giant sea turtle for which Fiji is famous. Even the swimming pool followed the design. The team were awarded the great honour of a royal welcome on the royal island of Bau and our enchantment began as we left Suva to be ferried over in dug-out canoes. Unfortunately it poured with rain and our uniforms were soaked, so upon arrival there was no choice but to change into *suluvakatangas*, the brightly patterned skirts that the natives wind so expertly around themselves. We wound them so inexpertly around ourselves that we lived in constant danger of them falling off.

The welcome ceremony involves drinking *carva* which is prepared from roots to a special formula by the elders of the village. It looks and tastes like muddy water, but fortunately only Handel Rogers, as manager, Brian Price, as captain, and Ivor Jones, the President of the W.R.U. who had accompanied us on the tour, were required to drink at the official ceremony. After the ceremonious concocting the honoured guest must drink down a bowlful of the liquid in one go and this is accompanied by various chants from the elders. Ivor Jones was the first to go and made a right mess of his clothes, face and arms as he struggled to get the bowlful down. He never quite succeeded and as he took the bowl from his face, still spluttering a little, the elders gave what appeared to be a deep rumble of disapproval. We thought that was the end of diplomatic relations between Wales and Fiji but the same concerted exaggerated sigh was also uttered when Brian Price and Handel Rogers downed their full quota successfully. We learned later it signified approval and not the opposite but for a moment, particularly as all the locals were in full and frightening costume, most of us were ready to make a run for the boats.

For the rest of the week it was back to preparing for the game. Enthusiasm for the local team was running high and they obviously fancied their chances on their own ground and in front of a partisan crowd. We soon learned to practise in the mornings before the daily downpour. On the first day we had left it until the afternoon and found that we had to share the field with thousands of large toads out to enjoy the wet grass. Nobody was anxious to fall over and hear that sickening squelch that meant a dead toad, but Keith Jarrett won the award for being the most squeamish. The toads improved his side-step no end, but it was difficult to avoid opponents when he had his eyes glued firmly on the ground five yards ahead. He refused to train again after a shower and I believe his revulsion for the toads would have even persuaded him to accept any punishment from the management, but the situation did not arise.

The other great experience in Fiji was a visit to the Indian market. There you can buy everything from a giant hi-fi set to local carvings and the name of the game is bartering. We all set off on a bus one day and spent a couple of hours negotiating with the stallholders for presents to take home. Everyone enjoyed himself and was totally happy that he'd beaten the trader down to his rock bottom price. Trouble began when we returned to the bus and Denzil noted that Brian Price had purchased some carvings and baskets that were the same as his.

Denzil: 'How much did you pay for those swords, Bri?'

Brian, determined that he was not going to be shown up as less expert in the art of barter than his old team mate and therefore lying through his teeth: 'One dollar fifty. [About half of what he'd actually paid.] Why?'

Denzil: 'Oh, you were done. I got mine for a dollar.'

By the end of the journey the whole coachload was lying, with everyone suddenly not so happy with their purchase. In fact we had all been conned. By the end of the week when the American luxury liner had left after its five-day stopover the prices began at the level we had managed to get the merchants to accept after fifteen minutes of skilled bargaining.

Buckhurst Park, Suva, is one of the most delightful grounds in the world. The grandstand is tiny and even the temporary seats erected for the game did not add to the capacity greatly, but it seemed as if every islander tried to get in. If they could not find room they saved themselves the cost of a ticket and climbed the palm trees outside the grounds to get a bird's eye view. Nobody was going to miss the great event especially as Freddie 'Needle' Allen the great New Zealand coach had been over to knock the forwards into shape and improve their rucking. He never really succeeded. The Fijians have a great talent for the game but their forwards do not like the tight pieces. Thank goodness, because if they could win ball as well as they run with it they really would be world beaters. In this match they kept their discipline for much of the game but, despite having humidity and temperature in the eighties on their side, eventually succumbed to the Welsh forward pressure. This set the backs free and Wales scored 18 points in the last twenty minutes to run out winners by 31–11.

The stars of the game from the Welsh point of view were Maurice Richards and Dennis Hughes. Richards, in his last appearance in a Welsh jersey, again had one of his unstoppable days, scoring one try after scorching up the left wing and then, at the end of two similar runs, handing inside to give me two of the easiest tries I can remember. Nobody ever discovered what an organisation and methods assistant (that was given as his occupation in the programme) actually did but the Tonypandy flyer had few equals on his day.

Dennis Hughes began the match at No. 8 with Mervyn Davies in the second row but after one half of torture 'Swerve' pulled rank and threatened to leave the field unless he could revert to his rightful place. Dennis readily acquiesced. It had been touch and go whether the lanky No. 8 would take the field at all. With his black curly hair and slim build he looked vaguely Fijian when he arrived on the islands. After a few days of sun the local people claimed him as a long lost brother and wanted him to play for them.

The Newbridge man still thought he had won the last laugh. Having taken his place in the second row he scored three tries, one from a scorching forty-yard run down the middle of the park, but his smiles turned to bewilderment when Mervyn declared it unethical for a No. 8 to score so many tries and Brian Thomas and Brian Price, the two specialist second rows, who were resting, promptly disowned him. Dennis had had a tremendous tour and even though he knew he was destined to play second fiddle to Mervyn Davies made the most of every opportunity he had to wear the red jersey.

Next day a chastened Welsh team returned home. If any other Welshman used the excuse that the New Zealand itinerary was madness and therefore the international results meant nothing not one of the actual party believed it. We all knew that we had been thoroughly put in our place. The tour might not have gone well in New Zealand, and the major aim had definitely been to defeat the All Blacks, but a number of players who were to form the core of the British Lions Test Team in 1971 had gained valuable experience and knew exactly what to expect the next time round.

4

CHICO HOPKINS' FINEST HOUR
1970

The 1970 international season began amid unparalleled scenes in rugby history. South Africa was making a major tour of the British Isles for the first time since the 1960/61 season. They were met by a highly organised campaign protesting that they should not be allowed to tour Britain because the policy of apartheid in South Africa meant that they represented the white minority in that country and were party to the suppression of the millions of blacks and coloureds relegated to second class citizenship. The demonstrators would stop at nothing in their determination to prevent the tour taking place and threatened to put tin tacks on pitches and halt matches by invading the field whenever possible. The result was a massive police presence at every game and some very ugly scenes. Those at Swansea for the game against West Wales were some of the worst when a vigilante force of 'stewards' was formed to ensure that the game was not disturbed. Their declared passive role became aggressive at the first opportunity and the demonstrators came off very second best as they were bundled unceremoniously from the ground and its surrounds.

The constant harassment also had its effect on the tourists. Although they had the hard core of the team that defeated the 1968 British Lions so comprehensively less than two years before, they returned home with the worst record for any Springbok side on a full tour of the British Isles. They had lost the matches against Scotland and England and drawn the match with Ireland before meeting Wales in the final international of the tour. In addition to this, they lost three other matches. Defeat in the opening match of the tour by Oxford University was explained away because it was the second team and the beginning of the tour. There could be no such excuses at Newport. They fielded what was virtually a test team and were well beaten 11–6 with Newport scoring two tries to nil.

South Africa started badly in their first match against Welsh opposition. Their forwards improved as the game went on and at the end they began to gain control of the set pieces but the backs were never a match for the Newport three-quarters. Billy Raybould had a tremendous game and cut big holes in the Springboks' defence throughout the game. At half time Newport led 3–0 from an Alan Skirving try and increased that lead to 8–0 when David Cornwall went over and John Anthony converted. Visagie pulled back one penalty and finished the scoring with another after Anthony had kicked a penalty to keep Newport safely ahead.

At Ebbw Vale the Gwent team, from all the Monmouthshire clubs except Newport, made it a double for the East Waleans. Games are usually won comfortably if one team is completely on top in the forwards, but Gwent won in spite of seeing very little of the ball. South Africa won six strikes against the head, which was an indication of their superiority, but their backs frittered away all the good ball they received. Visagie put the Springboks into the lead with a penalty goal but then Robin Williams, just nine-teen years old and a student at Cardiff College of Education, banged over two kicks to put Gwent in front. A Jennings try converted by Visagie gave the Springboks back their advantage at half time but Gwent managed the only scores of the second half to win the match. Robin Williams kicked a third penalty before Roger Beese, the Cross Keys winger, put them out of reach with a try which Robin Williams converted to make it 14–8.

When the Springboks came to play the last international match of their tour Cardiff Arms Park looked more like a prison camp than a rugby ground, with barbed wire strung above the walls and railings and a huge police presence. The touchlines were patrolled by sufficient numbers to form a cordon if necessary and there were patrols outside the ground with mounted police hovering in the background as reinforcements. In the event it all passed off quietly, probably because both demonstrators and those determined the match should go ahead were chastened by the events at Swansea.

It must be said that most of the rugby public and the players wanted the tour to go ahead. However, I found myself unable to come to terms with playing against the Springboks after my experiences in South Africa on the 1968 Lions tour and asked the selectors not to consider me for the game. Dennis Hughes replaced me, but that was not the only change in the Welsh team from the previous season. The side was almost unrecognisable from the team that played even in Australasia, especially in the back division. Not only Maurice Richards but also Keith Jarrett had turned professional and Gerald Davies had decided to make himself unavailable for international rugby because of his studies at Cambridge and the difficulty in attending practice sessions in Wales on Sundays from East Anglia. Thus three of the four regular three-quarters had to be replaced and there were no obvious contenders pushing themselves forward.

In the forwards the Australasian trip had seen the end of Brian Price and Brian Thomas. They had been great servants for Wales winning thirty-two and twenty-one caps respectively but there had been signs in New Zealand that they were no longer the force they had been. Brian Price retired from all rugby immediately and although Brian Thomas continued to put the fear of God into opponents as the anchor man for the Neath pack, he was never again considered for international honours. Jeff Young was also still unavailable because of his broken jaw.

Neither of the wings selected were specialists. Phil Bennett, who had won his first cap as a substitute, was chosen for the left wing and Ian Hall, the Aberavon centre who had won one cap against the All Blacks in 1967, was picked on the right. Billy Raybould, who had won seven caps in 1967 and 1968 was brought back to partner John Dawes in the centre. Vic Perrins, the Newport hooker, won his first cap and Barry Llewelyn displaced John Lloyd at tight-head prop. He had had a good tour of Australasia and as a big and very mobile player had forced his way in on merit. In the second row Geoff Evans from London Welsh joined Delme Thomas.

The game was a disappointment. Wales, despite their glorious achievements against other countries, had always lost to the Springboks and with the poor record of the tourists must have hoped to remedy the situation. Instead they were very nearly beaten and only a try by Gareth Edwards in the final seconds allowed Wales to draw the match 6–6. It was a typical Edwards try after a determined powerful burst for the line from a feed by Barry Llewelyn, Wales having won a ruck in the South African 25. Once again the scrum half's strength amazed everybody. The game had been played in appalling conditions. It had not stopped raining throughout and the mud was thick and slippery, yet he still found enough energy left to drive himself over in that vital last effort. He had been given the job of captaincy back again, having first taken it on against France in 1968 and it was typical of his approach when captaining the side. In desperate situations he would consider it his duty to pull the game out of the fire.

South Africa had led 6–3 from early in the second half when their left wing, Nomis, had scored a try in the corner. Edwards scored all the Welsh points because it was he who kicked a penalty in the first half to equal the one kicked by H. O. de Villiers for South Africa. The loss of Keith Jarrett caused a place-kicking problem that was to hamper Wales all season, although several unlikely kickers did well just when they needed to.

The experiment of playing Phil Bennett and Ian Hall out of position had not really worked and the reshuffled pack had shown a worrying lack of power, so nobody was surprised when the selectors made changes for the match against Scotland just two weeks later. To their credit they left the pack alone except for switching Denzil Williams and Barry Llewelyn to opposite sides of the scrum, but they began a bewildering series of changes in the back division that gave nobody a chance to settle down and work themselves into the team. For this match Laurie Daniel of Newport, a hard running wing who favoured going through people instead of around them, replaced Phil Bennett on the wing and he moved inside to centre, replacing Billy Raybould. Phil was an outside half but, such was his talent, the selectors believed they had to find room for him somewhere in the side. It was partly a reflection of their lack of understanding of the differences between the positions and partly a desperation measure because of the lack of centres around.

Scotland had a strong wind in their favour in the first half and it was obvious that they would need to turn round with a substantial lead to keep Wales at bay when it was our turn to make the use of it. They began promisingly and opened up a 9-point lead, all the points being scored by Ian Robertson. He started with a dropped goal from a scrum in front of the Welsh posts and then scored a try which he converted himself after John Williams had failed to find touch with a clearing kick. That lead lasted until almost half time but the Welsh forwards had been winning some useful ball and eventually the backs worked Laurie Daniel clear on the left and he squeezed in for a try in the corner. As a bonus kicking across the wind he converted his own try. To Jim Telfer, the Scottish captain, this was the decisive score. He felt that Scotland would have won had they turned around 9–0 in the lead, but four points was not enough of a buffer, especially as the Scots went into the interval a little deflated having given the score away so late in the first half.

In the second half Wales soon scored a second try when Barry Llewelyn charged over from a ruck. He had threatened on a couple of occasions in the first half from line out peels and on this occasion there was no stopping him. Daniel was left with an easy conversion from in front of the posts but nearly decapitated himself when he topped his kick and it rebounded from the bar. The Welsh forwards were now really putting the presssure on Scotland and some of the ball being fed back to the half backs was possession they could have done without. From such a pass Ian Robertson had his kick charged down and John Dawes dived on it over the line to give Wales the lead. Gareth Edwards took over the goal-kicking duties himself and added the conversion points.

Finally, when Welsh pressure had forced the Scots to minor the ball, Dai Morris was able to break from the back of the five yard scrum and dive over to set a seal on the victory. Gareth Edwards again converted.

Wales had won, but once again the Welsh backs' performance had been less than totally satisfactory and the selectors went back to the drawing board before selecting the team to play against England. The only man playing out of position who had come off at all well was Ian Hall. The Aberavon centre did not really have the pace for a wing but his defence was excellent and his appetite for work at least double that of a normal wing. Without looking a match winner, he had played steadily and effectively. John Dawes, too, having been in and out of the side since 1964, was beginning to establish himself as an essential part of the team. His support play, speed of thought and, above all, speed of pass were at last being appreciated and people became aware of the space he created for others rather than looking for devastating breaks which the uninitiated thought were still the prerequisite for a centre.

Instead of experimenting further, Stuart Watkins and Billy Raybould were recalled to replace Laurie Daniels and Phil Bennett. Daniel must have felt it a gross injustice, he had scored a try and kicked a fine conversion but was still discarded. Jeff Young was also restored to the pack, having fully recovered from the broken jaw he sustained in New Zealand.

England had not beaten Wales since 1963 and with the home ground advantage, and thus buffered to some extent against the singing of the Welsh supporters, they had high hopes of victory. These must have been even higher when twenty minutes from the end of the game, they were leading 13–6 and Gareth Edwards limped off injured. The man who had pulled the game out of the fire against South Africa had gone and they felt they really should be safe. Instead Gareth's retirement proved England's undoing.

He had not been playing at his best and those who knew him well were beginning to realise that the additional responsibility of captaincy did not suit his temperament. In attempting to stand apart from the game to evaluate what was going on he was thinking too much and robbing himself of his greatest asset, his intuition as to when to pass and when to go himself. He almost became hesitant which is the last fault that one would normally associate with Gareth Edwards.

When he went off he was replaced by Chico Hopkins from Maesteg, who had been busting his gut to get on the field for the previous two seasons and played as if he knew it might be his only appearance in the red jersey of Wales. Where Gareth had been hesitant, he was all bustle and thrust and undoubtedly won the game for Wales. We had gradually pulled ourselves back into the match, were beginning to dominate the game up front and for the first time looked like scoring a try. Then, we won a scrum ten yards from the English line and Chico darted away to the blind side and timed his pass perfectly to J. P. R. Williams who burst through Bob Hiller's attempted tackle on the line, to score. J.P.R. became only the third full back to score for Wales, following in the footsteps of Viv Jenkins right back in 1934 and Keith Jarrett in 1967 on his debut. The number of tries scored by full backs in international rugby since 1970 shows just how much effect the Australian dispensation law has had on the game.

Chico was not yet finished. Wales still trailed England by 4 points and a converted try was needed to take the lead. The Welsh forwards again drove to the English line, where the defending side was awarded the line out. Inexplicably, they threw to the back, a ploy which is normally considered an attacking rather than a defensive move, and as the ball bobbed back tantalisingly on the Welsh side the little Maesteg scrum half collected it and dived through to score in one movement. It was to be his only twenty minutes of international rugby for Wales but Maesteg knew they had the hero of the game.

However, Wales were still one point behind and with Gareth Edwards, who had been taking the place kicks, off the field, John Williams was called up to take the conversion. Although it was not a difficult shot it was not that easy and the one flaw in J.P.R.'s armoury was his place-kicking. Although he could occasionally kick magnificent goals, he was very inconsistent, but such was his competitiveness that there was no way he was going to be responsible for a Welsh defeat and the ball sailed straight and true between the posts. In the closing minutes Barry John dropped a beautiful goal to set the seal on the victory and J.P.R., who takes himself too seriously at times, was very upset that evening when the rest of the team kidded him his conversion was unimportant because Barry would have clinched the game regardless.

Every Welshman breathed a huge sigh of relief when it went over. It was already becoming unthinkable that Wales should lose to England.

The game was full of incident. Before Gareth went off the referee had been forced to retire hurt. Just before half time Monsieur Calmet, a diminutive figure, unwisely put himself in the firing line between the two packs and the ball. He was unceremoniously bundled out of the way and emerged with a broken left leg and dislocated shoulder. 'Johnny' Johnson, the very experienced international referee who was acting as the English touch judge that day, took over.

Earlier it had looked as if an England new cap would be the hero of the day. John Novak on the right wing had been brought into the side as a last minute replacement for Keith Fielding and he grabbed his opportunity with both hands, scoring England's first try and making the second. There was some controversy about his score because the move began with Roger Shackleton, the England outside half, juggling with the ball. The law had just been changed to allow an adjustment and, while the Welsh supporters thought he had done more than merely adjust, the referee ruled that his 'fumble' was within the law. Suffice to say he did not award a scrum and the ball reached Novak who had

Denzil and Delme make an impregnable wall while Dai feeds Gareth with perfect possession.

Hymns on the bus ride through Paris to Stade Colombes.

Preparing for the game is a serious business: a long hard look at the pitch before the last game at Stade Colombes. Below: the indefatigable Gerry Lewis in the changing room, Clive Rowlands creeping away and Barry John telling Arthur Lewis it will take more than speed oil to help him.

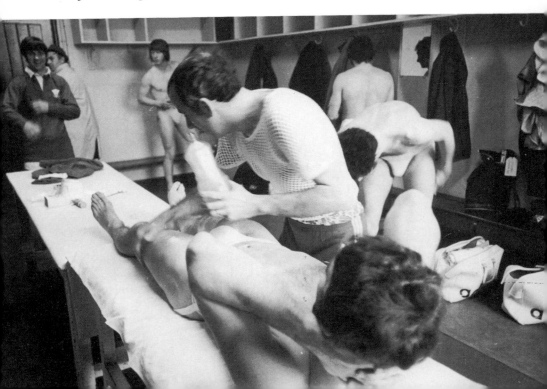

been put outside his opposite number and scored. Hiller, on his home ground, converted beautifully from the touchline.

The second English try was scored by David Duckham, put clear by a superb pass from the English captain, Bob Taylor, but Novak had created the situation. Shackleton had hoisted a kick which John Williams covered with his normal efficiency. As he caught it he was tackled by Novak, who was built more like a No. 8 than a wing three-quarter, and he was hit so hard that the ball spilled forward and England were able to launch the attack that led to the score. It was a rare occurrence for the Welsh full back to come off worst in a tackle but on this occasion he was well and truly flattened. Hiller again added the conversion points. He had also landed a penalty to give England their 13-point total.

With victories over Scotland and England safely, if not totally convincingly, in the bag, Wales now travelled to Ireland with the chance of winning the Triple Crown in successive years and, with France to be played at Cardiff, perhaps even a Grand Slam.

The selectors were still not entirely happy and this time it was Ian Hall who was replaced, not as one might think by a specialist winger, but by Keith Hughes, a medical student who had impressed with his elusive running for Cambridge University and, after the end of the Christmas tour, London Welsh. When at home in Llanelli, instead of playing for the Scarlets, he played for New Dock Stars and they proudly claim him as having been capped from their club.

Gareth Edwards and Barry John set a new record with sixteen appearances together at half back for Wales in this match, but it was Tom Kiernan, the Irish captain, himself setting a new record of forty-seven caps for his country, who had reason to celebrate. Ireland hammered Wales 14–0. It was Wales's heaviest defeat since 1951. There had been fears that there would be some attempt at retribution for the brawling that had taken place the year before but, sensibly, the players decided to forget that ill-tempered match and there was no violence. For a long time it was a very even game with Wales creating most of the scoring chances but elementary handling mistakes or poor kicking prevented them from building a lead. Barry John was one of the chief culprits and had what was probably his least memorable game for Wales, but he was certainly not the only player at fault.

The score remained 0–0 until fifteen minutes into the second half. Then Ireland were awarded the put-in at a scrum in front of the Welsh posts and Roger Young fed Barry McGann who dropped a goal. Soon after Wales were attacking and Barry John made a half break, only to pass behind his own three-quarters. There was no cover because John Williams had joined the line in the expectation of creating an overlap. Alan Duggan the Irish wing raced in to pick up the ball and sprint from half way to the line without a Welsh player getting near to him. With fourteen minutes to go Kiernan made the game safe with a penalty goal and three minutes later another Welsh mistake allowed Ken Goodall to rub salt in the wound. Once again Wales were attacking but an ill-directed chip ahead dropped straight into the arms of Goodall who was covering behind his backs. From well inside his own half he set off for the Welsh line. He ran, kicked ahead, and regathered before diving triumphantly over, and if the ball had not bounced favourably for him, Alan Duggan was the nearest player, so Ireland would still have scored. Kiernan converted to complete the rout and it was a humiliating defeat for the whole of Wales.

So yet again the selectors wielded their axe in an attempt to win, or at least gain a half share of the Championship with France, who had defeated Scotland and Ireland and still had England to meet in Paris. In the 1970 season the selectors came closest to abandoning their 'If he's good enough on a Friday night, he's good enough on a Sunday morning' philosophy. Clive Rowlands had by now replaced Vernon Parfitt on the Big Five and, as he was coach, one might have expected to see a drive towards consistency in selection, but it was not to be.

Three of the four three-quarters were changed, leaving John Dawes the only player to survive the season. They even allowed him to play in the same position. The three changes in selection were all winning their first caps. The two new wings were Jim Shanklin and Roy Mathias. Jim had arrived at London Welsh from Tenby and no doubt the folks from West Wales were delighted as there are not too many players honoured from there, while Roy Mathias had started life as a wing forward at Llanelli. Stuart Watkins had originally been selected, but had to withdraw because of injury. This was to prove the end of 'Paddy' Watkins' career. It had been a distinguished one for the big, long-striding wing, spanning the years from 1964 to 1970, during which time he scored nine tries for his country and won twenty-six caps. His critics have suggested he was not creative, and compared with Maurice Richards or Gerald Davies when he moved from centre to wing, he may not have been, but he was reliable and effective, especially on the short side or when he was given the ball directly from the line out in the set move that he and his club colleague, Brian Price, perfected, and he had proved himself a tremendous finisher.

The other new cap was Arthur Lewis from Ebbw Vale. It was significant that in the programme for the match he was the only player not to have his birth date printed in his pen picture. He claimed he was twenty-six, but few believed it. Nevertheless he had carved out a reputation for being a very hard tackler and specialised in taking crash balls and kicks ahead to set up the maul or ruck for his forwards. It was certainly a strong and steady three-quarter line, but as John Dawes said, 'We have to be the slowest back division ever picked for Wales.' This was particularly significant against France who had Jacques Cantoni and Jean-Marie Bonal on the wings with Jean-Pierre Lux in the centre. All three were specialist sprinters as well as rugby players, Bonal having recorded 10.6 for the 100 metres.

There were also changes in the forwards. John Lloyd returned for the injured Denzil Williams and Stuart Gallacher, born in Llanelli of Scottish parents so known to all and sundry as Jock, won his first cap to replace Geoff Evans. I was recalled as well. I was obviously delighted, not least since many people believed the Welsh selectors would never pick me again because I had made myself unavailable for selection. I must confess to fearing at times they could be right, but most of the time I felt sure that the W.R.U. would not penalise me for the decision that I believed, and still believe, was the correct one.

The evening that the team was announced Geoff Evans and I were driving to Wales from London. London Welsh were playing in Wales on the Saturday and Geoff's village, Pembrey, had arranged a presentation to him to celebrate his being selected that season for the national team. We had no radio and arrived at the Commercial, the inn that his mother and aunt, both tee-totallers, had kept for years, just in time for the presentation but after the announcement of the team had been broadcast. As we walked in big Dai Evans, Geoff's father, said very quickly and very loudly, 'Well done, John! Bad luck, Geoff.'

The room went silent but to Geoff's eternal credit it took him only a second to come back. Echoing the words that Max Boyce had not even written he said, 'At least I can say I was there. Two pints of Felinfoel, please.'

Forever afterwards he blamed being dropped on Keith Hughes' throwing in in the Irish match. Every time the pair of them have a few drinks together you can guarantee the subject will come up. Suffice to say that Keith Hughes never ever threw in for Wales or any other team again.

There was a further change on the eve of the match when Barry John had to withdraw and was replaced by Phil Bennett. In his fourth game for Wales he was at last picked in his proper position. John Dawes took over the captaincy from Gareth Edwards and not only was there a marked change in tactics but the young scrum half, still only twenty-two although he was winning his nineteenth cap, appeared relieved at being allowed to concentrate solely on his own game, instead of trying to dictate how the game should be played.

After the drawn game the previous year everyone expected a really thrilling contest, but on the day the match was something of a damp squib. France outscored Wales by two tries to one, but converted neither, so that John Williams's two penalty goals cancelled them out. The decisive Welsh try came almost immediately after half time when Paries, the French fly half, tried a speculative pass to Villepreux as the Welsh forwards steamed through on him. It never had a chance of reaching the full back and the new cap, Stuart Gallacher, could not have received a better pass had it come from one of his own players. He was already deep inside the French 25 and would probably have made the line himself, but responded to the shout of Dai Morris who touched down under the posts at a canter. John Williams had no problem with the conversion.

It had been a strange season. France had come into the final match unbeaten and having trounced England and Ireland in Paris. Wales, on the other hand, had only looked impressive against Scotland in the first match of the Championship. Many people expected a French Grand Slam but, far from playing like would-be champions, they had been diffident behind and weak up front. Against the odds Wales had won a share of the Championship, while never having looked totally convincing.

5

SLAM BY A WHISKER
1971

In a decade of success there are nevertheless some years that stand out above the others. The first of these in the Decade of the Dragon was 1971. At last all the pieces fitted into place and after promising much, only to disappoint their vast army of supporters, the Welsh team not only won the Grand Slam, but then provided the core of the Lions party that went to New Zealand and became the first British team this century to win a Test series abroad.

It was a truly amazing year to be a part of, not just because of the results, but because they were achieved in the grand manner with some of the most enjoyable rugby any of us had ever played. After years of apprenticeship the majority of the Welsh team were now hardened internationals, used to the special pressures of playing for their country and totally at home in the very different atmosphere of a national stadium packed with fervent supporters. In no other sport (except perhaps for the annual ladies' hockey international at Wembley) can there be a bigger difference between the week to week crowds you play before at club level and the 50,000 plus packed house at all internationals.

1970 had been a strange year (without referring back it would be a very keen student of Welsh rugby who could name the back divisions for the five internationals) but in 1971 the national team reverted to the shape most people expected. The main problem had been lack of pace in the three-quarters but now, fortunately, the selectors were able to call upon Gerald Davies once again. In 1971 he was in his last year at Cambridge and, apart from minor hurdles like his final examinations, he was anxious to return to duty for his country. His pace and sleight of foot made him an automatic choice, now on the wing rather than at centre.

Wales had not had a natural left wing since Maurice Richards had turned professional, but 1971 saw the emergence of John

Bevan. He was still only twenty and at the time was a second-year student at Cardiff College of Education. It was rumoured that he was the only man to beat Gareth Edwards in their various tests of strength relative to body weight and he used every ounce of his power on the rugby field. In addition, he was very fast which was the only reason he had been allowed to continue to play on the wing. Wanting to see all this power used more frequently, the National Under 15 Schoolboy selectors had made him play at No. 8. They tried again at Under 19 level, but John was committed to playing on the wing and refused to move. The selectors gave in and he won five caps at that level.

Barry John returned, having missed the last match of 1970 through injury, and Denzil Williams fought his way back after missing the last two games of the previous season. That in itself was a remarkable achievement. Having already won thirty-one caps and having had nagging injury problems, many people thought he would be content to rest on his laurels.

The only other newcomer to the side was Mike Roberts. 'Robbo' as he was known to everyone, hails from Colwyn Bay, and joined the small, elite band of players to be capped from what is generally considered a non-rugby-playing area (although I am certain North Waleans will protest that it is merely that they are under-represented). He had arrived in London via Trinity College, Dublin and Oxford University and at 6' 4½" and 16 st 12 lbs appeared ideally suited to take over the iron man of the pack role which had not been filled satisfactorily since the end of Brian Thomas's international career. The Welsh pack was now a very powerful unit with both props and both second rows over sixteen stone and only the two flankers, myself and Dai Morris, under fourteen stone.

The first match of the 1971 Home International Championship was against England. They had not won against Wales since 1963 and, although that victory had been achieved in Cardiff we were very confident of continuing our run of success, particularly as most of us could only remember the last two matches at the National Stadium as players and in both of those we had scored 30 points. Even the weather, it was one of those wet and cold January days, could not dampen our spirits. There was almost a feeling that we could not be beaten and we went out and played with the sort of confidence that can only come from believing totally in one another. The game began with a superb drop goal from Barry John. Delme Thomas won the ball from a line out, Gareth Edwards fed Barry and from thirty yards and well out towards the touch line, he stroked the ball immaculately between the posts.

England then attacked and won a line out just a couple of yards from the Welsh line. They threw long and I committed the cardinal sin of tapping the ball back in a defensive position. In fact I was being far too clever, as I hoped to knock it inwards for Mervyn Davies to clear up but it eluded him and Charlie Hannaford, the England No. 8, dived in for a soft try. At that stage of the game it could have been a crucial mistake but Merv just shrugged his shoulders, I shrugged mine back and the team accepted that the idea had gone wrong without recriminations. From that moment, we never looked back.

From the next Welsh attack, we scored our first try. It came from a perfectly executed back movement. Arthur Lewis had been brought into the side as a specialist on crash ball moves and one particular set piece was code-named 'Arthur'. This involved Barry John running flat across the field and feeding Arthur coming back towards the forwards or straight at the posts. In this case he did not make it through the English centre but set up the perfect maul. Wales won the ball cleanly, Barry John stopped the opposition by threatening to drop at goal again, and J. P. R. Williams joined the line. By the time the ball reached Gerald Davies on the right he had a clear run to the corner and admitted afterwards that he was looking for someone to beat. I was given the kick for the first time for Wales and slotted it.

The kicking arrangements at the beginning of the 1971 season were so complicated they are worthy of mention. Since Keith Jarrett's 'defection' it had been a weakness in the Welsh team. John Williams had had most success during 1970, but in the meantime I had started to kick for London Welsh and Barry John had begun to kick for Cardiff. We were both round-the-corner kickers and therefore tended to hook the ball a little. This meant that as a left-footed kicker, I had an advantage from the right as the draw on the ball would have the effect of straightening the angle and Barry, as a right-footed kicker, would achieve the same effect from the left. Thus we evolved a plan whereby Barry John kicked from the left of the posts, I kicked from the right, and J.P.R. took the long, straight ones with his toe punt style. It was very complicated and if there was a try scored under the posts you would see us all converging, but somehow Barry always seemed to win.

John Bevan was the next to score. He had already shown his strength with a couple of surging runs in unpromising situations and when Barry John gave him a clear run in he needed no urging to pin back his ears and join the surprisingly large band of men (seventy-six before him) who have scored a try on their debut for Wales. The try had started with an English tapped penalty. They worked the ball to John Spencer, but it reached him so slowly that he was tackled and the ball went loose to be snapped up by 'the King', as Barry was beginning to be known for his imperious approach to the game.

Before half an hour had passed the score was 16–3 to Wales. We won a scrum on the half way line and Gareth Edwards hoisted a monstrous up and under. Arthur Lewis again acted as the destroyer, this time hitting Rossborough just as he took the ball. One could not help but feel sorry for the England full back. The kick was so high that he had to wait underneath it for what seemed an age and then Arthur tackled him so hard that the ball was forced from his grasp. Arthur himself regained his feet and fed John Dawes who quickly switched it to Gerald Davies who again outstripped the opposition. I again converted.

Just before half time England's last chance of getting back into the match disappeared when they worked an overlap on the right wing only for Janion to drop Wright's pass.

Amazingly, the second half did not produce the flow of points that might have been expected. Mervyn Davies was playing the game of his life and dominated the back of the line out completely. Denzil Williams and Mike Roberts were dominating the tight loose, seemingly ripping the ball out of the mauls at will, and behind the scrum Barry John was carving great holes through the English ranks with his running, or testing them with probing, attacking kicks to the open spaces. But the tries would not come.

John Williams landed a straight penalty from forty yards and Rossborough replied from twenty-five yards. Then just before the end Barry John dropped another goal, but the nearest Wales came to a try was when John Bevan was finally tackled just short of the line after a ninety-yard run. It was a credit to the English defence, especially as their pack looked desperately weary in the closing stages, but it was disappointing for Wales. Having destroyed them in the first half we should have at least doubled our total in the second.

The second game of the 1971 campaign was against Scotland at Murrayfield. The selectors kept faith with the team that had beaten England but on the Thursday before the game, after the practice in Cardiff, Arthur Lewis had to withdraw with hamstring trouble and was replaced by Ian Hall. This highlighted one of the areas where the W.R.U. organisation fell down. Each player was entitled to a small allocation of tickets and naturally Arthur had made arrangements to give these to friends and relatives who wanted to see the match. As these were always handed out after the Thursday practice they were now given to Ian Hall. Worse to follow. The arrangements for travelling and accommodation in Edinburgh were so inflexible that Arthur had to pack his bags and return home to the valleys instead of taking a plane to Scotland. It was the sort of incident, there have been several others over the years, that made the players feel like poor relations in the Rugby Union infrastructure, even though they were the centrepiece of the occasion. Put this sort of occurrence alongside the thoughtlessness of not providing an hotel room for a player, let alone his wife, after home matches – a player was expected to attend the after-match banquet and dance and then return home if he actually lived in Wales – and some of the bitterness of the team towards officials can be understood. Fortunately, as players and selectors have grown closer together since the formation of the squad system, this situation has changed.

Nevertheless the team were in high spirits when they arrived in Scotland. The dominance of the pack against England had been so convincing that a repeat performance was expected. The mix in the back division also seemed right. With Gareth Edwards and Barry John now at their peak as attacking players and Gerald Davies and John Bevan equally dangerous, albeit in very different styles on the wings, it made sense to have steady centres who were solid in defence and very skilled at moving the ball quickly to create space for the wings to run. John Dawes in particular had become so adept at this that the ball moved so quickly it verged on sleight of hand. John Williams, too, was probably at his most devastating when coming into the line at this time. He had perfected his timing and his point of entry and the other teams had not yet learned how to counter the threat. After 1971 his incursions into the line to create the extra man became marginally less effective, although by no means worthless, simply because he had created so much havoc that the opposition practised stopping him as one of their top priorities.

On the day of the match there appeared to be even more Welshmen than usual on Princes Street and, on reaching the ground even more people on the great Murrayfield bank. The game turned out to be an epic with the lead changing hands six times. Even if it was not the greatest game I ever played in, it was certainly the most incident-packed one.

The game began conventionally enough with each side feeling out the other. John Bevan might have had a try after Smith, the Scottish full back, dropped the ball, but he hacked on too far and the ball went dead. Wales were on the attack again just before Scotland scored the first points. Barry John was trying to make room for a drop goal attempt but Frank Laidlaw, who had a memorable game for Scotland that day, charged down the kick. With the Welsh team committed to attack the Scots hacked on and although J. P. R. Williams got back to stop the rush he had no support and was penalised for not releasing the ball. Peter Brown the Scottish captain kicked a goal from thirty-five yards. How he did it, how he kicked any goals ever, remains a mystery to most who saw him. His awkward, seemingly unco-ordinated, style never seemed likely to succeed but often did.

Scotland took the initiative for the next few minutes but after Gerald Davies and John Bevan had both had their first dangerous runs Barry John levelled the scores with a left touchline penalty. Wales were not back on terms for long as Brown kicked another penalty for obstruction in the line out but on the field we felt as if we had the measure of the opposition. The forwards were by no means as dominant as against England but there were enough sweeping attacks to make us confident that the tries would come.

The first one came at a crucial psychological moment. Two minutes of injury time in the first half had already been played when Wales won a line out half way inside the Scottish half. The ball was moved quickly to J.P.R. who had joined the line and so sweet was the timing of the passes that a gap opened up for him. He swept through it devastatingly and with me screaming for the ball as if demented, he dummied to pass outside to Barry John and cut inside. With the Scottish cover still trying to cut off the impending danger on the wing he passed inside to me as he was swamped and I was able to cut further inside and score under the posts, despite Alastair McHarg's attempt to stop me with a soccer slide tackle. In typical fashion 'the King' took the conversion before even waiting for the Scots to get behind their own line.

Four minutes into the second half we were further ahead. A quickly taken short penalty gave Barry John space to run. He drifted through and across and then linked up with Denzil Williams and Jeff Young. A ruck followed and Gareth Edwards had enough room to move into top gear, having picked up from it. The Scots, like so many other sides, found him impossible to stop and he burst through several tackles before diving over in the corner. I failed with the conversion.

Most people, the team included, now expected Wales to pull away but ten minutes later it was Scotland who narrowed the gap. As against England, we tapped back a line out throw on our own line, this time from the middle not the back, and Sandy Carmichael scored a soft try. It might have been fortuitous but it gave Scotland the lift they needed. They attacked more ferociously and consistently than at any other time in the match and retook the lead when a Welsh forward did not move away from the ball quickly enough and stopped them winning a ruck. Brown again kicked the easy penalty and (incredibly to the whole of the Welsh team – it had felt as if we were winning reasonably comfortably) we were behind. The last twenty minutes were straight out of *Boy's Own*.

Wales regained the lead after sixty-four minutes. John Bevan set off on a run but was brought down just outside the Scottish 25. The ball ran loose and seeing Barry John outside me in space, I passed the ball to him soccer style. It made no difference to Barry whether the passes were on the floor or above his head and he scooped it up with ease and weaved his way through what looked like adequate cover to score a marvellous try. As he went over he was tackled by two defenders and fell heavily. Gerry Lewis had to attend to him before he could return.

Seeing that he was dazed John Dawes decided to take the kick himself – it was an easy one, probably only ten yards to the left of the posts – but Barry having been treated assured him that he was OK and waved him hack to the half way line. Knowing it was useless to argue with Barry, the captain went, but Barry hit the post with his conversion attempt. It was probably the easiest kick he ever missed and he was obviously still feeling the effects of the collision.

Two minutes later Scotland were back in the lead with another Peter Brown penalty and then Wales were in serious trouble as they went further ahead after scoring their second try. Again it came from a Welsh mistake. John Bevan took far too long to set himself up for a clearance touch kick and it was charged down, J.P.R. pounced on it but was tackled and as the ball went loose Chris Rea grabbed it and went hell for leather for the line. John Dawes got a hand to him and held on for a few moments, but was shaken off, and although the cover enveloped him as he reached the line, the Scottish centre scored just to the left of the posts. The conversion would take Scotland 6 points ahead with only five minutes plus injury time to go and it really appeared that we had made a hash of a game we should have won. Peter Brown came to our rescue by hitting the post with almost his easiest kick of the day and it was still possible to win with just one converted try.

The rest has become part of Welsh folklore and at last got me accepted even in those corners of Wales where they thought London Welshmen should be playing for England.

We attacked non-stop, running the ball from every situation and just as it seemed that we were going to go close but never score Delme won possession at a line out on the left and the ball was moved swiftly to Gerald Davies on the right with John Williams in the line. Ian Smith, the Scottish full back, was no match for the Llansaint Express and was left for dead. Gerald tried to run round to lessen the angle once over the line, but was cut off and I was left with a conversion about seven yards from touch.

All that I can say is that it went over and I've never hit a ball more sweetly ever.

Many people still ask how I felt. All I can remember is saying to myself, 'Well, after this you're either going to be the hero or the villain of the piece, so make sure it's the right one', and then trying to put everything else out of my mind. In a way there was less pressure because it was well out towards the touchline and therefore not a certainty, but I probably only thought about that later. When play restarted it seemed like an age until the final whistle. Indeed there must have been some minutes added on for

injury as there was still time for Gareth Edwards to go close with
a dropped goal attempt.

Afterwards in the dressing room there was a sense of relief. All
the boys reacted differently.

'You jammy bastard!' – Merv.

'Never in doubt! If you hadn't scored we'd have got another
one.' – Dawes.

'I couldn't look . . .' Delme.

'I could!' – Gareth.

'Why can't you kick like that all the time?' – J.P.R.

There was a subdued atmosphere as the closeness of the match
really sank in. The spell was broken when Clive Rowlands burst
in. Emotional Welshman that he is he arrived with fag in mouth,
raincoat collar turned up and tears streaming down his face.
When he admitted to leaving his seat and walking up the steps
with his back to the field when the kick was taken he was dragged
into the bath fully clothed as punishment for not having faith in
his team.

After a game the pundits will always spend hours on the 'ifs'
and 'buts'. They had a heyday after this one. The lead changed
six times in all and 'if' Barry John had not hit the post the try
would have been enough and 'if' Peter Brown had not hit the post
Scotland would have been out of reach. I must confess to being
quite pleased they both missed their kicks, it gave me my
moment of glory. Contrary to all the rumours that flew around,
my left boot is not on exhibition at the National Stadium. I wore
the same pair for the rest of the season and the left one is now in a
glass case at London Welsh. It is true that I still get abuse from
Scotsmen. Several times I have been sitting in a restaurant when
a stranger with a foreign accent has walked up and called me
something nasty. As they walk away I usually notice tartan socks
or a tam-o'shanter.

The game had certainly been exciting but, being in the business of winning, it had been too exciting for Clive. There were
five weeks before the game against Ireland and during that time
he emphasised that we could not allow our superiority to slip
away because of stupid mistakes and lack of concentration. He
was determined that the beating of Ireland should rely more
upon hard work than last minute conversions. He probably felt
that his 'ticker' could not take another Murrayfield.

The game went very much to plan after a couple of early

shocks. After half an hour Ireland were up 6–0 through two Mike Gibson penalty goals but then their scrum half, Roger Young, made a poor clearance and Gerald Davies scored a marvellous try, side-stepping the last two defenders after John, Edwards, Williams and Lewis had all handled. Barry John added a dropped goal and a penalty to make it 9–6, but then the Irish held on gamely until fifteen minutes from the end when the floodgates opened after tremendous pressure. Barry was at his best pushing kicks into the open spaces so that O'Driscoll, the Irish full back, was constantly struggling to get to the ball before flying Welsh wingers, and the forwards were winning a tremendous battle up front.

Gareth Edwards broke the stalemate when he robbed Roger Young as the ball squirted out sideways from an Irish ruck and forced his way over. Gerald then scored his second after Gareth had again made the running to leave him an easy run in. Barry weighed in with a penalty and then the effervescent Edwards, not to be outdone by his great friend and try-scoring rival on the right wing scored his second try. It was another solo effort but this time he broke away from a line out and used his speed and strength alternately to get to the line after a long run.

Gibson kicked a consolation penalty to make it 23–9 but it was undoubtedly the Welsh half backs who were the stars of the game. Edwards, lightning fast and with the power of a pile driver, was almost unstoppable in this mood and John had now achieved perfect harmony between his very astute footballing brain and his unique skills. He could put the ball on a sixpence with his boot, move it quickly but accurately with his very individual style of passing and drift through the opposition almost at will, never seeming to go very fast but always just out of reach.

The Triple Crown was in the bag and a share of the Championship was guaranteed but to win it outright France had to be beaten in Paris and a Welsh team had not done that since 1957. The French team were also unbeaten. They had defeated Scotland and had then played disappointingly to draw with England and Ireland. In those matches they had smouldered without ever really catching fire but at that time in particular, and even now to a limited extent, there was the feeling that France were never at their best until they felt the spring sunshine on their backs.

They certainly had the players: Villepreux at full back and a three-quarter line of Cantoni, Lux, Bertranne and the coloured winger Bougarel; Christian Carrère, the captain, alongside Dauga in the back row and the Spanghero brothers, Walter and Claude, in the second row. There was naturally apprehension in the Welsh camp when Gerry Lewis came round on his normal morning reveille and informed us that it was a beautiful day and, for late March, already very warm.

By the time we reached the Stade Colombes (everyone, especially the new boys, having been warned to complete their ablutions at the hotel because of the primitive French loos at the ground), it was even warmer. Everyone was on edge after the hair-raising drive through Paris. We always had a motorcycle escort of four policemen and they insisted on delivering us in the grand manner. They would throw their bikes down in front of the traffic at intersections and take us the wrong side of the bollards and through red lights. I never knew why we never left the hotel fifteen minutes earlier. An inspection of the pitch confirmed that conditions were perfect – perhaps more perfect for the French than for us.

When the game began our worst fears were confirmed. The French set off at breakneck pace. They won possession at will and began rolling the ball off mauls and releasing their big men who seemed to move as fast as their backs. Eventually when they were stopped the ball was channelled back beautifully and the backs were released. Cantoni and Bougarel both had early runs and after ten minutes I cannot remember Wales having touched the ball.

However, the Welsh defence held firm and there was a great determination already evident as the whole team gritted their teeth, hoping the French could not keep up such an onslaught. Bougarel made another storming run down the right and was only five yards from the line and going at full pace when J.P.R. Williams met him with the hardest tackle he has ever felt. Bougarel might have expected his momentum to carry him over the line. Instead he went backwards. Next Bertranne looked to have made the line under the posts but John Bevan swooped from nowhere and threw him back into the field of play before he could ground the ball.

Then the French inevitably did get through. The forwards, with Dauga and the Spanghero brothers prominent, broke away.

They won the maul and then Berot, the fly half, changed direction and took the ball back to his forwards. He found ready support from Biemouret and Dauga was on hand to score the try. Villepreux converted and many people thought that France had made the breakthrough and Wales would be swamped but the team's heads did not drop for a moment.

A few minutes later even Barry John, who usually considered tackling something to be done by his lackeys, the forwards, brought down Dauga as the French went on the rampage again. In doing so he took a bad knock in the face and all our hearts sank as he left the field. We knew that we would need his magic if we were going to pull this one out of the fire. He returned after ten minutes and, although we did not know at the time, played out the rest of the game with a broken nose. That, more than anything else, epitomised the spirit of the Welsh team that day.

Just before half time came the moment that turned the match. The French were still pounding away at the Welsh line and once again the ball had been worked out to the right wing. Bougarel was once more in full flight. About ten yards from the line he once again saw J.P.R. in front and, perhaps still feeling the effects of his previous collision with the full back, elected to hand over responsibility to someone – anyone else. He threw a wild pass inside and telegraphed it so badly that J.P.R. intercepted and was away. With Villepreux up in the attack, he made fully seventy yards before the cover began to close in and he looked inside for support, where Denzil Williams was chugging along trying to catch up. Then just as it looked as if he would have to pass to him Gareth Edwards appeared back on the outside. J.P.R. swerved in and passed out to a grateful Gareth who just made the corner.

It is a golden rule that a full back should never go for an interception but the mark of a great player is knowing when to break the rules and John Williams changed the whole match with his decision on that occasion. Instead of turning round 10–0 down we were only two points behind at 5–3 and the psychological advantage of scoring just before the interval was immense. It proved that the French were not invincible, even though we were meeting them on a day when they were trying to give a good impression of being just that.

From the start of the second half we began to take the

Above: Grand Slam 1971, v France: sheer determination won the match when it seemed the odds were stacked against us. Below: Final Test in Auckland: Mervyn Davies wins the ball for the Lions despite interference, not least from me as I try to stop Ian Kirkpatrick coming through.

'We've really done it!' Auckland after the Final Test. John Dawes, Doug Smith, Carwyn James and Gordon Brown take stock of the situation as Colin Meads accepts defeat with a brave face.

Time off on tour: left, Jack Nicklaus, Bob Charles (well I am left-handed), Gary Player and Arnold Palmer. Below, 'Snow' White carves at the final *hangi*, John Dawes still bears the scars of the Final Test the day before.

initiative. The French still had their moments and the tremendous defensive qualities of the Welsh side were tested time and again as the French forwards rolled the ball off the back of mauls and rucks to set up attacks but, unlike in the first half, they were having to back-pedal just as often as we mounted attacks.

John Bevan and John Dawes almost scored tries and then Wales took the lead with a Barry John penalty after the French handled in a ruck whilst desperately trying to stop us winning the ball. Having grasped the lead, there was no way the French were going to be allowed back into the game. Whenever there was a tackle to be made two or three players competed for the honour of making it and as the French fire began to die Wales looked the more likely to score.

From a scrum almost in front of the French posts Jeff Young won a heel against the head – to answer all those who had called for him to be replaced after giving away the penalty against Ireland – Gareth broke to the left and Barry John drifted through outside his marker to score a gloriously simple try. He could not convert but apart from a few anxious moments Wales were home and dry.

The post-match celebrations in France are always bizarre with the older players becoming the ringmasters and putting the youngsters through the hoop by making them over-indulge in the seemingly endless supply of rich French wine. On this occasion young John Bevan was the player not to last out the dinner. He need not have worried. Even Dai Morris, who was normally the most moderate drinker, went over the top. Feeling ill he rushed to the lavatory and lost his false teeth down the pan. John Lloyd, a substitute for that trip and always a good friend, went to help him but Dai mistook his intentions and answered his tap on the shoulder with a punch on the nose. It all worked out well in the end, but I cannot remember if Dai recovered his teeth.

Neither Morris nor Bevan missed anything by not hearing the post-banquet speeches. By the time the interpreter has had his say they are always drawn out and to make them more incomprehensible on this occasion John Dawes delivered his oration totally in French and Welsh. Before people get the impression that he is a superb linguist I should point out that he had to enlist the help of the hall porter at L'Hotel Normandy and Clive Rowlands. His French is non-existent and his Welsh is limited to

'Dim parcio'. 'Dim ginio', 'Dim beerio' (not even *cwrw*), or whatever else he has none of.

Later that night John Williams was to be seen serving behind the bar at the Churchill pub in the Place de General de Gaulle and even later Elie Cester, the immensely strong French lock forward against whom most of us had played the year before, was leaning over the counter at the Club Sunnyside and lifting the smaller Welsh players up to kiss them on both cheeks.

I like to think I played in many remarkable matches but France 1971 would be the one that I, and a number of other players on the field that day, would pick as the most satisfying. There is great joy in winning by a wide margin but it is even more exhilarating to win, and win deservedly, at the end of a battle where the opposition almost deserve to win and are within one score right up until the final whistle.

It was the last time Wales played at the Stade Colombes and a fitting match to say goodbye to the old stadium. It had an atmosphere all of its own created by the distance of the crowd from the edge of the pitch which was surrounded by an athletics track. Although there was never the intimacy of the National Stadium in Wales or Murrayfield in Scotland, the crowd always made their feelings obvious with high-pitched Gallic screams or ear-piercing whistles.

The 1971 team had realised one of the first great ambitions of any of the home players – a Grand Slam. Wales had only achieved it five times previously and only twice since the First World War. Four wins out of four does not sound that difficult but history has proved otherwise.

Instead of a long summer rest virtually the whole team now had to re-align their sights, become British, and prepare to do battle with the mighty All Blacks who had torn Wales apart so comprehensively only two summers before.

Barry Llewelyn, who had been such a tremendous success throughout the season, and Jeff Young were unavailable for various reasons and Denzil Williams and Dai Morris were not selected. Denzil had toured with the 1966 Lions and was, as it turned out, at the end of an illustrious international career that had begun in 1963. During that time he had set a Welsh record of thirty-six caps for a prop and it was probably felt that he would not last out a full tour after his back problems in 1970.

Dai never made a Lions tour. There was a feeling that he

suffered from homesickness more than most. He had certainly
not played at his best in Australasia in 1969, but he was a great
player and deserved the honour. I certainly consider myself lucky
to have been selected for two tours in front of him and it was only
because I was more of an open-side flanker. Dai was roughly the
same size as me and we were both often considered too small.
But whereas the Welsh selectors, who saw him week in and week
out, realised the phenomenal strength that he packed into that
slight frame, the Lions selectors did not. He would be in my team
every time. However, the Welsh contingent was still thirteen
because Chico Hopkins, who had been patiently understudying
Gareth throughout the season, won the second scrum half berth
and Derek Quinnell, the uncapped Llanelli back-row forward,
was called in to give height and weight to the wing forward
division.

At last a Welshman was also selected as captain. It seems
almost unbelievable that before 1971 Wales had never provided
a captain but there had persisted a belief that the Welsh were
bad mixers and in 1966 when Alun Pask was the only outstanding candidate for the post he had been bypassed and Mike
Campbell-Lamerton had been given the job. Perhaps it was felt
that Dawes being based in London was Anglicised enough to be
acceptable.

By this time John Dawes was known to all and sundry as Sid. It
is after all his first name, but the change came about because of
the number of Johns in the London Welsh club. Call out the
name John and Dawes, Williams and Taylor would turn round.
Initials became the first way round the problem, but when it was
discovered that the 'S' in S. J. Dawes stood for Sidney and that he
hated the name, everyone called him that instead. 'J.P.R.' of
course lasted for ever, as we know, even though it was abbrevi-
ated to 'Japes' by his team mates. 'J.T.' lasted a while, too but
half way through the Lions tour I was barking a bit too loud at
reluctant player choristers and Edwards crept round behind me,
then pulling his hair out in an imitation of mine, howled like a fox
and yelled, 'It's Basil Brush!' I have been 'Bas' ever since.

The selection was also a triumph for the London Welsh club.
Six players, John Dawes, John Williams, Gerald Davies, Mervyn
Davies, Mike Roberts and myself had played in all the Home
Internationals. Now we were selected to tour with the Lions.
When Geoff Evans was flown out as a replacement, the total of

seven players from the same club on a Lions tour was something no other club has ever achieved.

To make the Welsh feast complete, Carwyn James, the Llanelli coach was selected as Assistant Manager in charge of coaching the team.

Eight of the Welsh players had been on the 1969 tour and while we all wanted desperately to turn the tables and avenge the humiliation of those defeats, there was a certain amount of trepidation as we set off on a return visit.

6

CYMRU AM BLOODY BYTH
the Lions in Australasia, 1971

The previous two Lions tours may have been fairly disastrous but it was a happy and hopeful group that arrived in Australia. The worst fears seemed more than justified, however, when Queensland beat us in the very first match. Jet lag, or after our medical lecture from Dr J. P. R. Williams, circadian disrhythmia, was an impressive curtain to hide behind but we had not even reached the main destination, New Zealand. We had been given a toy lion by a well-wisher before leaving and were instructed to give it to the first provincial side that beat us. The last words of the dear lady were, 'I hope you bring him home with you.' He never even made New Zealand. Ironically, had he survived that match she would have seen him again. Queensland were the only province to beat the Lions.

In Sydney I was greeted by referee Craig Ferguson with the words, 'I'm still a cheat, but I'm looking forward to our verbal battle on the field tomorrow, John.' We survived his decisions, beat New South Wales, and at last made New Zealand.

Thankfully, the first few matches in New Zealand passed uneventfully and the team was able to find its feet under Carwyn's studious and careful supervision. The forwards, always the key to success in New Zealand, were developing well. Willie John McBride, now on his fourth Lions tour, and Ray McLoughlin were invaluable aides to him – Willie with his wealth of experience and Ray with his great technical knowledge of scrummaging. The grizzly group of pundits who scrutinised every training session began to be impressed with the tight play but emphasised that the provincial teams played so far were amongst the weakest.

The first real test was against the Maoris. They were particularly incensed because there had been a move within New Zealand for their traditional right to play the Lions to be withdrawn. It was argued that they were now so well integrated into the community that the fixture was meaningless. They took the field anxious to prove a point but took it all too far and the game became ill-tempered as they continuously punched and obstructed in an attempt to thwart the superior side. The tactics did not succeed. Instead they highlighted another area where the Lions were growing in strength. Barry John was able to kick six penalty goals as well as a conversion. He had already kicked 32 points and with this haul, pushed his tally over the 50 mark, which was quite remarkable in six games when you consider that he had left Britain as a makeshift one side of the field kicker. It was vitally important because many of the previous Lions teams had failed in Test matches for lack of a reliable place-kicker. The only specialist in the party was Bob Hiller and it had already become obvious that J. P. R. Williams had to be included for his all round play.

The only try in that game was scored by John Bevan and he too had begun his first Lions tour in remarkable fashion. He had now scored six tries in three games in New Zealand and the record by any previous Lion was only seventeen by the great Irish wing Tony O'Reilly.

The following game was against the first of the really top provinces. We were to play Wellington at Athletic Park. Many of the locals thought that this time the Lions were about to be put in their place, but to their horror the local team were smashed by 47–9. They could hardly believe it, and still few people agreed with Graham Williams, the Wellington captain, when he said that the tourists were the greatest team he had ever played.

The Lions party were not surprised. The forwards continued to go well and behind the scrum the razor-sharp running of Mike Gibson in partnership with the superb passing of John Dawes was paying dividends. A win of that proportion had been on the cards for some days. To achieve it against Wellington was a bonus. John Bevan scored another four tries to take his total to ten in four games in New Zealand and Barry John weighed in with another 19 points. This included five conversions of the nine tries scored and, unbelievably, he retired as place-kicker in disgust after missing a fairly simple one and J. P. R. Williams and Mike Gibson converted the final two tries. Barry had now scored 66 points in four games in New Zealand, just 7 short of the record 73 scored by Malcolm Thomas.

For the first time the dour New Zealanders began to understand why we called him the King. He certainly did things in style
and in jest he even treated the rest of the players as his subjects.
Before the tour Chico Hopkins had asked him about the arrangements for assembling. Barry John could not resist an imperious
reply, 'Well, you lot are going to Eastbourne for a week to get
yourselves in shape but I'm off to the South of Spain for a break.
The plane's going to stop in and pick me up on the way.' Nobody
else could have got away with a reply like that, but because he
was so modest in reality everyone laughed. He had, after all,
been put on the throne by the rest of the players – not by himself.

The tour now entered the crucial period. There were five
games before the First Test match and these included Otago who
had an incredible record against touring sides and Canterbury,
the Ranfurly Shield holders. Our party was beginning to feel that
we might just be in with a chance of making history by becoming
the first British and Irish touring team to win a series in New
Zealand or South Africa since the turn of the century. Otago
were easily beaten, despite their great traditions, Barry John
breaking Malcolm Thomas's record by scoring 12 points. Then,
after David Duckham had taken his chance to go into the record
books by scoring six tries in the 39–6 defeat of West Coast and
Buller, the team moved on to Canterbury.

The Ranfurly Shield is the challenge cup played for by New
Zealand's provincial sides and a province holds it until another
province beats them in an officially recognised challenge. This
makes the approach gladiatorial and the Canterbury team, as
holders, were used to this approach. They treated the game
against the Lions as a war, the invader to be repulsed at all costs.
The game was a disgrace to rugby and the cost to the Lions
was enormous.

Sandy Carmichael was literally battered out of the tour.
Always a believer in non-retaliation, he soaked up so many
punches from the Canterbury pack that he ended the game with
multiple fractures of the cheek. Fergus Slattery had his teeth
loosened by a punch and Ray McLoughlin broke his thumb when
retaliating to try and prevent more mayhem being committed in
the name of rugby. In addition Mick Hipwell twisted his knee
and tore a cartilage and he and McLoughlin were both out of the
tour as well as Carmichael.

In between fist fights the Lions won the match. Arthur Lewis

brought off a perfect 'Arthur' to his delight and scored a
marvellous try and John Bevan demolished a wall of defenders as
only he could to score an equally good one. The final score was
14–3. There had been no Barry John to kick the frequent
penalties. Fortunately we had been warned of Canterbury's
intentions and the management had sensibly decided not to risk
him.

Nevertheless, the cost could have been enough to sink all
chances of winning the series. Carmichael and McLoughlin were
undoubtedly the first choice props and they were now out of
contention for the rest of the tour. This was all just one week
before the First Test match and few of us could believe it was a
coincidence. It was at this point that Carwyn James coined his
now famous phrase, 'Get your retaliation in first.' It was not a
question of abandoning his faith in the skills of rugby and
advocating new and violent tactics, as some people have tried to
construe it. It was simply telling us that if this sort of thuggery
occurred again there was no point in taking the punishment that
Sandy Carmichael had taken. The referee appeared powerless to
stop it and therefore each player must look after himself
whatever that involved.

Out of the debris the team had to be picked. When it was
announced Mick Hipwell was included in the back row with
Mervyn Davies and myself. When he dropped out it meant that
three Test players had been lost as a result of the Canterbury
match. Mervyn and I were also in trouble. He had not played
since the match against Wellington, and I had pulled a hamstring
against West Coast and Buller (thereby fortunately missing
Canterbury). The training session to prove our fitness was
probably the hardest, longest, most gruelling I have ever taken
part in. The normally gentle Carwyn had been criticised for
selection because we had been unfit and was determined that if
we were going to break down it would be before rather than on
the day. We both lasted out, but the other players cursed us for
the rest of the day as they had had to go through it all too. It was a
total contrast to the fun and games sessions that Carwyn often
used to break up the routine. We often played soccer to the
disbelief of the local experts who had turned out to criticise the
British approach to preparing a rugby team. We all thought it
funny when the press carried derisory remarks about our training, but the locals at Mosgiel saw what they thought a training

session should be like and went home happy.

On the morning of the match among the many telegrams that arrived there was one that was very special. It read 'VICTORY WILL MAKE US AS IRRELEVANT AS DINOSAURS. WILL PRESS FOR WELSH AS UNIVERSAL LANGUAGE IN COMMON MARKET. YOU CAN WIN. YOU MUST WIN. CYMRU AM BLOODY BYTH.' Only Tony O'Reilly and Andy Mulligan, the arch clowns of the 1959 tour, could have sent it and several of the older members of the party had their names on their lips before the words were out.

The twenty-year-old John Bevan said, 'Isn't he the guy who's record I'm just about to beat?'

He played his only Test at Dunedin. Having started off magnificently, both he and Chico Hopkins began to suffer from homesickness. Both were young and both were from the valleys, John from the Rhondda and Chico from the Llynfi. The *hiraeth* was obviously too great. Chico also played in the First Test. Gareth Edwards had had a bad hamstring pull which was still giving trouble and, sure enough, as soon as he set off on a typical surging run and put it under real pressure, the muscle gave way and he had to leave the field. We went on to win the match 9–3 and the heroes of the day were an Irishman and a Scot, Sean Lynch and Ian McLauchlan, the two props. They anchored the scrum so well that, although the All Blacks exerted great pressure elsewhere, the Lions always had a strong base from which to defend. McLauchlan also scored his only try of the tour after charging down a clearance.

There were now only three matches before the Second Test at Christchurch. They were duly won, although Taranaki proved to be the most stubborn opposition up to that point and were only beaten 14–9 after much nail-biting. Geoff Evans had by now arrived and played his first game in that match. This meant that Mike Roberts had to play for the rest of the tour as a prop, much to his disgust, and the two great friends, partners in the London Welsh second row, spent a lot of the time ribbing each other about their various strengths and weaknesses. Robbo was never quite sure whether he was pleased that Geoff rather than a specialist prop had been sent out to replace Sandy Carmichael.

The Second Test was a terrible setback. Perhaps it was the effect of returning to Christchurch, the scene of the Canterbury game, or perhaps it was the way the All Blacks lifted their game. Whatever it was, we were soundly beaten, with Ian Kirkpatrick scoring one magnificent try for New Zealand and Gerald Davies, of all people, giving away a penalty try.

A defeat by 22–12 seems convincing but Carwyn James, with that great ability to say the right thing at the right time, immediately gave the whole party a lift. After pinpointing the weakness – we had become preoccupied with scrummaging so that the back row were not alert enough to the running of Going – he said he felt happier than after the First Test because we had created many more chances of scoring. He now felt he could work on the defence and expect to win through a superior attacking strike force. As usual he turned out to be right.

One of the greatest joys of a Lions tour is the chance to indulge in activities that were not normally available at home. For Willie John McBride this usually meant a day's shooting. For Arthur Lewis it was golf, much to the sadness of various greenkeepers around New Zealand. Arthur was very much the life and soul of the party. He did an amazing job as social secretary, practical joker, trip organiser and many other tasks, always smiling when he must have been very frustrated about the playing part of the tour.

Mike Gibson had been selected as a fly half but it soon became obvious that he was going to make the Test team as a centre and therefore he had to play in that position in some of the provincial games as well. Thus, there were less games to go round between the four selected centres. The situation was made worse because one of them was John Dawes, the captain, and traditionally the captain plays more than any other player. Dawes played in seventeen of the twenty-four matches in New Zealand, while Barry John played in sixteen and Mike Gibson in fifteen. This left only twenty-eight possible appearances to be shared between John Spencer, Chris Rea and Arthur. All were magnificent and contributed greatly to the success of the tour but Arthur took out his frustrations on the golf courses of New Zealand.

He could never understand why he was not an instant success and everything came to a head on a day off between the Second and Third Tests at Castlepoint, a seaside complex forty miles from Masterton. A river meandered its way through the local golf course and Arthur hit several balls into it. Then, to make him even angrier, he hit one over the river. He could see it sitting up beautifully and, ignoring shouts of 'Out of bounds', insisted on walking a quarter of a mile back to the ball. The inevitable happened, he topped his recovery shot and lost the ball in the river.

At moments like these Arthur could indulge in some heavy Anglo-Saxon oaths and we were most embarrassed when two ladies emerged from behind a bush on the adjoining fairway. They walked off the course and Arthur kept cursing. By the time we had finished the ladies had obviously forgiven him. One of them, who turned out to be the lady captain, accepted his apology with a smile and thanked him. She said that she too had been having an awful round and that he had persuaded her to give up for the day.

The highlight of the four games between the Second and Third Tests was a dazzling performance by Gerald Davies against Hawkes Bay. The match was rather ill-tempered but Gerald was above such things and scored four of the best tries one could hope to see. Having side-stepped, swerved and outsprinted all opposition on the wing for three of them, he moved into the centre and split the defence wide open for the fourth with his unique ability to side-step at full pace and then continue in the direction in which he was first travelling. Geoff Evans, too, scored a fine try against Auckland, much to Mike Roberts's annoyance, and then the party moved up to Waitangi for a few days of quiet preparation before the decisive Third Test.

When the team was announced Peter Dixon and I had both been dropped after the failure of the back row in Christchurch and Derek Quinnell and Fergus Slattery were selected to replace us. It was a great moment for Derek Quinnell. Although he had continuously struggled with a knee injury, fluid appearing every time he played, he was lean and fit, much lighter in fact than at any other time in his career and extremely mobile.

I was naturally disappointed but the night before we left Waitangi there was a sensational 'South Sea' party, complete with very beautiful dusky maidens. The Test team were not allowed to attend, but the rest of us could, so I felt that there were some compensations. The next day my recuperation was complete. Poor Fergus had a virus infection and I was back in the Test team – not only the game but the party too.

From the moment we arrived in Wellington thoughts were only on rugby. We all knew that this was the most important match of our lives. Seventeen minutes gone and the score New Zealand 0, British Lions 13. We could not believe it and failed to score again in the match despite undoubted superiority. However, it had been a glorious seventeen minutes. A Barry John dropped goal began it, a Gerald Davies try in the right corner was converted via the left post by Barry John and then came a Barry John try and conversion after Gareth Edwards had run straight through Bob Burgess, the New Zealand fly half. Here were three Welshmen exacting revenge for the humiliations of 1969.

The All Blacks managed a solitary try in the second half but we won the game 13–3 and suddenly had created history. No other Lions team had ever managed to win two Tests in a series in New Zealand, and now we could not be beaten.

Everything had worked as planned, except that our attacking nerve went when we were well on top and therefore we let them back into the game. However, even then the defensive plan was adequate and New Zealand seldom looked dangerous. The introduction of Quinnell had been a total success and Going barely had a run all day. Burgess was also pressured to such an extent that he seldom managed to put the ball in front of his forwards and perhaps most significantly the Lions' line out performance was the best of the tour. Delme Thomas had found that New Zealand referees were not so strict on interference as at home, so he was never as effective as he could be. He was replaced for the Third Test by Gordon Brown, who became a far better player on tour than when playing for Scotland and the combination of him with Derek Quinnell and Mervyn Davies behind was something New Zealand could not combat. By pushing Mervyn in the back I even managed to win some ball myself.

After the celebrations at Wellington, the team moved on to Palmerston North and the stay was to be an eventful one. Barry John took over the bar at the hotel for the lunchtime session of the Sunday School. This was a not too elite group – anyone could join by attending regularly – who met for Sunday morning cocktails and to discuss the ways of the world. It was the only day we did not train, so it seemed a natural thing to do. On this occasion, however, we had a barman who was too slow and we installed Barry John. With his normal incisiveness the King decided that the way to speed things up as regards service was to dispense with payment. Although all the players attended this particular session, a unique occasion in itself, the bill which was presented next day was staggering. It was thirteen hundred dollars but was paid with a wince and a weak smile. The Sunday School disclaimed responsibility, as the party went on all day and all evening.

J. P. R. Williams and I were two of the last to bed. We are both convinced that we took a lift to our rooms but neither of us could find it again during our stay.

The next day training was a shambles. As each player shuffled out on to the pitch it became obvious that the coach could have a rebellion on his hands if he tried to organise a really hard session. Several of us were grateful when Carwyn quietly suggested that we go for a very gentle long run. Once again, it showed his ability to understand what was needed and we all knew that it was his way of patting us on the back for the performance of the previous Saturday.

Willie John McBride was made captain for the match against Manawatu and Horowhenua to the delight of everybody. It was his fourth tour and he had been an inspiration to the whole party. His Northern Irish brogue was always ready with a joke or a rallying call.

'We'll take no prisoners!' – after Canterbury.

'There won't be many going home . . .' – in the difficult time between the Second and Third Tests.

'What have I done to deserve the man from the Bible?' – a reference to the length of my hair, when he found that we were to be room mates.

The game itself turned out to be a triumph for John Bevan. Having scored eleven tries in six games, he had scored only one try in the previous six weeks. Injury had restricted him to four games but most of it was caused by the mid-tour melancholy that he found so difficult to handle. It was only resolved when he received a letter from 'My girl', as he called Rhiannon, his childhood sweetheart. It was almost as if he could see the end of the tour in sight. To celebrate he scored four tries which once again put him on a course for equalling or beating Tony O'Reilly's record of seventeen tries in New Zealand.

He equalled it in the last minute of the next game, against North Auckland to make sure of victory for the Lions. We were now very conscious that we could become the first Lions to beat all the provincial sides, but North Auckland, with a team built around the three Going brothers, almost spoilt that dream. Eventually tries from David Duckham, John Williams and that

long-awaited one from John Bevan saw us home at 9–5. The last
provincial game against Tauranga was also won after a few
hiccups and some excellent goal kicking from Bob Hiller. For the
second tour running he had scored over one hundred points
without playing in one Test match. He played really well on both
tours but was dreadfully unlucky to understudy the captain,
Kiernan, in South Africa in 1968, and John Williams now.

Our one remaining hurdle was the Final Test against New
Zealand. Although we could not lose the series a draw or better
would mean that we could become the first Lions since the turn of
the century to win a series in both South Africa and New
Zealand. The team originally selected was the same as that which
played in the Third Test but, after his exertions in the North
Auckland game, Derek Quinnell had to withdraw because his
swollen knee was too painful. Peter Dixon deputised.

The game itself was an anticlimax, primarily because we were
so full of tension at the thought of what we were about to achieve
that once again we froze. After twelve minutes New Zealand led
8–0 and the chance of glory seemed to be slipping away. It
seemed even more remote when Barry John, having already
scored 172 points mainly through his round-the-corner kicking
style, elected to kick an easy fifteen-yarder with his toe and
missed. However, John Dawes coaxed the side back into the
game and by half time we were level with the wind at our backs
for the second half. Dawes told us at half time that we now
could not possibly fail.

We should have won comfortably but in the end needed an
unlikely J. P. R. Williams score to draw the match 14–14. Some
full backs are renowned for their drop-kicking, others are not
and J.P.R. is in the latter category. Therefore, when he let fly
from the ten yard line, it was not only his London Welsh
colleagues who were sceptical. But the ball sailed over. J.P.R.
has always been the man for the big occasion but his triumphantly raised fist signalled his own surprise as much as his
delight.

All the records were broken, the series was won and Barry
John with a massive 180 points was the King of New Zealand as
well as Wales. Exhausted but delighted, it was time to go home.

After the victory over Wellington the cynical local response
had been, 'Wait until you get to Otago!' After Otago it became,
'Wait until you get to Canterbury!' and so on through Taranaki,

Auckland and finally North Auckland. Bob Hiller, our very dry resident comic, could not resist a parting shot as we left, 'Wait until you get to London!' However, it was the incomparable Willie John McBride who had the absolute last word.

'Men,' he said, 'it's great to have travelled with you.'

That said everything and we all knew that although everyone would be all out to win for their respective countries just as much as ever in 1972, games against each other would never again be quite the same.

7

O YE OF LITTLE FAITH!
1972

Nothing could have been more different from the return home after South Africa in 1968 than the return from New Zealand in 1971. Instead of three men and a dog there were thousands at Heathrow and the television cameras were out in force. There followed a number of celebrations and everybody took a month or two months off before starting to play again. However, by November virtually all the Welsh players were back in action and looking forward to the Five Nations Championship.

The new season had brought several changes, the most important of these was the change in the laws that made a try worth four points. The argument still rages about the number of points that should be awarded for a penalty goal as against a try. This move at least tipped the scales towards the try, even if not enough.

There were also some changes in personnel. John Dawes, having first been capped in 1964, decided it was time to rest on his laurels. Who could blame him? After years of being a voice in the wilderness, his methods and ideas of playing the game had been adopted by both the Welsh side and the Lions. The result had been a Grand Slam for Wales and the first ever Test series victory for the Lions. In addition he had at last been recognised as a wonderfully talented player and not just a good captain. It was a fitting time to go, especially as it became apparent later that he was already being groomed to succeed Clive Rowlands.

The other player to depart the scene after a long and distinguished career was Denzil Williams. He had first been capped in 1963 and took a lot of stick from the rest of the team as being the only player who had played in a side which lost to England. Since then he had won a total of thirty-six caps which is still a record for a Welsh prop forward. He was a remarkable player in many ways but particularly because he played much of his club

A typical Edwards try. He plunges through a wall of defenders to begin the scoring spree that ended in Wales's highest score ever against Scotland, 1972.

Below left: Give him a sight of the line and John Bevan won't notice a tap on the shoulder, even when it's from Pierre Villepreux, at Cardiff, 1972. Below right: 'I'm glad we won, my wife would have had my neck if we hadn't – she hasn't seen me for ten weeks.'

A tale of two scoreboards: final score at Stradey, 1972; and below that last kick v the All Blacks in 1972. Despite his optimism the scoreboard operator didn't have to change the Welsh total.

rugby at second row. Many players holding down a place in the national side would have refused to play elsewhere but Denzil was always ready to sacrifice himself for the greater good. If his beloved Ebbw Vale wanted him to play in the second row then that is where he would play.

He had a wicked sense of humour, as most of his young team mates found when Wales played in Paris. Probably because he had been caught himself right back in 1963, he would always take the chair at a post-match wine tasting. There was only one difference from the real thing – every drop tasted had to be swallowed. Few first-timers in France lasted out the dinner. However, he was basically a big quiet man whom everyone respected. To J.P.R. he was always 'Uncle Denz' because they shared the same surname, to the rest of us he was certainly a father figure. Twice before it had seemed that he was finished but he fought his way back and it was only injury that stopped him going for another campaign. He had to withdraw from the final trial and at the age of thirty-two at last found it impossible to make a comeback. Nevertheless, he continued to play for Ebbw Vale, at whatever position they wanted him, for several seasons. Denzil was a true man of steel. Incidentally, his replacement in the trial was a twenty-year-old prop from Pontypool, Graham Price.

After the heights of success reached by the team in 1971 the critics might have been expected to remain silent but not a bit of it. The trial was won by the Probables but only by a score of 35–25 and the doubts crept in.

Delme Thomas, who had decided he needed a longer break than most, had not played enough rugby to be fully match fit said the pundits. I was still too small. (I had naively believed that after five years of enduring that particular old chestnut the New Zealand trip might have changed things.) Barry John and Gerald Davies apparently did not have the physique to stop big players if they were run at continuously. The Lions tour had suddenly become an ogre that had affected us all so deeply there was no possible way, it was said, that we could have regained our appetite for the game.

In the end most of us shrugged our shoulders and put it down to overkill. We had been wined and dined on a scale unheard of in rugby circles previously.

My own chances were not helped by Morrie Evans of Swansea.

On the day after Boxing Day he splattered my nose across my face when Swansea played London Welsh (referee and ball were all of forty yards away). However, the selectors picked me against England, providing that I played on the Saturday before the match, just ten days after the injury. I played, tentatively, and took my place with the rest of the team. But it gave the pundits another chance to have a go, as they doubted whether I could possibly go flat out with the nose still broken.

The new captain was John Lloyd. He had already won nineteen caps but had not played since the 1971 Championship. However, he had been captaining Bridgend with a great deal of success and therefore had the right pedigree for the job. John Dawes not only had to be replaced as captain but also as a centre and Roy Bergiers, a twenty-one-year-old still studying at Cardiff College of Education, training ground for John Lloyd, Gareth Edwards and John Bevan, was chosen. Bergiers had played well for Wales B against France B the previous October and had impressed with his hard, direct running and fierce tackling. The other change from the 1971 line-up was in the second row where Geoff Evans replaced Mike Roberts. Having arrived in New Zealand as a replacement on the Lions tour, he had played so well that he was in contention for a Test place and his good form had continued on his return home.

Perhaps the critics were right and we did expect to win too easily but whatever the reason Wales had much the worst of the first half in that first game against England. The forwards were constantly under pressure and found particular difficulty in the scrums. By the end of the game John Pullin, the English hooker, who had had such a marvellous tour of New Zealand with the Lions had taken eight strikes against the head.

At half time England led but only by a solitary penalty goal from the ever-reliable boot of Bob Hiller. Based on forward superiority the lead should have been greater but this was Barry John's first game on the international scene since returning from his triumphs down under and he was determined to show the home spectators his full range of skills. Although he did not have much chance in attack he made a couple of telling runs but in defence he was immaculate. Time and again as England pressure threatened to overwhelm the Welsh he pushed them back deep into their own territory with raking touch kicks which curled over the line only when they had just run out of steam from inside his

25 and beautifully placed chips which unerringly bounced into touch from outside it.

By half time the Welsh pack had weathered the storm and began to re-establish themselves. Nobody had seriously considered that we could lose and now the team was confident that Wales would turn the screw in the second half. Barry John kicked a penalty when England were penalised for lifting Ralston and then kicked another, again given against the English forwards, this time for handling in a ruck. Wales were ahead but all the scores had been penalty goals. It had been a drab game and badly needed a try.

Eventually it came. Once again, the initiator was Barry John but not quite in the way he would have wished. With the English pack fading and the Welsh forwards now beginning to exert pressure, Wales drove deep into English territory and Barry dropped for goal. The ball was deflected but still crossed the line and Alan Old, the English fly half touched down, thereby giving a five yard scrum to Wales. A perfectly-controlled heel gave Gareth Edwards the chance to run to the right, the short side, and with perfect timing J. P. R. Williams appeared outside him to take the pass going at full tilt. He brushed aside Keith Fielding and dived triumphantly over the line as Peter Dixon managed to tackle him. It was a classic J.P.R. intervention, a sudden surge of pace which caught many a defence unawares and then a dive for the line making full use of that fourteen stone. It was an almost unstoppable combination especially when he timed his entry into the line perfectly as he did on this occasion. The score was only five yards in from the right touchline, Barry John's wrong side but, as we had come to expect, he converted with ease and Wales had won 12–3. It had never been a sparkling game but at least it had silenced the Welsh doubting Thomases.

Any lack of drama on the field was immediately compensated for by the appearance of the smiling Irishman with the big red book, Eamonn Andrews, in the players' tunnel. Only those players who had been involved in setting up the programme knew about it and to the rest of us it was as much of a surprise as it was to Barry. Who else could they possibly have chosen?

The power of television is quite amazing. There we were just off the field and suddenly instead of savouring our victory, we had to change quickly, get back to the hotel and put on our dinner jackets ready for the post-match banquet at the Hilton and then rush off to the television studios to make the programme. Several of us felt that it was not quite right somehow, but nevertheless we fell into line and joined the rest of the team on the show. It turned out to be great fun and the very fact that Barry had attracted the attention of the 'This Is Your Life' team was a reflection on how rugby had increased in popularity.

After the match there was once again a call for the dropping of Jeff Young, but the selectors resisted it and chose the same team to play Scotland. Most of Jeff's critics did not realise how important his scrummaging was to the team. Although he was not particularly big, he weighed on 14 st 2 lbs, he was incredibly strong and was vital in keeping the scrum really tight. His hooking was usually efficient as well, but he and Gareth had had troubles with their timing against England and it had taken some time to sort out. He had also been up against John Pullin, probably the best hooker in the world.

There were also doubts about Barry John. During the year after the Lions tour I received nearly 200 invitations to speak or appear at various functions, so he must have received many more. He had tried to fulfil too many of them and by the time of the England game, was mentally exhausted. The Wednesday after the game he flew off to Majorca for a rest on the advice of his doctor. It was unheard of. Apart from anything else he would miss the squad session the following weekend and many people in Wales thought he was taking the role of prima donna too far. He recalls the anxiety in his own mind – wanting to play, but knowing that it would be impossible unless he gave himself a rest, yet at the same time appreciating the pressures on the selectors because some people would not realise just how tired he was.

Once again the selectors did not allow public opinion to influence them. They knew that Barry would not go on holiday as an act of defiance and picked him. Barry still remembers the relief when he picked up the paper in Majorca and read that he had been retained. Having missed the practice the previous Sunday he took his place on the Thursday before the game feeling a new man. He played like it on the Saturday too, contributing 15 points to the Welsh total of 35 points, the most ever scored against Scotland.

There was still one more scare before the match. Mervyn Davies had bruised his hip badly and it was not responding to treatment but eventually, after hours with the indefatigable Gerry Lewis, he was passed fit.

Memories of the match the previous year were still fresh and the first half gave promise of another equally close encounter. Jim Renwick kicked a penalty for Scotland and Barry John replied with a beauty from the right-hand touchline. Then Wales scored a classic try. Mervyn Davies won a line out absolutely cleanly and palmed direct to Gareth Edwards. John Williams came into the line to make the extra man and gave Gerald Davies the space to go around Alastair Biggar. Everyone was now waiting for the side-step but seeing too much cover defence even for him to elude, he chipped over the top of the full back, raced through and collected the ball on the first bounce to score. It was again a beautiful example of his awareness of the total situation and what it required.

Peter Brown narrowed the gap with a penalty but Barry again took Wales four points clear when he also kicked one. Then Scotland regained the lead which they had held until half time. In a set three-quarter move they sent Frame on a dummy crash ball run. They then passed behind him and although he appeared to obstruct the Welsh defence the move was allowed to continue and took play to within ten yards of the Welsh line. Scotland won the maul and MacEwan fed Clark, his hooker, who scored. Brown converted to make it 10–12.

Amidst all the excitement J.P.R. broke his jaw. Midway through the half the Scots were attacking strongly and their speedy winger, Steele, was put clear on the right. The full back was the last man to beat and Steele elected to try to run around him, not an easy thing to do. J.P.R. had him covered but at the last moment the Scots winger appeared to try to jump the tackle. He did not succeed but his knee caught John in the face. In just three years he had established a deserved reputation for being the rock at the heart of the Welsh defence and the dismay of the crowd and players was only too apparent but he was replaced by Phil Bennett and the talented Llanelli outside half gave another exhibition of his great versatility, playing in his fourth different position for Wales.

The second half was a complete revelation. Gareth Edwards tore the heart out of Scotland with two tries and from then on there was no stopping Wales. Whilst Scotland could not add to their first half total the Welsh added 25 points to theirs.

The first Edwards try was a typical effort. Barry Llewelyn, who did this better than any other forward I have ever played with or against, took a peel from Mervyn Davies at the back of the line out and drove to set up the maul. As usual when he took in the ball, but unlike many other prop forwards, it emerged on our side and, with the opposition back row tied in, there was no stopping Gareth as he hurled himself over the line.

His second try was a gem and I would rate it as the most determined piece of football I have ever seen in an international match. We were defending and Mervyn Davies set up a maul which we won. Everyone expected a kick but Gareth darted around the blind side and, shaking off a high tackle in the manner of a judo expert going for a shoulder throw, made forty yards up the touchline. He then kicked ahead over the remaining opposition and continued the chase. At no time until he actually touched down with a last desperate dive did he look to have outstripped the cover defence but somehow he overhauled them. At that time there was always a patch of reddy brown marl in the right hand corner which was used for treating the greyhound track. It was a wet day and he surfaced from the dive with his face covered in the stuff, so that his huge grin showed brilliantly, Black and White Minstrel-style, as the referee awarded the try.

Roy Bergiers then scored his first try after the forwards dispossessed Frame. As so often happened it was Dai Morris, who was not only quick enough to tackle him but also strong enough to rob him of the ball, who led the charge.

The final try came from me. We took a quick short penalty just inside the Scottish half and Bergiers took the ball to the 25 and handed on to me. I made some ground and looked to pass to Gerald Davies but he was obscured by one of the opposition so I held on to the ball. All the best dummies are the ones that are not predetermined and this one worked like a treat. Suddenly I had a clear path to the line. Barry John converted three of the four second half tries and kicked a penalty and that was 35–12 after having been down 10–12 at the interval.

The only cloud to mar our enjoyment of such a convincing and spectacular win was the injury to John Williams. A fractured jaw is always one of the nastier injuries and can be very serious. We should have known better. The Iron Man had lived up to his reputation and had returned to the reception by the end of the meal. There he chewed lamb on the unbroken side of his jaw and held court for the benefit of the press, explaining the medical technicalities and exact extent of the injury.

This should have caused J.P.R. to miss his first international since gaining his first cap in 1969 but politics yet again intervened in sport and the Irish match was cancelled which gave him seven weeks to recover before the game against France. The 'troubles' in Northern Ireland were going through a particularly active period but nobody had ever felt there was a problem in the Republic. Suddenly the Provisional IRA became active down there and achieved a worthless but spectacular success by blowing up the British Embassy. Nobody was hurt, and most people expressed amazement that the building had lasted that long but it proved that Belfast was not totally remote from Dublin. Thus when some of the Scottish players received anonymous letters threatening their lives before the Ireland v Scotland game a few of them refused to travel and the game was called off. This game was scheduled to precede the Ireland v Wales game and therefore it came as no surprise when similar threats, purportedly from the Provisional IRA, were received by certain Welsh players before we were due to travel to Ireland. A couple of players were unsettled by the threats and, despite the fact that most of us were quite prepared to go, the match was called off.

It was a great pity as it should have been the match of the season. Ireland had already won their two away matches of the Championship, beating England 16–12 at Twickenham and France 14–9 in Paris. Dublin has often been the graveyard for Welsh aspirations, but there was not a player in the 1972 side who did not believe that we would have recorded our first win in Dublin since 1964. Those players who had been involved in the farce of 1968 and the humiliation of 1970 were particularly determined. Whatever players believed all thoughts of a second successive Grand Slam had to be forgotten. There was talk of the game being re-arranged but nobody really believed it and the players had to concentrate on the match against France which was for a very devalued fourth consecutive Championship.

As expected by all of those who knew him, J.P.R. was fit for the French game. He even had time to prove his fitness by playing for London Welsh the previous week and therefore the Welsh team was unchanged.

France fielded a mighty pack with Walter Spanghero, Benoit

Dauga and the giant Alain Estève at the centre of it, but it was Wales who put on the early pressure. Then against the run of play, France took the lead. Pierre Villepreux, playing in his last match in the Five Nations Championship, landed a penalty from inside his own half. Nevertheless, Wales were still exerting most of the pressure and earned a stream of penalties as the French defended desperately. Barry John kicked three of them before Villepreux emulated his own earlier feat and kicked another monstrous penalty from his own half.

The score remained at 9–6 until half time but just before the interval Gerald Davies prevented a French try that could have changed the course of the match. It was once again an example of his tremendous awareness of every situation in the game. Sillières, the French left wing had been put clear, Gerald having been drawn in as they created the overlap. However, he managed to get back on terms as the Frenchman got within five yards of the line. A conventional tackle would have been praiseworthy but ineffective as Sillières would still have scored in the corner, so Gerald took a gamble. Although not a big man, he took his opposite number round the shoulders and then twisted him and flung himself beneath him. Then, using his own body as the fulcrum he threw the winger over the top of his own body. By the time Sillières touched the ball down he was over the line but he was also in touch in goal.

As was by now the Welsh pattern, we took over in the second half. Ten minutes into it Jeff Young heeled against the head and Gareth Edwards put Arthur Lewis through the gap. He linked with Gerald Davies who scored. Barry John could not convert, but soon after kicked his fourth penalty to beat Jack Bancroft's record of 88 points for his country which had lasted for over sixty years.

The second Welsh try came from a superb solo effort from John Bevan. He had a unique mixture of power and elusive running because, whereas most of the power merchants chose to go through their opponents and were therefore always vulnerable to the good tackler, he was able to half beat his man and then use his immense strength to go through what remained of the tackle. Receiving the ball thirty-five yards out, he used exactly this technique to beat his opposite number, Duprat, the Frenchman never seeming beaten but suddenly grounded in his wake. Even then a try did not appear likely because Villepreux had him covered and the French defensive cover was storming across but Bevan had another ace up his sleeve. For such an ungainly runner (he resembled Bob Hayes the great American sprinter when in full flight, all legs and arms and no style), he was remarkably balanced and could kick a ball with great control. As he came up to Villepreux he chipped to the left corner, surged past the full back and collected the ball on the bounce to score what had looked an impossible try.

The game was now safely in the bag but the French resistance remained spirited and eventually, in winning yet another ruck, Mervyn Davies took yet another knock on an injury he had carried into the match and had to leave the field. It was only five minutes from the end but the buzz from the crowd grew as they realised that the replacement was Derek Quinnell. Derek had been on the verge of the Welsh team since before the Lions tour and he had played on the flank in the Third Test on that tour, but he had still not won a full cap for Wales.

Replacements are not allowed on until the doctor in charge of the match has certified that the player who has left the field is unable to continue. To judge this, he obviously has to examine his patient. The minutes were ticking by and it seemed that the final whistle would go before Derek would be allowed on the field. Then, with just seventy seconds to go, the South Stand (opposite the players' entrance tunnel) and the lads in the North Enclosure, overlooking the tunnel, erupted and Derek Quinnell could be seen fighting his way through policemen, St John Ambulance Brigade members and anyone else in the way. He knocked a couple of policemen over but avoided arrest and the crowd roared at the referee until he noticed him and allowed him onto the park. It was hardly an auspicious first cap as he did not touch the ball but at last that elusive first cap had been won and Derek's beaming face acclaimed the fact as he trooped off triumphantly with the rest of the team barely a minute later.

Victory by 20–6 was impressive by any standards but it was particularly satisfying because it was against a good French side with players like Maso, Lux, Estève, Spanghero, Dauga, Skréla and Biemouret at their peak. It was also a game where supremacy had not been inbuilt. It was fought for and not won until the first Welsh try ten minutes into the second half.

Wales had won a sort of fourth Championship in as many years but none of the players felt any real elation. In the 'seventies there was only one key match in the Home International Championship in most seasons and it was generally accepted that the Championship winners would come from that game. Just as in 1980, everyone knew that the game was England v Wales. In 1972 it was obviously Wales v Ireland. It was just a great pity that it never took place. As London Welsh proved when they went to Dublin at the end of the season to play in the Old Belvedere International seven-asides, the welcome in Dublin would have been anything but hostile and the danger to sportsmen was minimal. Even the Provisional IRA seem to realise that they will win no support by committing atrocities against sportsmen as they have never even attempted to disrupt a game in Belfast let alone Dublin. It was an even greater shame because, unbeknown to most of us, Barry John had decided early in the season that it was going to be his last. He, more than any other player, had been under the spotlight since the Lions tour and he felt that he could no longer take the pressure. He had, incidentally, been one of the players threatened in the anonymous letters, but had been quite prepared to go to Ireland.

Those who knew him well had noticed that he had played far more games than usual once he had rested after the tour and he now explained that this was because he was conscious that it would be his last visit to many of the famous Welsh club grounds as a player. He recalls being in a state of high anxiety because he had to go to Newcastle on business and a cancelled flight had prevented him playing against Swansea at St Helens. Not unnaturally the offers for promotional work, for television and for press work poured in and Barry retired in style just as he had played the game. A few seasons later he admitted that he had stopped playing too early, but having seen what the pressures could be like he had decided early in the season that it would be the last and from then on there had been little doubt because the idea was so firmly fixed in his mind.

It is unfair to compare players of different eras and it is often unfair to make comparisons of players only a couple of years apart because they may be playing with a weaker team or against stronger opposition. However, having played with three great fly halves, David Watkins, Barry John and Phil Bennett, I have no hesitation in naming Barry as the best at the peak of his career.

He had every skill in the game at his command, including tackling when it was necessary, and with those skills, a tremendous rugby brain. If you won him good ball it would be run and not returned to touch just because Wales were in their own 25. Similarly, there would be a look of disgust and a quick return to the tight situation if he was given bad ball in the opposition 25.

He even created a new sort of pass, flipping the ball on with his wrists and fingers instead of swinging it on with his arms in the traditional manner. It worked for him beautifully but many of his imitators found it impossible without running across with the ball. He was therefore cursed by quite a number of coaches, as every schoolboy modelled himself on the first rugby superstar.

In fact his whole style was unique. Touch-kicking became an art form – it was almost sacrilege to waste effort by allowing the ball to cross the line until it had run out of steam. Running was a question of teasing the opposition into thinking they had him covered and then drifting away; and while others prepared long and carefully for difficult shots at goal, place-kicking was made to look as easy as taking a corner in soccer.

By the end of his career, the world saluted his play.

8

SCARLETS RULE OK
1972/73

There were high hopes for the 1972/73 season despite the retirement of Barry John. Phil Bennett had been playing inspired rugby for Llanelli and had already gained five caps in various positions, so he seemed to be the King's natural successor and the whole of Wales was convinced that Max Boyce's fly half factory was working well. The first opposition of the season was the All Blacks and with the Lions having beaten them in New Zealand the previous year the people of Wales were looking forward to a great victory from the National side who, despite the constant criticism, most believed were better than the full British Isles team.

Optimism was increased when Llanelli, living up to their reputation as the scourge of touring teams, beat Kirkpatrick's All Blacks 9–3 at Stradey Park. The team read as follows:

R. Davies, J. J. Williams, R. Bergiers, R. Gravell, A. Hill, P. Bennett, R. Hopkins, B. Llewelyn, R. Thomas, A. Crocker, D. Thomas (captain), D. Quinnell, T. David, G. Jenkins and H. Jenkins.

Many of the players were to make a huge contribution to Welsh rugby over the next few years, Roy Bergiers had played his best game for Wales in the last match the previous season when the strength of his tackling had been a revelation, Phil Bennett, Chico Hopkins, Barry Llewelyn, Delme Thomas and Derek Quinnell (by the skin of his teeth) were internationals already and J. J. Williams, Ray Gravell and Tommy David were to play for Wales in the future. It was a tremendous line-up, especially when coached by the man who planned the defeat of the All Blacks in New Zealand with the Lions, Carwyn James.

They played a storming game, never allowing the All Blacks to settle down, with every man running his heart out and tackling everything that moved for the full eighty minutes. Typically in such a game the Llanelli try came from pressure. Phil Bennett struck the bar with a penalty attempt and as Lyn Colling, the New Zealand scrum half, tried to clear the ball Roy Bergiers stormed through to charge down his kick and follow through for the touch down. Bennett this time made no mistake with the kick. Although Karam kicked a penalty to reduce the leeway Andy Hill, who has scored more points than any other player in history for Llanelli, kicked a magnificent penalty in reply from fifty yards and Llanelli were home and dry.

The two most significant comments afterwards came from captain and coach. Carwyn, always a student of the game, gave his considered verdict: 'After watching them play against Western Counties we felt that if we could contain the All Blacks at the back of the line out and take the game to them, they would react badly under pressure. It had to be a physical contest all the way.'

Delme allowed himself a little more emotion. 'I'm glad we won, my wife would have had my neck if we hadn't – she hasn't seen me for ten weeks.'

The build-up to the Wales v New Zealand game did not go that smoothly. Roy Bergiers was injured in the trial match and there were doubts about his fitness until the last moment. When he was passed fit Arthur Lewis, his centre partner, had to drop out of the team with a pulled hamstring. It was a great shame because he had been named as captain for the first time. Jim Shanklin the London Welsh centre who had been capped against South Africa in 1970 replaced him.

The obvious replacement as captain was Delme Thomas after the tremendous performance from Llanelli and he was joined in the second row by Derek Quinnell, the first time he had been selected for Wales. There was also a change in the front row. John Lloyd, having captained the side very successfully in 1972, went out and was replaced by Glyn Shaw the tearaway loose-head prop from Neath. His rise to prominence was quite remarkable. He had only joined Neath in the New Year of 1971 from Seven Sisters where he had learned the rudiments of propping in the hard school of West Wales League rugby. At the time he was capped he was still only twenty-one, an amazingly young age for a prop to be considered good enough for his country (Barry Llewelyn on the tight head was considered too young by many people in 1970 when he was capped at the age of twenty-two). Unlike most props, he was tall and slim and few of the players believed the match programme which gave his weight at fifteen stone. However, all the players respected his strength and his ability to out-scrummage much heavier men. That strength came from his work as a self-employed coal screener, he earned his money by sifting the tips to reclaim the good coal that had been deposited with the waste. The more he sifted the more he earned and the stronger he became.

The build-up to the game was indicative of the importance everyone in Wales attached to it. Instead of the normal excitement and confident boasting there was a seriousness that is seldom seen when a match against one of the home countries is about to happen. It was almost as if privately the two countries had agreed that this was for the World Championship.

Clive Rowlands gave his usual rousing team talk, constantly referring back to 1969 and the chance to avenge the humiliation of two 19-point defeats. Delme Thomas then gave us his own build-up. Always a man of few words, it was often hard to tell what Delme was thinking, so when he appealed to our Welshness, our pride, our belief in each other and our duty to ourselves in quiet, impassioned tones, it was very moving and, just as Llanelli had been a couple of weeks before, we were now prepared to give our all for him.

There was also the intriguing prospect of actually playing against Keith Murdoch for the first time. The Otago prop had occupied a lot of newspaper space on the 1971 tour but had never made an appearance against the Lions. New Zealand could not have had a better start to the game. After seven minutes they were 6–0 up from two penalty goals from their new full back Joe Karam. It might have been his first cap but he showed nerves of steel as he hit both dead centre when Welsh forwards strayed offside. Then Keith Murdoch left his mark on the game by scoring a try. Going had made the initial thrust and Murdoch followed in support. He was brought down well short of the line but the referee, 'Johnnie' Johnson, had no doubts that his momentum had carried him over. It was now 10–0 to New Zealand and things looked bad for Wales. The All Black forwards had won most of the possession and Wylie, Sutherland and Kirkpatrick had controlled the loose play because they usually had possession and kept it tight. Phil Bennett reduced the lead with a first penalty goal, but then just before half time Karam kicked another goal to keep the margin at 10 points.

I cannot actually remember what Delme said at half time but the look on his face as he saw our chance of victory being thrown away by stupid mistakes – all the penalties had been avoidable – was enough to make the side even more determined and right from the beginning of the second half the Welsh pack was a completely different unit. In the first scrum New Zealand were hurled backwards and it was Wales's turn to attack. Suddenly we were winning good ball and the backs were given a chance. Soon John Bevan scored a typical try. Having been put away fifty yards out, he set off like a sprinting tank for the corner. Bryan Williams, the great All Black wing, and Duncan Hales, the centre, both homed in on him but were brushed aside as he scored in the corner. It was again an awesome exhibition of pace and power from the Ferndale Flyer.

When Phil Bennett kicked a penalty goal a minute later Wales were only down by three points and the noise in the stadium became deafening as the Welsh forwards continued to take the initiative away from the All Blacks and time after time launched their backs into the attack.

Then disaster struck with two more stupid penalties being given away in mid-field, both for technical offences. Karam, appearing more and more like a latter day Don Clarke to Welsh supporters, made light of the forty-five yard kicks and Wales were back to 19–10. The Welsh forwards were by now completely in control, winning rucks and mauls at will as they powered forward but the New Zealand defence somehow held out. Phil Bennett landed a penalty as their methods became more and more desperate and then landed another as they became blatantly illegal.

In the closing stages we thought we had pulled the game out of the fire when John Williams forced his way over the line. As a try it looked very similar to the one scored by Murdoch in the first half but this time Mr Johnson decided that J.P.R. had been stopped short and then 'rabbited' his way over. Even then the drama was not over. We were now getting very upset with the All Blacks' tactics. They were resorting to any means at their disposal to stop us scoring and were quite happy to give away penalties for obstruction and short arm tackling as long as they were outside kicking range. Eventually, almost on the final whistle they were forced to short arm tackle J. P. R. Williams as he surged through just thirty-five yards out to the right of the posts. Phil Bennett had that kick to tie the game but hit the ball just wide of the right-hand post. It was curling in all the way and had the kick been ten yards further back would have gone over, but it wasn't and we had lost.

In retrospect it was our own fault. The penalties that had been given away should have been avoided at international level where penalty goals play such a large part in deciding games. Joe Karam kicked five goals in six attempts, Wales had more attempts but on the day Phil Bennett could not match his reliability. Losing is always hard to take but there are times when you know you are well beaten and it makes it easier. We did not deserve to beat Ian Kirkpatrick's All Blacks because we contributed so much to our own downfall but we did deserve to win in many ways and had there been the differential penalty, as we have today, we would have won. It was certainly the most difficult defeat to take in the whole of my career. I felt sick and so did most of the other players.

Delme just kept repeating, 'God, boys, we had 'em. We had 'em . . .'

The All Blacks should have been happy but instead of being generous in victory a group of the more senior players, including Keith Murdoch, arrived at the dinner in an ugly mood. Murdoch himself ploughed through all the autograph-hunters waiting in the corridors of the Angel, knocking several of them down as he made his way to the Banqueting Suite. At the dinner they were equally surly and the evening culminated in the big prop thumping a security guard. Next day he was sent home and disappeared into the mining area of North Australia. It was a great pity, on a first acquaintance the Welsh front row thought he was a good player.

On the Sunday evening, after a day of depression in Cardiff I drove down to stay with friends in Garnant in the Amman Valley. Just above Gwaun-Cae-Gurwen, the birthplace of Gareth Edwards. I picked up a hitch-hiker in the pouring rain (it always seemed to rain in the Amman). It transpired that he was still on his way home to Ammanford, having been to the match on the Saturday and then having had far too much to drink in trying to drown his sorrows. Naturally, we talked about the game and by the time we reached my destination, the Amman United Rugby Club, he had realised who I was. He intended to catch the

Arthur Lewis scores from an 'Arthur'. Gareth Edwards, having made the crossfield run before the scissors, looks back triumphantly with Roy Bergiers.

Gerald Davies takes out the last of the opposition and pivots to put in Gareth Edwards. The team came first, even if it meant Gareth went on ahead in their try-scoring battle.

An unusual shot – Delme Thomas grounded and Mike Roberts in the air. Jeff Young, at the front, Glyn Shaw and Phil Llewellyn stop the Irish coming through, in 1973.

Terry Cobner uses his immense strength to stay on his feet until help arrives from Trevor Evans and Gareth Edwards, against England, 1975.

bus from there, but as he put it, 'To 'ave a lift in the rain is worth a pint, to have one from someone who was actually out there on the Park is worth two.' It was only then about 8.30 p.m. but he missed the last bus.

The first of the home internationals was against England and the only change in the Welsh side from that originally selected for the match against New Zealand was that John Lloyd came back to replace Barry Llewelyn who was suffering from a knee injury. Although few of us would have believed it then he had played his last game for Wales. He was still only twenty-four and had justly gained a tremendous reputation as an intelligent running prop. He was one of the few players ever to make a successful conversion from back-row to front-row forward. At 6' 2½" and 16 st 4 lbs he was ideal as a prop and was one of the fastest front-row forwards that I ever played with. He did make one attempt at a comeback and were it not for illness would have made it, but he had set up a business of his own and the time he needed to spend on that, allied to the time he felt he should spend helping his wife bring up a young family, left too little time for the sort of commitment needed to play international rugby. His was a sad and premature loss to the Welsh team. Many props do not fully mature until they are thirty and he could have spanned the decade.

Arthur Lewis, having recovered from his hamstring injury, took his place as captain. It was not that Delme had done a bad job but by this time the squad system was so organised that the captain for the season was announced in November.

The Welsh forwards began the match as they had finished against the All Blacks and exerted enormous pressure but the penalties that resulted were not converted. Phil Bennett sprayed two wide and unluckily hit the post with the ball rebounding instead of going over on the third attempt.

As often happens when a side has survived a period of pressure without giving away a score, England took the lead. They won a ruck in front of the Welsh posts having established virtually their first attacking position and Cowman dropped a goal. That was after fifteen minutes but three minutes later Wales were in the lead. Derek Quinnell had become a favourite with the Stradey crowd because of his powerful bursts for the line, knocking opponents out of the way with his dropped shoulder. Already he had made two such runs and had only just been held. Now he did it again and, although stopped, managed to feed John Bevan to his left. The Cardiff winger, not to be outdone, powered his way through two more tackles to score wide out. On the half hour, we went further ahead. Jeff Young won a heel against the head, Phil Bennett dummy scissored with Roy Bergiers and set John Bevan free on the left. He was stopped in the English 25 but from the scrum that followed, Bennett put in a beautifully angled kick and Gerald Davies scored in the right-hand corner.

England came back through a penalty from the late Sam Doble but Gareth Edwards then slipped through close to the ruck in typical fashion to make the score 12–6 to Wales at the interval.

Phil Bennett was having another poor day with his place-kicking so I was given a kick again after a year of deferring to Barry John. It was for a line out offence and I put it over safely. Doble then kicked another penalty before we scored twice in the last five minutes to make the score line as convincing as had been our superiority.

Arthur scored with his favourite 'Arthur' move, bouncing away two tacklers as he took the ball. He was one of the best examples of someone who never took his eyes off the ball until he had safely caught it, even if he was about to receive the man as well. Phil Bennett converted this try but then John Bevan closed the scoring as he had opened it, with a try. This time Gareth Edwards did the spade work and made an overlap for him. 25–9 was a convincing win and Wales looked all set for another good season.

Between the England match and the game against Scotland the Barbarians played the All Blacks in the traditional final game of their tour.

Seven Welshmen were included in the side, Bennett, J. P. R. Williams, Dawes, who was brought out of international retirement (he continued to play for London Welsh) to captain the team, Bevan, Edwards, Tommy David from Pontypridd but playing for Llanelli and Derek Quinnell who came in as a last minute substitute No. 8 when Mervyn Davies had to withdraw with influenza. In a superbly open game the Barbarians beat New Zealand 23–11 and Gareth Edwards scored a try that many people consider the greatest ever seen on a rugby field. Perhaps not entirely coincidentally six of the seven Welshmen playing were involved in the movement. It began with Phil Bennett fielding a ball just to the right of his own posts. Shaking off the tensions that at the time inhibited his play in full internationals, he set off on the counter-attack instead of kicking, and with two superb side-steps left the All Blacks trailing before linking with J. P. R. Williams on the 25. By now the move was going towards the left-hand touchline and when J.P.R. handed on via Pullin to John Dawes, he switched it inside to Tommy David who stormed on and gave the ball back on the outside to Derek Quinnell. Finally Edwards came from nowhere to take the final short pass and sprint the last fifteen yards before diving over in the corner.

1973 was the year in which the Scottish R.F.U. celebrated their centenary. It made their celebrations all the more sweet to record their first victory over Wales since 1967. It was the first time that we saw Andy Irvine who had won his first cap against New Zealand and it was the first time that Ian McLauchlan, the 'Mighty Mouse' of the 1971 Lions tour, captained his country. He made his forwards play with as much energy as he always expended and, using himself and Sandy Carmichael as the linch pins of the exercise, persuaded them to scrummage as they had never scrummaged before. They caught the Welsh pack on the hop and won so much good ball in the first twenty minutes of the game that they scored two tries and put 10 points on the board, which was enough to see them home.

They had first use of the strong wind blowing down the pitch and soon pinned Wales back into their own 25. They then pushed Wales in a set scrum and Dougie Morgan launched Colin Telfer. He went for the outside break, sold a dummy and was over. Morgan converted to make it 6–0. Then from another scrum Telfer went blind, having first tried the open side, carved his way through a static Welsh defence and found Billy Steele clear on the right. The winger scored in the corner, 10–0.

By this time the Welsh team had great confidence in itself, perhaps too much confidence, because we still expected to win and perhaps did not work hard enough to make it happen. Certainly the forwards tightened up their game to gain an equal share of the ball but the Scottish pack were not about to relinquish their advantage and, behind, the Welsh back division was not working with the same fluency to which we had become accustomed. Nevertheless we began to pull the Scots back. Phil Bennett kicked a penalty and then just before half time I kicked one and we felt reasonably happy about the state of the game with the prospect of playing with the wind in the second period.

Arthur Lewis was certain that the second half surge which had become so much a feature of the Welsh team would carry us home. His half time talk was punctuated with appeals to each individual player.

'C'mon, Del, it was a slow start but we'm got 'em now.'

'C'mon, Merv, we'm a got 'em.'

'Gareth, we'm a got 'em.'

'Bas, we'm a got 'em.'

He was wrong. Hard as we pressed, the Scots pack were equal to the situation and although the vital try was almost scored on several occasions the backs were never really in total harmony and all we managed was another penalty goal from Phil Bennett. Although we were close enough to snatch a dramatic victory as in 1971, there was not the same belief within our own ranks that it would happen. Sadly we had to concede that we had lost to the better side on the day and by two tries to nil.

The performance of the forwards had been so lacklustre against Scotland that changes were inevitable for the game against Ireland. John Bevan was unavailable because of injury and was replaced by Jim Shanklin. John Lloyd who had captained the side throughout the 1972 season had finally played his last game for Wales. He won twenty-four caps and developed from being a very mobile forward who was perhaps suspect as a scrummager into a really powerful prop. Perhaps all those steaks in Argentina had helped. Always quiet off the field, he led by example and was a vital contributor to the success of the Welsh team in the first half of the decade. He was replaced by Phil Llewellyn from Swansea.

Derek Quinnell was also dropped. He played much of his rugby at this time at No. 8 for Llanelli and his critics said that he played far too loose a game for a second row forward and blamed him for some of the lack of drive in the Welsh pack. To counter this the selectors reverted to Mike Roberts. The big London Welshman had had a disappointing Lions tour two years previously, but had now recovered his appetite for the game. (He had never lost it for food and that was part of the problem.) His weight and undoubted mauling ability were hopefully going to add some steel to the pack.

The first half of the game was completely shapeless with the packs almost cancelling each other out and neither back division able to string their movements together. Phil Bennett kicked two penalties for Wales and Barry McGann, the tubby but very talented outside half from Lansdowne, kicked one for Ireland. Suddenly in the second half the game blossomed and all the running rugby that had been missing in the first half was there in abundance.

Phil was having his best game at outside half for Wales. In the first half he had kept us in control, with shrewd probing kicks and accurate touch finders and now he began to show the sort of confidence in his own running ability that he had not carried on to the National Stadium previously except when playing for the Barbarians. Just as he had a few weeks earlier for them, he started a counter-attack from his own 25 and linked with Glyn Shaw who had done remarkably well to get back with him. Glyn carried the ball to half way and I took it on from there and set up a maul with Mervyn Davies. Dai Morris ripped the ball free and gave it to Gareth Edwards who wriggled through on the blind before linking inside to Jim Shanklin who scored.

The Welsh forwards were beginning to dominate the loose with Mike Roberts particularly effective in the mauling at close quarters and another Welsh try had to come. Almost inevitably it was Edwards who scored it. I stole the ball from the Irish and moved it left to Phil Bennett. He broke back to the right and passed to Edwards to give on to Arthur Lewis. He scissored with Gerald Davies who then found Gareth, with his marvellous instinct for space, back outside him with a clear run in. 'Benny', as Phil was now universally known, converted and Wales suddenly had a handsome lead of 16–6.

Ireland still had one more ace up their sleeve, Mike Gibson, that superlative centre, cutting through on the short side and beating five Welsh players before scoring. McGann converted to make it 16–12, but Wales were home and dry.

It had still not been a happy performance from the Welsh side. Our forwards had only dominated in short spells and seemed to lack the fire that had been so much part of the successful period since 1969 and outside the scrum the backs were moving without any real fluency. Gareth Edwards and Phil Bennett were not combining as effectively as Gareth and Barry had done and generally the cogs in the Welsh squad machine were not running smoothly. Something needed oiling.

For the game against France there were further changes. Arthur Lewis was dropped and replaced by the London Welsh centre, Keith Hughes, and Dai Morris and I were also axed because of the lack of drive in the scrums. We were replaced by the much bigger pairing of Tommy David and Derek Quinnell. However, upon arriving at the squad session at Afan Lido the following Sunday, feeling very unhappy at being made a scapegoat, I learned that I was back in the side. A very disappointed Derek Quinnell congratulated me and told me that he had arrived with a cold and, with still a week to go before the game, was immediately withdrawn. We shrugged our shoulders and managed weak smiles but wondered what the hell was going on. Since the formation of the squad it was very untypical behaviour by the selectors. Arthur Lewis was also brought back into the side as Keith Hughes was injured.

Tommy David did replace Dai Morris which was the first change in the back row line-up since 1970 when I had elected not to play against the Springboks. Dai, Mervyn and I played eighteen times together for Wales which remains a record for a back-row combination and it was obviously sad to see it broken up but sentiment has no part in the selection of international teams. Although we had plenty of rugby left in us, we were perhaps becoming a little complacent and less hungry after such a long run in the national side.

The squad session did not go well. Gareth, who had been reinstated as captain for the first time since 1970, had by now perfected a huge spin pass but it was not launching the line as well as a shorter, quicker pass. We practised for ages but Phil Bennett was still taking the ball standing still and then running sideways which was clogging up the midfield. We finished the practice without the problem being resolved.

We arrived in France to find ourselves staying at the Hotel Terminus, a massive old railway hotel, instead of the quiet and small Hotel Normandy where we had always stayed previously. It was something of a let down but we found that we could not return to the Normandy because of a dispute about the W.R.U. bill two years previously. On returning to the hotel after the match the players had gone to the bar for a few drinks and had been followed there by a hoard of supporters. The supporters had remained after we had left to go to the banquet but had seen several players signing for drinks. They decided it was worth a try and the barmen accepted their signatures even though they were not staying at the hotel. Three hundred pounds worth of booze later, they left. The W.R.U. rightly refused to pay the bill and the Normandy insisted that they should. The money is probably still owing today.

The game was also at a new venue, the Parc des Princes, a superb new stadium shared by the rugby and soccer federations. All spectators are seated and much closer to the action than at Colombes. Even the loos are of the highest standard and comfort.

With the spectators so much more enclosed the full Gallic temperament of the French rugby supporter was immediately more apparent and it was enhanced by the town band from Dax. They managed to get permission to play on the pitch but there was none of the formality of a military band for them. They just belted out their traditional songs and even arrived with a spare conductor, apparently because the first one was usually drunk before the end of the day and therefore unable to last the course.

France had made ten changes in their side after having been defeated by England at Twickenham and therefore we should have had the advantage with a far more settled side but we never really moved out of second gear and Romeu, the French fly half, took his chances to kick the goals so that France drew away to win with some ease in a game that was something of a non-event. Even the Welsh place-kicking was a disappointment. I missed an early chance which I would normally have expected to kick and later in the first half Phil Bennett missed a sitter. In the meantime Romeu had kicked two penalties and then dropped a goal after Badin, the French centre, had latched on to an Edwards pass that went astray and had put away Cantoni who had set up a perfect maul in front of the Welsh posts.

At last in the final quarter of the game the Welsh pack began to find some fire and put on the pressure but we still looked unlikely to score as the Edwards/Bennett combination was still not working well and Benny was tending to run across the field and crowd up the centre. Even John Williams' incursions into the line would not work smoothly and there were several embarrassing tangles as players found themselves in the way of each other. The only reward was a well taken drop goal from Phil Bennett but that was not until the seventy-fourth minute of the game and any hopes of a dramatic last-minute try and conversion to save the match were dashed when Romeu kicked a forty-five yard penalty to make the score 12–3.

There was only one piece of exciting play for Wales throughout the whole game. In the last few minutes Arthur Lewis was injured and had to leave the field. Jim Shanklin moved into the centre and J. J. Williams took his place on the left wing to gain his first cap. In his only chance to attack he sprinted down the left, kicked ahead and took off like a rocket after it. It was a ploy that was to become his trademark and earned him many tries. In this case the French cover defence just beat him to the ball but it almost earned him a try in his first international.

It was a disappointed Welsh contingent that arrived at the banquet that night, disappointed not just because of the result on the day but because of the season as a whole. What had begun with a storming performance against New Zealand had degenerated into a side that had lost its direction by the time the season ended. The evening was saved by the unscripted arrival of the band from Dax. Suddenly the doors burst open and in the middle of a speech from Monsieur Pompidou, in they marched. Black and red berets were given to all the players and the dinner disintegrated in good-humoured chaos. Unfortunately, Gareth still had to make his captain's speech and as most of us were marched out by the band we could see his imploring looks begging someone to stay behind and wait for him. We had no choice and had to follow the band.

It had been a strange season. Each of the countries in the Championship had won their two home matches and therefore for the first time ever there was a five-way tie for the Championship. As far as Wales was concerned, we had played as if we expected to win without putting in the effort that is vital, no matter how good the team is. It was time for a re-think.

There is no better time to introduce new blood into a team than when it is on tour and in the summer of 1973 we went to Canada on a sort of missionary trip. Nobody expected any of the Canadian sides, including the national team, to give us a hard game but the tour was designed to stimulate interest in rugby in that vast country.

We also took Gerry Lewis, the team physiotherapist, along for the first time. It had always seemed strange to me that he was not the first person selected. At home internationals he always did such a good job, doubling up as baggage man as well as looking after the minor injuries of the players, that I would rate him as one of the most important members of the administration.

Everybody was delighted for him. He deserved the trip as a reward for all his work at home and he proved invaluable on tour. Playing twice a week means that players are more vulnerable to injury and continuity of treatment is impossible when you are moving from town to town, unless you have someone medically qualified as a member of the touring party. If you rely on local facilities, time is wasted, and going to see different doctors often means a new diagnosis in each town, as I found to the cost of my knee in South Africa in 1968. On top of all this it is vital for a player to have faith in the man who is treating him and all the players trusted Gerry completely. Always ready with a new story and always interested in the tales of the players' social lives, he was and still is a very popular character and a great aid to the management in keeping up morale. It is unbelievable that the Lions still go abroad, and for a much longer period, without a physiotherapist.

Gareth was chosen to captain the party and Ken Gwilym was made the manager. All those who had played against France were selected with the exception of Jim Shanklin. In addition John Bevan returned after injury. Keith Hughes who had originally been selected against France was included and the reserve half backs were Ian Lewis from Bridgend and Clive Shell from Aberavon. Dai Morris was the extra back-row forward and Allan Martin, the young Aberavon lock made his first tour. Gerry Wallace from Cardiff was the third prop and Bobby Windsor, then still at Cross Keys, provided cover for Jeff Young at hooker.

In contrast to all the other national team tours we had been on it was a wonderfully relaxed itinerary. We did all the normal tourist things. In Vancouver we had snowball fights and watched people ski on Grouse Mountain and then swam in the Pacific on the same day. In Alberta we were all given enormous white stetsons from the Calgary Rugby Club (unfortunately we were too early for the rodeo season). In Ottawa we were shown around the Parliament and from Toronto we took a trip to see Niagara Falls. It really was a holiday but we played some good rugby as well, even though we gave the manager and captain a hard time when they tried to enforce discipline in the same way as if we were in New Zealand.

British Columbia were beaten 31–6 and then Alberta were thrashed 76–6 with Allan Martin giving a superb display of goal-kicking. Eight conversions and four penalties gave him a tally of 28 points, a Welsh record. We then beat Quebec 44–9 and Ontario 79–0. Both of these games were played on Canadian Football (virtually identical to American Gridiron Football) pitches which are narrower than rugby pitches and therefore cramped our passing movements!

In between the matches Clive Rowlands made us work fairly hard on the practice ground and managed to persuade Phil Bennett that we really could not afford to play soccer at every session, but the holiday mood continued until the build-up for the big match of the tour against the Canadian National XV.

Off the field everyone had enjoyed themselves, the after-match gatherings were far more informal than in some of the more traditional rugby playing countries and you would often find yourself explaining the game to people who were about to see or had just seen their first match. Inspired by the stetsons, we had one group within the party who organised themselves as a branch of the United States Cavalry and Corporal Windsor and Trooper Shaw refused to take orders from anyone but Captain Arthur Lewis. It could have been a major problem but Captain Lewis was only interested in captaining the social side of the tour so there were no real difficulties and Ken Gwilym found them no threat to his authority, except when they wanted a week off to go Indian hunting.

The biggest crisis was over Jeff Young's telephone bill in Ottawa. He became very melancholy one evening and decided he just had to 'phone his wife, Pat. Once he had contacted her he became very amorous and stayed on the 'phone for half an hour. He even went as far as to discuss what he would do if she were with him at the moment. Pat, realising he was drunk kept telling him to put down the 'phone but to no avail. In the morning Jeff's room mate Gerry Wallace reminded him of some of the things he had said to Pat and in a fit of remorse Jeff insisted on calling her again to apologise. He was stopped as we booked out of the hotel by an anxious official who gave him the bill. We were not told exactly how much it was but suffice to say Jeff did not have enough with him in Canada. The future seemed to hold nothing but washing dishes for him, but fortunately between the rest of us we just had enough to get him off the hook.

Broke he might have been but at least he could take his place in the team to face Canada in a game that was doubly important for them as it was the first to be televised live, coast to coast in that country. J. J. Williams played on the right wing because Gerald Davies had pulled a hamstring. The match was a good exhibition for the Canadian public. In the first half the Canadian team held us well and it was only just before half time that we scored our first try but then in the second half we gained clear superiority in the forwards and we moved away to win by 58–20.

Phil Bennett almost beat Allan Martin's record of 28 points in a match but had to settle for one try, seven conversions and two penalty goals, 24 points. Tommy David and Keith Hughes each scored two tries and Phil Llewellyn, John Bevan and J. J. Williams one each. I kicked a conversion and also scored a try, despite threats from J. J. Williams and John Bevan that they would not pass to me because they did not like flank forwards scoring as many tries as wingers. We all ended up with seven tries for the tour, much to their disgust.

Apart from the fear that we would never get out of Canada – we had to wait twenty-four hours in Toronto airport for our charter to arrive from Vancouver and the Canadian R.F.U. had not enough money to book us back into an hotel – it had been a breath of fresh air as a rugby tour. There were times when we were four to a room in hotels and times when we were given just five dollars a day for food, so that we could not afford to eat in the hotel, but the enthusiasm we found everywhere for the game, and the enjoyment of helping spread its popularity throughout the world made it very worthwhile. It is also a very beautiful country and few of us would have had a chance to go there had it not been for rugby.

9

BLIND IRISH REFEREE
1973/74

I could lay claim to being the most successful captain of Wales ever. It would be a spurious claim but if you counted matches against non-International Board countries as full internationals and judged the success of a captain purely on the points scored in games when he was in control, it would be true. Who else can claim a record of: played 1, won 1, points for 62, points against 14?

All of which is a rather long-winded way of saying that the first match of the 1973/74 season was against Japan. Wales did them the honour of selecting a full international side but as Gareth Edwards had delayed his return to the game and was taking a late holiday, I was chosen as captain. Clive Shell deputised for Gareth.

The game was one-sided because the Japanese could not win line out ball. They tried all sorts of variations, some of them quite original but the height of Derek Quinnell, Allan Martin and Mervyn Davies was too much to overcome and therefore the match was never in doubt. Had line outs been replaced by scrums every time the ball went into touch they would have fared much better, as their technique was superb. On the Welsh loose heads they timed their push perfectly, their togetherness was admirable, and on their own ball they locked the scrum most effectively. However, the line out is a part of our game, and long may it remain so, although perhaps in different form to the present untidy and unnaturally spaced compromise which is supposed to allow for jumping and effective blocking but does neither.

So from the abundant flow of ball against Japan we had a festival of running. The centres understandably became a little self-indulgent even though Gerald Davies and J. J. Williams were screaming for the ball, but nevertheless we ran in eleven tries and Phil Bennett converted nine. He scored two of the tries to set a new points record for a home match with 26. The other scorers were J. J. Williams, Roy Bergiers, Clive Shell, myself, J. P. R. Williams, Gerald Davies, Bobby Windsor and Keith Hughes twice.

The biggest cheers were reserved for the Japanese when they came back right at the end of the game to score two tries both touched down by Itoh their right wing. The second one in particular was a little gem, with the winger dummying two experienced Welsh internationals before going over in the corner. Yamamoto could not convert either of them but did kick two penalties. Afterwards, their ever pragmatic manager, Shiggy Konno, was completely unbowed. He knew he had wanted to play against the best to show his players just how far rugby in Japan still had to go. Now they knew exactly what they had to do. Try as they might they had not succeeded in overcoming their lack of height and therefore needed to recruit some bigger men. Contrary to popular opinion, said Shiggy, they were around but preferred to take up sports like Sumo wrestling. Knowing just how much he had been responsible for the growth of the popularity of rugby in Japan, none of the Welsh players doubted that he would find his men.

Having built myself up as the most successful captain of Wales, I must also admit to being the most unsuccessful. No other captain has ever led a side to such a resounding victory and then been dropped. Even more ignominiously I was the only change from the side that played against Japan except for the return of Gareth Edwards who was reinstated as captain.

The next game was against Australia who also made a short visit to Britain in the autumn of 1973. They played eight matches in England and Wales with Tests against both those countries. It was a disastrous tour, as they beat only two provincial sides and lost both internationals heavily.

I had been vice-captain in East Wales's victory over the tourists and thought I would probably continue in that role for Wales (which is always a dangerous assumption). But Dai Morris had started the new season with all his old determination and enthusiasm and was selected in front of me with Tommy David, who had recovered from a shoulder injury that caused him to leave the field against Japan, on the other flank. I can remember feeling very hurt, but then nobody likes to be dropped and in retrospect I had had a longer run than most.

The game against Australia gave Bobby Windsor his first full cap. He had moved from Cross Keys to Pontypool at the beginning of the season and the extra competitiveness of their game pushed him ahead of Jeff Young who he had been pushing hard for the whole of the previous year. Jeff Young had won twenty-two caps which is remarkable in itself, considering the number of critics he had in Wales. He occasionally gave away silly penalties but was also blamed for a number given away by Gareth Edwards as he learned the scrum half trade. He also had a couple of bad matches when he lost too many loose-head heels to his opposite number. Again, that was often only half his fault, as every hooker relies on a steady and consistent relationship with his scrum half. Only those who played with him know his true worth. Suffice to say he was vital to the scrummaging power of the Welsh pack from 1969 to 1974.

The game was all over by half time because Phil Bennett was in superb kicking form and punished some rash moments by the Australian forwards. They had shown that they were not strong enough as a unit to compete with a good British pack and tried to compensate with what, at its kindest, can only be called over-vigorous play. They literally paid the penalty and at the interval were down 12–0. The last three kicks were all given away in the ten minutes before half time as they began to lose the forward struggle and Benny made no mistakes, even though the first two were mammoth kicks from well over forty yards. He and Barry John more than any other players proved the point that timing is everything in kicking. They are both small men but could kick goals from as far as any of the siege-gun merchants.

After five minutes of the second half, Wales went further ahead with a try from Dai Morris and it was worth waiting for. Wales had developed a counter-attacking move, usually between wing and full back, but this time between Gareth Edwards and Bennett, in which the player receiving a kick in his own 25 would sprint towards a touchline, hopefully taking the opposition with him only to give to a man coming back to the open. With opponents, especially in safety first international matches, really expecting a touch kick it was and still can be capable of totally splitting the other team. On this occasion Phil Bennett set J. P. R. Williams free and the full back made fifty yards into the Australian 25 where he was bundled into touch. Wales won the line out and from it set up a ruck which they also won to allow Dai

Morris to pick up and dive over. Phil Bennett hit the post with his conversion attempt.

Wales's second try came from a well-executed crash move. Having won a line out they moved the ball to Roy Bergiers, there for his power more than his ability to beat a man, and the Llanelli centre set up a ruck. Wales won it and with the Australian defence in disarray it was a simple matter to move the ball right via Edwards, Bennett and J. P. R. Williams to the master finisher, Gerald Davies, who scored.

Almost on the final whistle Gareth Edwards had to leave the field with a hamstring pull and while Wales were down to fourteen men they scored again. Phil Bennett went to scrum half and with J. P. R. Williams outside him they moved the ball to Keith Hughes. He cut back inside on the sort of stuttering side-step run which is wonderful when it comes off but more often goes up a blind alley and found support from Tommy David and Glyn Shaw. They eventually worked the ball to Bobby Windsor who stormed in to become the first hooker ever to score on his debut for Wales. His smile showed that he was probably aware of the fact.

As Phil Bennett converted there was a very anxious Clive Shell on the touchline trying to attract the referee's attention. The game was moving into injury time and if the referee blew up for no side he would have been deprived of his first cap. He made it on to the field to a huge cheer from the crowd but had no opportunity to make the same sort of impact as Chico Hopkins at Twickenham in 1970. However, he did go one better than Derek Quinnell when he won his first cap as a substitute against France. He at least managed to touch the ball as he put it into the final scrum. He deserved his cap, having understudied Gareth since Chico had become a professional.

It had been a convincing 24–0 win but Australia had been woefully weak and before the Home Championship Wales decided to hold a trial, even though they had had two international matches upon which to judge the form of the players. It seemed unnecessary and was made even more pointless by several injury problems. Steve Fenwick, a promising youngster from Bridgend, withdrew with a groin strain which made the problem of replacing Roy Bergiers even more difficult and Derek Quinnell was not available because of a cracked cheekbone. Tommy David was also still suffering from a troublesome shoulder injury. Before the team was announced both Quinnell and David had to prove their fitness by playing for their respective clubs. Derek could not fit in a game for Llanelli, but in good Welsh tradition a game was found for him with the local steelworks side. Also in the squad was Barry Llewelyn. Having had a cartilage operation on his troublesome knee, he had returned to Llanelli full of zest and had made a remarkable recovery.

When the team was announced it was learned that Tommy David had not been considered as his shoulder had not recovered. He did not win another cap until 1976, yet two months earlier had appeared set for a long international career when he had played a storming game against Australia. Luck always plays an important part in whether or not a player has a long international career or a few glorious moments. Luck was not with Tommy but it was with Terry Cobner.

After the trial he had been omitted from the squad and as he put it, 'I thought it was all over for me – perhaps they wanted a chap with more hair on top.' But now he was back from the wilderness and into the team. He grabbed the chance with both hands and gave Tommy David no chance of a comeback. To make the occasion even more memorable for him the game was against Scotland at Cardiff on his twenty-eighth birthday. Therefore he would receive his cap at the after-match banquet, a present he will never forget. Gareth Edwards was given the captaincy and Mervyn Davies became pack leader but the most remarkable selection must have been that of Ian Hall. He had won his first cap against New Zealand back in 1967 and had won another four in 1970 and 1971 on the wing and in the centre. Without being the most subtle player in Wales, he was always brave in attack and defence, the man to turn to in a crisis and perhaps the ideal foil for the tricky running of Keith Hughes, his co-centre. There had been doubts about Gerald Davies. He had not played since December 27th because of a pulled hamstring and was having treatment right up until the match.

The game itself was a dreadful disappointment with just one score after twenty minutes. Bobby Windsor won a tight head and Gareth fed Phil Bennett with a beautiful reverse pass going to the short side. Phil made ground and gave the ball on to Gerald Davies. He cut inside his opposite number and looked as if he would score himself but as he went to swerve around the full back

Two great back-row forwards – Terry Cobner scores the only try in his debut international against Scotland 1974; and below, Mervyn Davies eventually gets one on his twenty-ninth appearance.

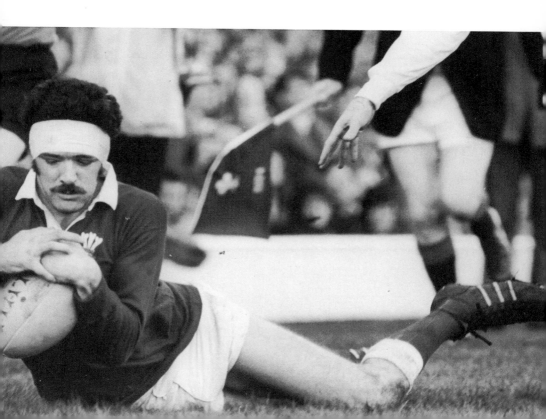

Above: Undoubtedly strong and sometimes silent – Graham Price, Bobby Windsor and Charlie Faulkner, the Pontypool front row. Below: John D. Bevan and Steve Fenwick work a scissors against England, 1975.

he lost his footing. One of Gerald's greatest attributes was always his ability to change his mind quickly and as he fell he twisted onto his back and popped the ball up to Terry Cobner who was steaming up like a train. Terry ran in unchallenged from less than ten yards for the try. Phil Bennett made the difficult conversion right-footed from close to the right touchline.

Thereafter it was a tale of unsatisfactory possession, too much pressure from the Scots forwards and bad passing from the backs when the ball was good enough to move. Ian McLauchlan and Sandy Carmichael again anchored the Scottish scrum and for the second year running the Welsh crowd had to watch their pack go backwards on too many occasions. Outside the scrum it was becoming very difficult to find space. John Williams was by now a totally marked man and his entries into the line were less effective and therefore it was as necessary to miss him out as use him, but the passing was not slick enough to release the wings.

In the second half Mervyn Davies went close to scoring and so did Gareth Edwards but there were enough near misses at the other end to leave the Welsh supporters in high dudgeon: Barry Llewelyn had to come back into the front row; Derek Quinnell should never have played because of lack of fitness; Phil Bennett always took the ball standing still; Gareth Edwards was trying to pass the ball too far and so the criticisms went on.

They had some substance to them, but there had also been some plusses. The back row had played magnificently with Mervyn Davies covering acres of ground to tackle Scottish three-quarters and Terry Cobner a tower of strength in the loose. Wales had also won.

Nevertheless, there were bound to be changes in the game in Ireland. Keith Hughes wrote to the selectors asking not to be considered. He had not been playing at his best and had taken a lot of criticism from the lack of cohesion behind the scrum. It was certainly not his fault alone but he took most of the stick and as he was at a crucial phase in his medical studies he understandably opted out. He was replaced by Alex Finlayson, the big Cardiff centre who was similar in style to Ian Hall. In the forwards Phil Llewellyn was replaced at tight head by Walter Williams, the hard man from Neath, and Derek Quinnell was dropped from the second row. His place was taken by Geoff Wheel from Swansea who had played soccer for Swansea Reserves. He had only been playing rugby seriously since 1972 but played for Wales 'B' in 1973 and was gaining a reputation for being one of the best maulers in the game. At well over sixteen stone he also had plenty to give in the scrums and with the National Coaching Organiser, Ray Williams, an advocate of the maul rather than the ruck he was a natural selection. On the Thursday before the match Wales had to make one further change. Gerald Davies again pulled his hamstring at the practice session and was replaced by Clive Rees his fellow London Welshman.

Wales had not won in Dublin since 1964 and were desperate to regain the support of the fans with a resounding win. As it turned out they were lucky to finish with a draw. Ireland had a total of twelve shots at goal and managed to kick only three of them. Welsh commentators reflected that Mr Pattinson, the referee was over-zealous and that two of the penalties that were kicked should never have been. They also pointed out that Wales scored the only try but most independent observers felt that had the Irish selectors picked McGann instead of Quinn at outside half (and they have been criticised heavily for dropping him despite his figure) then the match would have been won.

As it was, Ensor gave Ireland the lead after five minutes with a penalty when the Welsh forwards were adjudged to have picked up the ball in front of the hindmost foot. Wales replied with a well executed try. They wheeled a scrum on the Irish 25 and Dai Morris grabbed the ball and broke to the open, interchanging passes with Gareth Edwards. Dai then fed Phil Bennett who switched play to the blind side. J.P.R. came into the line and made an overlap for J. J. Williams to go over in the corner. Phil Bennett kicked the vital conversion from the left touchline against the wind. Ensor replied with another penalty and in spite of one promising break from Clive Rees the sides turned round with the scores level.

Ten minutes into the second half J. P. R. Williams was penalised for not moving away from the ball when he was pinned to the ground at the bottom of a maul and Ensor kicked the goal to make it 9–6. Once again it looked as if the Welsh were going to be unsuccessful at Lansdowne Road but with fifteen minutes left Phil Bennett kicked a penalty to level the scores and the score stayed at 9–9 until no side.

The overall performance by the forwards had still been unsatisfactory and three changes were made for the match against France. Barry Llewelyn was selected at prop. It was a magnificent achievement to fight his way back to fitness so quickly after a cartilage operation but typically the bad luck which ruined his career at international level struck again and on the Thursday before the game he withdrew because he was suffering from influenza. It was also bad luck for Wales. They needed his contribution in the loose while sacrificing nothing in the tight. His withdrawal caused the recall of Walter Williams and the same front row eventually took the field as that against Ireland.

Both second rows lost their places. Allan Martin and Geoff Wheel were both young and perhaps lacked the physical hardness that only comes with age and experience. With France fielding the very experienced Cester and the giant Estève, who was the backbone of the mighty (but some people felt overphysical) Beziers pack, the selectors brought in Ian Robinson from Cardiff for his first cap. It might have been a risk to give a player a first cap in those circumstances but Robinson was known to be able to look after himself. His partner was Derek Quinnell, a strange choice as he had been dropped for not playing a tight enough game against Scotland in the first international of the season.

The flu bug that had forced Barry Llewelyn to withdraw almost knocked out Phil Bennett as well and for a time on the morning of the match it was unclear who was playing. At one stage John Bevan of Aberavon had been called up to replace him but then Phil felt better and after a run out at the National Stadium declared himself fit to play. Even then some of the medical advisers advised against it but Benny was determined to take the field. Right at the start of the match he had a kick charged down and the selectors feared the worst but after only two minutes he kicked a penalty to make it 3–0 to Wales. Another charged down kick signalled that all was not entirely well but after that he settled into his normal game.

France took the lead through a Lux try after a dummy crash move in the centre that was so effective it carved a huge hole in the Welsh defence and Romeu made the score 3–7 when he kicked a penalty. The forward contest which many people had felt would be a torrid one was strangely muted with neither pack looking like dominating the other. Phil Bennett kicked a second penalty to bring Wales back to within one point of France and

when Gareth weighed in with a beautifully taken dropped goal
Wales were back in the lead.

After the early try which had resulted from exciting three-
quarter play France might have been expected to run the ball but
Romeu, a fly half who kicked almost as much as Clive Rowlands
had as a scrum half, was content to keep the ball in front of his
forwards. Estève and to a lesser extent Cester were dominating
the middle and front of the line out but Mervyn Davies was
redressing the balance at the back.

Romeu kicked two penalties to put France back into the lead,
but then just before half time Wales scored a try to level the
scores. The ball was worked out to J. J. Williams on the left and
just as he had done a year before in Paris he chipped the ball over
the defence and gave chase. This time he reached the ball before
the defence and before it went over the try line. Still moving like
the Commonwealth Games sprinter he had once been he used his
knee to knock the ball into the in goal area and collapsed on it for
the try. That was two tries in three games and five minutes for
Wales, a promising start for the lad many people criticised for
being more of a sprinter than rugby player.

In the second half Phil Bennett gave Wales the lead again with
a penalty and for a while it looked as though we might hold it. But
whatever Romeu might have lacked as a runner he made up for it
as a kicker. As the game went into the final quarter, Cester, the
French captain, was urging him to go for dropped goals. Appropriately from a good line out ball he let fly from forty yards to give
France a share of the spoils. It had been a strange match, somehow lacking in excitement even though the lead had changed
hands on five occasions, as well as being all square at the interval.
Just a penalty and a drop goal in the second half to make it 16–16
was disappointing after 26 points in the first session.

Nevertheless, Wales were still unbeaten and favourites to win
the Championship, even though the remaining match against
England was at Twickenham. England had not beaten Wales
since 1963 and had not won at home since 1960, so 'HQ' held no
fears for the Welsh boys. The added incentive for Wales was that
the team knew it was the last match for Clive Rowlands as coach.
He had decided to step down at the beginning of the season and
hand over to John Dawes and the squad would have dearly loved
to make it a rousing finale. Since he had taken over the side in
1969 Wales had always had a share of the Home International

Championship and had won two Triple Crowns and the Grand Slam.

The selectors made several changes after the French game. Roy Bergiers returned to replace Ian Hall in the centre and Phil Llewellyn won back his place from Walter Williams. Delme Thomas returned to the second row, for what was to be his last match for his country, at the expense of Derek Quinnell. However, the most important change was forced upon them. J. P. R. Williams damaged his knee ligaments in a club match and was not fit so he was replaced by the Swansea full back Roger Blyth. It was the first match J.P.R. had missed since he was first selected in 1969. He had won twenty-eight consecutive caps since then.

The day began to go wrong right from the start. As if to pay back the tiny minority of Welsh people who boo in Cardiff when the English national anthem is played the Rugby Union decided not to play 'Hen Wlad Fy Nhadau' for the first time in memory. As the whistle signalled the start of the game there were thousands of enraged Welshmen still singing the anthem without any help from the band. To make matters worse, the game also went badly from the off. The English pack began to put on the pressure in the tight scrums and after ten minutes England scored a good try. The English centre with the Welsh name, Geoff Evans, cut back inside after an orthodox passing movement and linked up with Uttley (then playing in the second row) and Ralston. They gave the ball on to Duckham who jinked inside Blyth to score. Five minutes later it was 7–0 when Old kicked a penalty.

Wales got back into the game when England tapped back badly at a line out near their own line. Dai Morris got a boot to the ball and Mervyn Davies followed through to tap the ball over the line and score wide out. Phil Bennett converted beautifully in difficult conditions and then kicked a forty-yard penalty to give Wales a 9–7 lead. Just before half time Wales had a good chance to go further into the lead but J. J. Williams dropped the scoring pass. It was to prove a vital mistake, although by the end of the game no Welshman would believe the referee would have given a try had it been scored.

In the second half the England forwards again exerted a tremendous amount of pressure on the Welsh scrum which made Bobby Windsor's feat of winning six tight heads against two in the match even more creditable but he could not prevent

England from scoring direct from a five-yard scrum. They heeled perfectly, held the ball in the back row and began to push, then Ripley picked up and dived straight over on the open side to score. Old converted.

Phil Bennett then brought Wales back to within one point with a penalty but it was here that dissatisfaction with the referee began. England were penalised for obstruction after Phil Bennett had broken clear with Gerald Davies outside him and just one man to beat. A try for one of them under the posts seemed a certainty but instead Wales had to settle for three points. However, that kick did take Phil Bennett's tally of points for the season to 36, one better than Barry John's previous record in 1972. There was one big difference. In 1972 Wales had won three matches out of three whilst in 1973–74 we had won only two out of five.

Worse was to follow. Old kicked another penalty to make it 16–12 and then Wales made a desperate effort to pull the game out of the fire. We attacked constantly and eventually managed to work J. J. Williams free on the left-hand touchline. He made ground and then cut inside and, seeing his way blocked, reverted to his favourite tactic of kicking ahead and chasing the ball. It was a perfect kick, straight ahead and he used his pace to get to the ball before Squires and Duckham, who were covering desperately. Unfortunately, the referee had been left miles behind and J.J.'s look of jubilation turned to disbelief as he realised that the referee had not awarded the try. He had quite clearly reached the ball first (as the television cameras showed when they played the incident back in slow motion a hundred times afterwards) and the referee had no quarrel with the touchdown, he had simply been too far away to judge which player reached the ball first. It is one of the only times I have ever seen rugby players rush up to the referee and complain or even try to get him to change his decision. Of course it had no effect and Wales had lost.

After the immediate post-match bitterness Mr John West became the butt of a number of Irish jokes and was then immortalised when Max Boyce wrote a song about the 'Blind Irish Referee'. Two years later when he was in Cardiff to referee the Wales v France match (many people thought he was brave to accept the game), the Cardiff Referees Society invited him as guest of honour to a dinner. After the meal they presented him with a copy of the record and a white stick.

It was a sad way for Clive Rowlands to finish as coach. His contribution to the Welsh successes of the previous six years had been enormous. He might not have been a great coach of technique but the spirit he produced within the squad was such that it was the envy of every other rugby-playing nation. Under his guidance Wales played twenty-eight full internationals, won seventeen of them, drew four and lost seven. In all that time they lost only once in Wales, against the 1972 All Blacks. John Dawes certainly had a difficult task on his hands to follow him.

10

LIONS WORLD CHAMPIONS
the Lions in South Africa, 1974

Although Wales had had a disappointing season, with only one championship win, they provided more players for the Lions touring party to visit South Africa than any of the other home countries. It surprised some people, especially as Gerald Davies had declared himself unavailable. J. P. R. Williams, Phil Bennett, Gareth Edwards and Mervyn Davies were certainties while Bobby Windsor, J. J. Williams and Roy Bergiers had emerged as world-class players during the Home International Championship. However, Tommy David and Clive Rees who made up the Welsh contingent of nine had not been able to command a place in the national side. David had lost his place through injury at the beginning of the season and had been unable to win it back, while Clive Rees had won his only cap when Gerald Davies was unfit for the match against Ireland.

The manager was also Welsh. Alun Thomas, who had resigned from the Big Five in 1968 because David Nash, then Welsh coach, was not selected to go as assistant manager to the Argentine, had the ideal background. He had played thirteen times for Wales and had been a Lion in South Africa himself in 1955. The coach was Syd Millar who had been on the previous tour of South Africa in 1968 as a player and the captain was Willie John McBride. There could be no other choice. He had proved an inspiration in New Zealand and had just led Ireland to the Five Nations Championship. There must have been a few worried faces in South Africa. In 1968 the big man had not had a particularly successful playing tour but had been one of the leaders of the 'wreckers' whose escapades off the field were difficult to handle for the South African Rugby Board, South African Railways and various hotel managers.

At last the four Home Unions had been persuaded that it was unfair on the players and virtually useless to the coach to spend a week practising at Eastbourne or Bournemouth. Carwyn James had said in 1971 that he had been scared to involve the players in any real contact work for fear that one might get injured and not even make New Zealand having been selected. For the first time the team set off a week early and spent their 'getting to know each other' period in the country they were visiting.

As it turned out even that nearly caused a casualty. The team went to stay at Stillfontein, a small mining town in Western Transvaal near to Pochefstrom where the first match was to be played. It might have been ideal for training and practice but it was very lacking in social life and one of the Casanovas in the party decided that the only lady he found attractive was a married member of the hotel staff. He eventually persuaded her, no doubt with original chat like 'Come and see my etchings', to go with him to his room and set about trying to seduce her. After some time there was a knock on the door and the lady screamed something original like 'Oh, what shall we do, it must be my husband.' At which the gallant Lion jumped from the first floor window. He landed badly but, forgetting the pain, punched a St Bernard dog on the nose because it threatened to reveal his sudden arrival by starting to bark loudly, and ran for the hills. He limped back into the hotel some time later, complaining of having slipped on a rock while out for a walk, only to find that the knock on the door had been his room mate who wanted a handkerchief and had grown tired of waiting. The management were not amused.

The first match also provided a departure from normal rugby routine. Instead of the usual track-suited official taking on the oranges at half time, the task was given to two local beauties sporting hot pants and tee-shirts. The Lions approved and managed to regain their concentration enough to win comfortably by 59–13. From that beginning the Lions went from strength to strength. Jan Ellis, the veteran Springbok flanker, almost led the South West Africa team to a surprise victory in the second game but the tourists rallied and won 23–16. From there the build-up to the First Test was straightforward but it included a remarkable 97–0 win against South Western Districts at Mossel Bay. The Lions were expected to win easily but when the captain of the home team said that he felt it would be a moral victory if his side held them to a hundred points most people thought he was joking. In that match J. J. Williams equalled David Duckham's record of six tries in one match for the Lions and Alan Old, the English fly half, set a new record for points by scoring 37 in one match. The total of sixteen tries was also the most scored by any British Isles team abroad.

From then on the records continued to tumble but Syd Millar, the coach, knew from 1968 that there would be a vast difference between the strength of South African provincial rugby and the international team itself. There had already been a punch-up in the match against Eastern Province and the feeling in the Lions' camp was that the Springboks would stop at nothing if it meant the difference between winning and losing.

Six of the nine Welshmen were chosen for the Test team and all six were to retain their places throughout the series. J. P. R. Williams, Gareth Edwards and Mervyn Davies were veterans of the 1971 tour and they were joined by J. J. Williams, Phil Bennett and Bobby Windsor.

The First Test was played at Newlands in Cape Town on a wet day, yet the South African Rugby authority still went ahead with two curtain-raisers before the main match so the ground was a quagmire before the Lions and Springboks took the field. This suited neither side but the Lions were far more used to such conditions than the South Africans. They settled down to play a tight game with Edwards and Bennett kicking for position and all depended on whether the forwards could hold their own. South Africa played with the wind and after J. J. Williams had almost scored from an Edwards chip ahead, they took the lead. On this occasion J.J. failed to clear the ball after a penalty attempt and had to concede a five-yard scrum. The Springboks won it and Snyman, the fly half, dropped a goal.

After that the Lions forwards began to dominate in all phases of play and just before the end of the half Phil Bennett landed a penalty for offside at a line out to make the scores equal. With the wind at their backs, the Lions were soon in the lead. Only four minutes of the second half had passed when a Springbok forward fell offside at a maul and Bennett kicked another penalty from the touchline. Fifteen minutes later he did it again and five minutes after that Gareth Edwards dropped a goal after Mervyn Davies had set up a ruck. The Lions were now safe and controlled the rest of the match without increasing their lead. The Lions forwards had mastered their opposite numbers in the lines out and scrums, where Bobby Windsor had won three strikes to two against the head. It was probably at that moment that they knew they could become the first British Isles team to win a series in South Africa and, with the 1971 Lions having won in New Zealand, stake a claim to be world champions.

The three matches before the Second Test were all won, even though there were some anxious moments against Transvaal as the return to the high veld caused a number of players problems with the thin air. During an illicit visit to Rhodesia, Mervyn Davies contrived to get himself bitten by a crocodile, fortunately only a baby on a crocodile farm, and by the opposition prop, who was a bit bigger, but recovered from both.

The Second Test was at Pretoria and for it South Africa made eight changes to their team, with only two of the backs retaining their places. The Lions kept faith with the same XV.

Just how important the match was to them revealed itself in the tension of the first minutes when Phil Bennett missed a penalty he would normally have kicked with his eyes shut. However, the Lions were soon in front. Gareth Edwards kicked over a scrum into the box and J. J. Williams fly hacked the ball on and over the line to score in the corner. After half an hour he scored again, the first ever player to score two tries in a match against the Springboks in South Africa, after Phil Bennett had counter-attacked from his own line and Bennett converted to make it 10–0.

Bennett then scored a truly memorable try. Receiving the ball from Fergus Slattery just inside the South African half, he took on the defence and left everyone in his wake as he jinked and side-stepped his way through. Somebody must have touched him because he found he had a nasty gash on his instep as he walked back but although it needed five stitches afterwards there was no way that he was going to leave the field.

Gordon Brown stormed over for a try in support of an Edwards run to stop the scoring in Tests from being a Welsh monopoly and then Ian McGeechan dropped a goal. Bennett at last kicked a penalty and Dick Milliken crashed through two defenders on the line for the final try. In between the Springboks had kicked a dropped goal and two penalties but they had been beaten by the biggest margin ever in their history.

It was really Phil Bennett's day. J. J. Williams's second try which he had made, and then his own amazing individual effort, came at a vital time and took the Lions into a commanding lead.

The Lions were already assured of a share of the series and only the 1955 Lions had previously achieved that in South Africa. Another win would make them the most successful major Lions tour this century. When John Pullin's England side had visited South Africa and won the only international in 1972, after having lost all four matches in the Home Internationals, there were obviously signs that South African rugby was not as strong as it had been but nobody had expected a rout.

The players went off for their traditional rest in the Kruger Park in high spirits. They flew there, taking their own supplies of beer in case there was a shortage. One plane full of players and one full of booze sounded about right for a few days off, but the celebrations were so heavy the supplies lasted only the first night to the amazement of the local liaison men.

Phil Bennett revealed himself not only as a fine player but also as a practical joker at Kruger. The accommodation there is in rondevals, native mud huts, and the locals take great delight in telling stories of snakes and other nasty forms of life finding their way in while people are asleep. Quite a number of the party found furry or slimy objects in their beds and when the panic had died down they were usually traced back to Benny. The other Welsh boys had also made their mark. Bobby Windsor, carrying on in the tradition of Ray Prosser, shared the role of comedian with Mike Burton, while Roy Bergiers gained the reputation of being a marathon talker. Normally on a Lions tour players arrange a signal, such as a surreptitious tug of the ear lobe to ask the others to rescue them if they are landed with what is universally known as a 'heavy', someone from outside the party who has cornered them and will not allow them to get away. By the end of the tour the 'heavies' were tugging at their ears to get away from Budgie.

Only Clive Rees had a really disappointing trip. He broke a bone in his hand and then in the first match after it had mended broke it again and had to be replaced by Alan Morley of England.

Having returned from their short holiday, the tourists suddenly found the rugby very much more difficult. Three of the five games before the Third Test were tough ones and all proved to be very close. The Quaggas, an invitation side similar to our Barbarians, fielded four internationals and were only beaten 20–16, and two days later only an injury time try by

J. J. Williams, after Gareth Edwards had been put away on the blind side by Mervyn Davies, saved the day against the Orange Free State. Certainly it helped to bring the Lions back down to earth and out of the holiday euphoria with a bump which was probably a good thing.

Northern Transvaal, often referred to in South Africa as the Fifth Test, were beaten 16–12 in front of 55,000 people at Loftus Versveld and now it seemed that the 1974 Lions must emulate the team of 1971 and go through the tour beating every provincial side. Those three hard games also gave the Lions a tremendous competitive edge for the Third Test. Cunning old Danie Craven, who decides virtually everything in South African rugby, might have put them all together to soften the tourists up before what is always the most crucial international, as neither side can have won or lost the series until that point. The problem with 'loading' the itinerary in that way is that the opposition come through with tremendous confidence if they win the matches.

The Lions were now certainly ready, while the South African selectors proved just what a mess they were in by making another eleven changes, having made eight between the First and Second Tests. This made it particularly difficult for the forwards, another completely new unit (although from the way they played that is the wrong word) against the British and Irish pack that was unchanged for the third time running. Only Hannes Marais, the captain, and the veteran flanker, Jan Ellis had been selected for all three games against the Lions.

South African pride demanded that this team gave its all and they began by swarming everywhere, so that Gareth Edwards had two kicks charged down and the Port Elizabeth crowd sensed that for the first time it would be a real contest, but the Lions gradually took control. The Springboks took the lead with a penalty but then Irvine, the only change in the side from the Second Test, as he had forced his way in on the wing through his brilliant attacking running at the expense of countryman Steele, equalised from nearly fifty yards. Realising the game was slipping away the Springboks went over the top and as the punching began Willie John McBride called '99', the signal for "All for one and one for all', and the game degenerated into a travelling brawl. When that was over the Lions moved slowly but surely towards complete supremacy. Gordon Brown, the Scottish lock who played so much better on his Lions tours than he ever did for

Scotland, scored a record eighth try on tour direct from a line out. Leading 7–3 at half time, Andy Irvine landed the killer blow with a fifty-eight yard penalty soon after (and this at sea level not in the rarefied air of the high veld). Again there was an interlude for a brawl before Bennett dropped a goal.

J. J. Williams set the seal on things, repeating his feat in the Second Test and scoring two tries, both set up by J. P. R. Williams and Dick Milliken, the Irish centre, but leaving the Llanelli wing plenty to do before going over. For the first he showed he had added a side-step to his attacking options and for the second he reverted to his favourite kick ahead and chase. No wing can ever have used the ploy more successfully. Irvine converted one of the tries, Snyman kicked two penalties for the Springboks and appropriately Phil Bennett finished the rout with another snap dropped goal.

The score was 26–9 and became the second biggest defeat suffered by the Springboks. The series was won, the first time a Lions team had achieved it this century, and the players understandably went on a bender.

Having won the series it was difficult to concentrate on rugby, but they managed well enough to win the last three provincial matches, the one against Natal again turning nasty as J. P. R. Williams and the local hero, Tommy Bedford, set about each other. The other players were all for letting them sort it out and did not think much of the shower of beer cans that were thrown at them. In the Final Test in front of 75,000 people, the Lions just failed to make it a clean sweep, although Fergus Slattery appeared to have scored a perfectly good try at the end which was disallowed and would have made the draw a win.

Cronje scored South Africa's only try of the series and Snyman kicked three penalties while Uttley and Irvine scored tries for the Lions, one of which Bennett converted. Irvine also kicked a penalty. 13–13 kept the Lions' unbeaten record but a few of the players admitted that they found it hard to concentrate, having already won the series. Once again it had been a great team effort and the Welsh contingent had played their full part. Gareth Edwards, J. P. R. Williams and Mervyn Davies returned home as the undisputed world number ones in their respective positions and Bobby Windsor, Phil Bennett and J. J. Williams had taken the leap from promising international players to great ones.

British rugby was on top of the world and the 1974 team set a host of records. Apart from those already mentioned their total of 729 points is the most scored by a British side abroad and included 107 tries, which is a record in South Africa. They became the third side in history to go through a long tour unbeaten; the others were the 1891 Lions and the 1924 All Blacks. Finally, they scored 79 points in the Test series which is also the highest number ever against South Africa.

11

THE PONTYPOOL FRONT ROW
1974/75

Wales had visited and received a touring side from Fiji but until the autumn of 1974 had never played against the other South Sea island rugby-playing nation, Tonga. The Tongans were making a short tour of Britain with ten matches in all, but the itinerary was based on Wales with six matches culminating in a game against a National XV at the National Stadium.

They began auspiciously with an 18–13 win over East Wales but could not repeat that form and lost their other nine matches. In Wales Llanelli beat them 24–15 and North Wales won 12–3 before they went to Scotland and were hammered 44–8 by a Scottish XV. On their return to Wales they fared no better and lost 14–6 at Newport and by the same score to West Wales before their big day against the Welsh team. To help them prepare they enlisted the help of Carwyn James and he worked with them on wheeling the scrum and shortening the line out to try to counter their weaknesses in those areas. Wales did not select any of the Lions who had been in South Africa but otherwise put out the strongest team with Gerald Davies as captain. Unfortunately, the day of the match was wet, which did not suit either side as they had both expressed intentions to play a running game.

Wales won 26–7, having led 10–0 at half time. Alex Finlayson scored two tries and Steve Fenwick, John Bevan and Terry Cobner one each. None of them was converted but Allan Martin kicked two penalty goals. For Tonga Valita, the full back, kicked a penalty and the loudest cheer of the day was saved for Talilotu who ran forty-five yards to score an excellent try.

As soon as the Tongans left another touring party arrived. The Irish R.F.U. was celebrating its centenary and to mark the occasion they had arranged a visit from a side a little stronger than the Tongans, the All Blacks. While they were around the British Isles the powers that be could not resist slipping in one

Two of the best – Gerald Davies is once again too fast for the cover against Ireland in 1975 and J. J. Williams makes the line in spectacular fashion against Australia in the same year.

Mike Gibson can do nothing to stop Charlie Faulkner from scoring and Charlie, arm already aloft in triumph, knows it, 1975; the following year against Scotland, he proves you're never too old to run, as Ray Gravell waits to join forwards, Terry Cobner, Trevor Evans and Allan Martin in another Welsh attack.

match in Wales. It was played on a Wednesday and curiously was billed as New Zealand versus a Welsh XV and did not count as a full international even though New Zealand and Wales put out their strongest sides. It was fortunate for Wales that it was not considered a Test or the record against New Zealand in recent years would be even worse, as New Zealand won 3–12. It was a disappointing game, perhaps because it was on a Wednesday and because it was not a full international. The only scores were penalties, four to Joe Karam, against one to Phil Bennett, but one cannot help wondering whether it would have suddenly been elevated to Test status if Wales had won.

Again the selectors decided that they needed a trial and were rewarded with a resounding success for the Probables. They won 44–6 primarily through an incredibly powerful forward display that gave their backs so much ball that they could not help but score. Disregarding his success on the Lions tour, Phil Bennett had been demoted to the Possibles and his place was taken in the Probables by John Bevan, the Aberavon outside half. At the time many people thought it was just a move to remind Phil that his selection was by no means a certainty, but after playing an important part in such a victory, Bevan was selected. It became clear that the Big Five saw his generalship and ability to launch the back division as an important asset because they named him vice-captain. In South Africa the Edwards-Bennett combination had worked better than at any other time, but had not proved itself at home. John Dawes, now fully in command, felt that the Welsh back division had failed as an attacking unit the previous season and saw the static half back play as the major reason. He had quickly shown that he had his own ideas and was prepared to fly in the face of popular opinion in order to play the game in the way he thought it should be played.

There were five other new caps. Trevor Evans came into the back row, having been close to a cap in 1972, but then having taken a year off to concentrate on his studies, and Bobby Windsor was joined in the front row by his team mates Charlie Faulkner and Graham Price. It was a unique achievement and a great tribute, not only to the club who were carrying all before them with their powerful forward play, but also to their coach and mentor, Ray Prosser. Until then he had been Pontypool's most famous son, having won twenty-two caps between 1956 and 1961. He had also toured Australia and New Zealand with the 1959 British Lions and, although part of his approach demands that he pretends not to know the meaning of words such as 'mentor', his influence on his players goes far beyond the bounds of pure coaching.

The achievement of providing the whole of the front row for the national team from one club was made all the more special because Charlie Faulkner should really have retired from senior rugby before he won his first cap. He slyly admitted to being almost thirty-two in the programme with a birth date of 27th February 1943, which became 1945 in the 1976 programme. But nobody really believed him and John Reason, a stickler for detail in all such matters, actually checked the birth records at Somerset House, a task not made easier by Faulkner's seldom aired first names appearing as Aubrey George in some programmes and Anthony George in others. Suffice it to say no trace of him was found within three years of 1945. Even after retirement from the international scene, he has not revealed his true age (probably because he is considering a come-back), but most people close to him accept that he was over thirty-five before he was capped and some people put it nearer forty. Graham Price's selection was no surprise. Since that first trial in 1973 he had been knocking on the door and at the age of twenty-three now had the power to hold his own with any prop in the world. With Terry Cobner in the back row, Pontypool supplied half the pack.

There were also two new centres. Roy Bergiers had been ruled out because of injury and his clubmate, Ray Gravell, and Steve Fenwick ('It's spelt Fen-wick and that's how it's pronounced.') of Bridgend were brought in. They were both big powerful centres and provided a strong defensive mid-field, even if their styles were so similar that they sometimes lacked variety in attack.

1975 was the beginning of the second half of the decade, not just chronologically but also in the make-up of the team. J. P. R. Williams, Gareth Edwards and Gerald Davies were to span the whole period, as would have Mervyn Davies, had he not been forced to retire, but by 1975 the bulk of the 1971 Grand Slam team had been replaced. It had been done gradually so that the public were forever praising the selectors for keeping a settled team but, using the squad system to allow the newcomers to acclimatise themselves to the international scene, it had happened.

The new team could not have had a better start. The rotation of fixtures in the Five Nations Championship took Wales to Paris for the first match. France are always difficult to beat at home and to get them first was a testing initiation for the new boys. They strode through it with flying colours winning by 25–10, the biggest margin in Paris since 1911. It was also the first time in the Championship since 1972 that a country had won away from home.

The restructured pack was an enormous success and the match was tied up by half time through their domination of the tight and loose phases of the game. The scoreline at the interval was 17–7 and the Welsh total included three tries. Steve Fenwick made an auspicious debut by scoring the first to give Wales a 4–0 lead. It was a fortuitous try but immediately established one of his main virtues, the invaluable knack of being in the right place at the right time. From a scrum to the left of the posts Gareth Edwards moved right and let fly with a drop kick at goal. He sliced it badly and it flew across the face of the posts towards the right corner flag. Steve Fenwick had taken up the chase where many would not have bothered and was on hand to score. The lead was soon reduced by a Taffary penalty and then France took the lead with a Gourdon try. It was Fenwick again who equalised with a fine penalty. The Welsh pack were making their strength tell in the set pieces and Gareth Edwards was softening up the French forwards by pushing them back constantly with kicks down the touchlines or into the spaces behind the backs. He had by now perfected his rolling kicks and was almost infallible at making the ball pitch inside the side lines before bouncing into touch. Because they had a top spin on them the kicks were low and hard which very often caused the opposition to knock on even if they did manage to reach them.

When Gareth did let the ball out, John Bevan kicked equally accurately or moved the ball quickly and incisively so that the Welsh supporters began to appreciate why he had won his place. He was certainly not as elusive as Phil Bennett in broken play, but as a pivot and link man he was ideal. After half an hour, instead of kicking, he gave the ball out to Gravell on the right who, grateful at being given his head, steamed outside his man to make the half break and then linked up with Fenwick who passed on to Gerald Davies. The winger then linked back inside to his new captain, Mervyn Davies, who found Terry Cobner clear inside him and 'Cob' was able to score under the posts. Fenwick converted to make it 13–7.

In the thirty-sixth minute Wales completed the first half scoring when J. P. R. Williams came into the line with the ball going right. Instead of his usual charge he grub-kicked through and Gerald Davies raced after the ball. Taffary seemed to have it covered but underestimated the speed of the Welsh winger and Gerald, who had returned to the Cardiff club from London Welsh at the beginning of the season, booted the ball almost out of his hands. It popped up obligingly on the line and he picked it up to score with ease.

In the second half Gareth Edwards scored a typical try to keep in touch with Gerald Davies in the private battle they were having to become Wales's top scorer. Gerald had now scored thirteen tries and Gareth equalled that number, but they still had some way to go to beat the record of seventeen held jointly by Ken Jones of Newport and Johnny Williams of Cardiff. Gareth's try came from a maul. Geoff Wheel ripped the ball free and Gareth broke to the right. At one stage the cover seemed to have enveloped him but with a wriggle and a swerve, plus his incredible acceleration, he was through and over.

In injury time, Graham Price made the celebrations complete. Geoff Wheel booted the ball through when it fell loose at a line out around the Welsh 22*. Taffary, the French full back, and J. J. Williams gave chase. J.J. got there first and continued to hack the ball on. Taffary again tried to come across and fall on it, but his heart was not in it. The Welsh wing worked the ball loose and found Price. Showing remarkable pace and stamina for a prop at the end of an international, he picked up the ball and ran on the three yards to score. It was an amazing effort but there was not a flicker of emotion on his face as he ran back with the ball. What was even more amazing was that he had joined his clubmates, Cobner and Windsor, as one of the elite band of forwards to score in their first international. The Pontypool legend was already beginning to grow.

After the match John Dawes was philosophical. He found it hard to suppress his enjoyment of the victory but felt that there were large areas for improvement and told the press, 'You won't see the best of this side until March.'

The next match was against England at Cardiff and the selectors naturally kept the same team. Everything had worked well

*Even rugby has been forced to keep up with the times and went metric in the 1974/75 season.

and the back division had shown more cohesion than throughout the previous season. Five tries against France away from home was testament to that.

Nevertheless there was plenty to work upon in the practice sessions at the Afan Lido. By now the pitches at the back of the sports centre were usable even though they were marked out for soccer and the sands were rarely used, unless John Dawes had had too many GTs the night before and some foolish player stepped out of line. Nevertheless the pattern had been set and the crowds still turned up to watch. At some sessions there were more spectators than at a top English club game. It was not until Rod Morgan became a selector and introduced the squad to the delights of the cuisine at the South Wales Police club that practice sessions moved there. The players were delighted, now they could upset the coach without fear of the sands.

It was at the Lido in 1975 that Gareth Edwards set his own intelligence test for the forwards. They had been working on back row moves and decided that they needed a code to tell the rest of the pack which way the ball would be worked. Terry Cobner was from Pontypool and Trevor Evans from Swansea, so it was suggested that any word called that began with 'P' signalled that the break would be on Terry's side and a word beginning with 'S' would mean that the move would be worked towards Trevor. Gareth and the back row would already have set the move for each other by visual signals. At the next scrum Gareth picked up the visual signal and before putting the ball into the scrum shouted to the rest of the pack, 'PSYCHOLOGY!' When they broke up half went one way and half the other and that was the end of another good idea.

Forwards can work some things out, as Allan Martin showed in the match itself. With Phil Bennett out of the side Wales were not happy with their place-kicking cover. Steve Fenwick had managed only one penalty and one conversion in France, so Allan Martin was given his chance against England. He began magnificently with a fifty-yard penalty after ten minutes to give Wales the lead and then landed another after half an hour from nearly forty yards to make the score 10–0. In between Wales scored a well worked try from a set piece move. John Bevan scissored with Ray Gravell and the big centre ploughed through the middle and then straightened his line of running and looked to the outside again for support. There were defenders between him and Steve Fenwick but he found his centre partner with an overhead pass and the Bridgend player threw a long pass to his wing, J. J. Williams, giving him a clear run to the corner.

After twenty-five minutes Geoff Wheel dislocated his shoulder and was replaced by Derek Quinnell who soon made his presence felt. In the injury time added on at the end of the half because of Wheel's departure, he played a big part in a second try for Wales. Gravell made the initial thrust once again from a line out and set up the maul. Quinnell was quickly on hand and freed the ball, passing it back to Edwards. A quick long pass from John Bevan to J. P. R. Williams allowed the full back to put Gerald Davies in for a try in the corner. Allan Martin converted and Wales looked set for a high score with 16 points already on the board and the whole of the second half to go.

Instead we relaxed badly and in spite of the prompting of Mervyn Davies and Gareth Edwards who had had magnificent games, leading by example as well as encouragement, the game went to sleep. The pack were content to hold England and the backs attacked badly, over-elaborating or being downright greedy. There were no further scores until the last five minutes when Nigel Horton caught a ball two-handed in a line out just short of the Welsh line and dived through a gap to score. This at least roused Wales out of their lethargy and after a run by John Bevan, Trevor Evans, Bobby Windsor, Allan Martin and Ray Gravell all handled before Steve Fenwick was on hand to score in the corner. Allan Martin hit the post with his conversion attempt and Wales had won 20–4.

Dawes was worried about the relaxation. 'We can't afford to do that against Scotland,' he commented prophetically. The game had shown that the team was perhaps not as strong as some had believed after the game against France. Cobner had confirmed that he was a tireless forager, Martin had shown that he could kick goals in the international arena as well as at club level and Fenwick with his two tries in as many games was already establishing a reputation as one of those players who are always in the right place at the right time but some of the newcomers still had to prove themselves.

Scotland had out-scrummaged Wales in 1973 and with Ian McLauchlan as captain were determined to do the same again. 'We'll give Wales hell,' was his battle cry before the game and leading his men from the front he inspired them to do just that.

The Welsh side was disrupted through two important injuries, but it was the Scottish forwards who won the game. John Bevan had to leave the field after twenty-six minutes with a dislocated left shoulder, the third to a Welsh player in one season, and he was followed six minutes later by Steve Fenwick. They were replaced by Phil Bennett and Roger Blyth respectively. It proved to be a disastrous day for Benny, who coming into the match cold from the substitutes' bench never atuned himself to the pace of proceedings and just could not put his game together. All those who thought he should be in the team instead of John Bevan had their faith in him shattered as he kicked badly and constantly ran into trouble. It was the memory of this match that caused a major incident in the following season.

Before he quit the field Steve Fenwick had left his stamp on the game by kicking a couple of penalty goals to bring his total number of points to 19 in three internationals. Not bad considering he had not taken the place-kicks in one of them and missed an hour of the third. Unfortunately, his goals were sandwiched between three from Dougie Morgan, the Scots scrum half, and Wales turned round at the interval three points down.

The Scottish forwards had shown more fire in the loose and despite the presence of Mike Roberts, who had been brought into the second row as Derek Quinnell had dislocated a shoulder in a club game, the Welsh pack also found it tough going in the scrums. They did slightly better in the second half and held Scotland until five minutes from the final whistle when Ian McGeechan, the Scottish fly half who had played as a centre in all the Tests for the Lions in South Africa in 1974, dropped a goal. At last Wales realised that they were on the verge of losing and won a ruck out on the left. Edwards whipped the ball to the right via Gravell to Gerald Davies and his magical side-stepping took him back in field past three men. Unfortunately, there was too much cover still around him to go all the way but he found Trevor Evans back outside him and the flanker crashed over in the corner. Another touchline conversion against Scotland in the last seconds of the game – this time Allan Martin was entrusted with the kick to save the match but, although his effort was a good one, it drifted wide and Wales had fallen to the Murrayfield bogy again.

All chances of a Triple Crown and Grand Slam had now gone

but the Championship was still there for the taking. All the other sides had lost at least one game and therefore a win against Ireland would ensure at least a share for Wales. Wheel had recovered fitness and replaced Roberts, while Roy Bergiers who had originally lost his place through injury now came in for the injured Fenwick and Phil Bennett was retained as fly half, despite his nightmare at Murrayfield, because John Bevan was unfit. The inclusion of Roy Bergiers gave special pleasure to Queen Elizabeth's Grammar School, Carmarthen. With two other former pupils, Gerald Davies and Ray Gravell, also in the team they could boast that they had provided three of the four Welsh three-quarters.

Ireland had an identical record for the season to Wales, having beaten France and England and having lost to Scotland at Murrayfield. If they could win at Cardiff for the first time since 1967, they would be champions for the second year running. It should have given them all the motivation in the world and they could hardly have expected the fate awaiting them.

John Dawes had forecast that his team would be at their best in March and he was proved right as they beat Ireland by 32–4. Even the most biased Welsh supporter could not have foreseen a win by that margin at the interval. The first half had been hard fought with the Welsh pack responding to the National Stadium crowd and just eclipsing Willie John and his men. Phil Bennett kicked a penalty after thirteen minutes and Wales scored a try after half an hour. Yet again it came from Gareth Edwards running from the base of the maul. John Moloney, his opposite number, was caught after an Irish heel at a scrum and from the maul that followed the tackle Bobby Windsor fed Gareth with room to move. As always he took off like a rocket and dropped his shoulder to knock over two would-be tacklers who were standing still as he hit them. To take Edwards head on unless you were going forward hard to meet him was almost impossible. Phil Bennett converted and the score remained 9–0 until the teams turned round for the second half.

Even when Gerald Davies scored his fifteenth try for Wales, the game was not safe. Geoff Wheel had set up a maul on the left and the ball had been passed swiftly to the right to allow him to squeeze in at the right corner flag. Phil Bennett converted from the touchline. The forward battle was as hard as ever and nobody foresaw the collapse that occurred in the last twenty minutes.

The game was just moving into the last quarter when Bennett kicked another penalty to make the score 18–0 and that was the signal for Wales to start playing irresistible rugby.

It was Benny, already having shown that his play at Murrayfield was nothing like his true form, who created the next try. Gathering the ball deep in his own half he suddenly changed direction, just as he had for the Barbarians against the All Blacks in 1973 and counter-attacked down the left-hand side of the field. J. J. Williams carried the move on before giving inside to Bobby Windsor. The 'Duke' could see the try line ahead and only Tony Ensor between him and another try. There were no frills with Bobby and he decided to try to go through him. The full back did well to stop him but was powerless to prevent the pass to Charlie Faulkner trundling (it would be inaccurate to use any other word) up on the outside and screaming for the ball. He just made the line and flopped over it before the cover could reach him and the grin on his face bettered any of the 'first try' triumphant smiles on any player's face before or since. He had become something of a cult figure even after only four caps and half the Welsh side rushed up to congratulate him. It had been nine games since Bobby Windsor won his place in the team and four games since Graham Price and Charlie Faulkner joined him but, unbelievably, the Pontypool front row had all scored tries. The legend grew, even though Charlie had to take some ribbing about his age from the other two. They claimed that had he been younger he would have scored sooner.

Next it was Roy Bergiers' chance to set up a try. He did so by dragging several of the Irish backs into a maul while still controlling possession for Wales. When Terry Cobner fed Gareth he had Phil Bennett and J. P. R. Williams outside him going left and they were able to feed J. J. Williams so that he could score in the corner. Bennett's conversion attempt hit the post. When a side is 26–0 up they are bound to feel arrogant and Wales began to run the ball from everywhere. Once again Bennett split the defence and gave the ball out to Gareth Edwards. He almost strolled up to the right touchline, trying to draw the opposition to him. When they were about to engulf him he was able to slip the ball inside to Roy Bergiers who scored. It had been 'Budgie's' best game for his country and the try was a fitting finale.

Bennett converted to complete the Welsh scoring but over-confidence in the last minutes allowed Willie Duggan to score a consolation try for Ireland. Wales won the ball badly from the middle of a line out on their own 22 and Edwards went back to collect it. Normally he would have cleared safely to touch but instead tried a blind reverse pass to his half back partner. Duggan, who had run through from the back of the line out, intercepted cleanly and was over the Welsh line before anyone could move. Gareth shrugged his shoulders and grinned, victory really had been that comprehensive. That final score prevented the winning margin being the greatest ever between the two teams but Wales scored more points than ever before and only in 1911 when they won 29–0 was the points gap bigger.

The game was a personal triumph for Phil Bennett who scored 12 points to take his total for Wales to 79, only 11 short of Barry John's record. It was also a triumph for John Dawes. He had adopted very different methods to those employed by Clive Rowlands, emphasising technique more than motivation. Having won the Championship in his first season in charge he now had a short summer tour to Japan to really work on the younger players and prepare for an even more successful second year.

The tour to Japan was another missionary trip and a way of thanking the Japanese for visiting Wales. The party chosen was the strongest available with Mervyn Davies as captain, John Dawes as coach and Les Spence as manager. Wales may have educated the Japanese on the rugby field but most of the players found that the country was an education in itself. At first they found it difficult to leave the hotels without running the risk of not finding their way back. They could not recognise the street names in Japanese for the most part and were certainly incapable of pronouncing them. Most overcame those fears and discovered some of the traditional Japanese delights.

The tour had actually begun in Hong Kong where Phil Bennett continued as he had left off and scored 21 points in their 57–3 defeat of the Hong Kong combined team. In Japan the first match was against Japan combined and 50,000 people turned out to watch Wales win by 32–3. Japan B were beaten by a similar score, 34–7, before Wales met the full Japanese National XV for the first time. Although the temperature for the match was 90° the team were now thoroughly acclimatised and put on a mar-vellous rugby display to score ten tries in the 56–12 victory. In the first half the two wings, Gerald Davies and J. J. Williams, had scored two tries each and Steve Fenwick kicked two penalty goals and two conversions to give Wales a 26–9 lead. In the second half Ray Gravell and Trevor Evans scored twice each and John Bevan and Clive Shell also added tries. Fenwick converted three of the tries.

There was one problem. Mervyn Davies had found his shoulders becoming so sore towards the end of the match that he could not push. When he came to take his shirt off, half his back came with it and only then did they discover that the pitch markings had been in lime and several of the players were suffering from burns. Mervyn's discomfort turned into unbearable pain when his coach, a former science teacher, decided to take a hand. The theory according to Dawes went something like this. 'Lime is an acid. To neutralise an acid one requires an alkali. What alkaline liquids do we have at our disposal? Answer – aftershave solutions Q.E.D.' The captain abandoned his dignity and screamed upon their application. After soothing balm had been applied, he was to be heard muttering about the educational standards of Aberystwyth University, the institution which had been stupid enough to grant Sydney John Dawes a degree.

Derek Quinnell was to be heard muttering in the same way about St Mary's Hospital, Paddington, the medical school where Dr J. P. R. Williams had trained. Derek had picked up an ear infection and as the ear also bore great resemblance to a cauliflower the nasty by-products of the infection could not escape. The young doctor decided that the answer was to lance the ear and that the ideal substitute for a scalpel would be a razor blade. That was bad enough but having survived the operation Derek literally hit the roof as Dr Williams also applied that tested cure all, aftershave, to stem the bleeding and told his patient not to be a baby.

The biggest trouble away from the rugby scene was the night the team decided to take up cycling. They had been to a reception and, as it was raining, decided that they should really get back to the hotel as quickly as possible. Allan Martin spotted a pink bicycle and convinced himself that the owner would not mind if he borrowed it. He sped off to the hotel but was met on arrival by a Japanese policeman. John Dawes who was already back at the hotel was called and managed to smooth things over until Graham Price also arrived on a pink bicycle, closely followed by Phil Bennett. Benny, having toured before, assessed the situation quickly and disappeared into the hotel never to be seen again. However, the policeman was now very unhappy and insisted that John Dawes accompany him to the station. Eventually it was explained that all the cyclists were members of the Welsh rugby team and the station sergeant agreed to forget the incident providing that they made a signed statement apologising for their actions.

Allan Martin, nicknamed 'Panther' some time before because of his line out jumping but now called 'Pink Panther', and Graham Price were present but Phil Bennett had hidden himself so well that responsibility for the third statement fell upon the captain who was dragged out by assistant manager Dawes, even though he had been at home all evening nursing his bad shoulders. He still blushes as he remembers the humiliation he felt as the station sergeant addressed him in perfect English, having read his confession complete with name, age and occupation. 'Do all schoolteachers in Britain behave in this kind of manner?'

The final match was against the Japanese National team once more and 40,000 spectators went to the Olympic Stadium in Tokyo to watch. They saw Wales score a record 82 points against their team. All the fit players who had not played in the First Test played in this one. Appropriately the captain still smarting from his sore shoulders and the humiliation of his confession, scored first and before half time Charlie Faulkner, Gerald Davies, Ray Gravell, J. P. R. Williams and Phil Bennett also added tries. Bennett, having reappeared when the fuss was over, kicked four conversions and a penalty to make the score 35–6. In the second half J. J. Williams, Graham Price and J. P. R. Williams all scored two tries, while Gerald Davies and Phil Bennett scored another one each. Benny converted six and kicked a penalty to create a new record of 34 points in a game.

The tour had been a great success. Wales had played rugby of the highest quality, albeit against inferior opposition, but John Dawes on his return felt able to say that he now felt he had twenty-five players who were all good enough to represent their country.

12

BENNETT, P., THIRD CHOICE
1975/76

Having made a short tour of England and Wales in 1973, the Australians returned for a major tour of the British Isles in the autumn of 1975. They played twenty-five games in the United Kingdom and won eighteen of them, including the international match against Ireland. It was a much more impressive record than that they achieved in 1973, but the result against Wales was much the same.

The Welsh team showed three changes from the side which had played against Ireland in the last match of the Home International Championship the previous season. Phil Bennett was selected but withdrew with an injury and was replaced by John Bevan, while Steve Fenwick, who had missed the Irish match because of a fractured cheekbone, returned at centre. Gerald Davies was also injured and was replaced by Clive Rees. He in fact played on the left wing with J. J. Williams moving over to the right. J.J. had something to prove. After little more than a season of international rugby he had found that life at the top is not always easy and was being accused of having lost his sparkle.

Although Clive Rees might have been awarded a penalty try, as he was felled after kicking ahead over the line with a clear run in front of him, there was only one score until the last minute of the first half, a mishit penalty from Steve Fenwick. From thirty yards the ball somehow swerved its way over the bar on a very flat trajectory, looking more like a banana than a rugby ball. The score should have been greater because even at that stage of the game the pack had assumed complete control, but the break-through came at the vital psychological moment, just when the Australians must have been waiting for the whistle and a chance to regroup and rethink with only three points against them.

Rees was almost over once again but the referee awarded a scrum five to the attacking side as he was unsighted on the touchdown. From a well controlled heel there was no prize for guessing Gareth Edwards' intentions, but even though the Australians were ready for him, he handed off McLean and flung himself for the line, ploughing straight through two would-be tacklers as he went. Fenwick converted and Wales carried a healthy 9–0 lead into the second half.

After eleven minutes J. J. Williams scored an excellent try created by John Bevan who looped around Ray Gravell to create the extra man. Fenwick converted again, this time from the touchline and without their skipper, Hipwell, who had left the field with a knee injury, the Australians had no chance.

Wales went further ahead when John Bevan found the time and space to drop a goal after Mervyn Davies had tapped the ball cleanly to Edwards from the back of the line out, and from then on it was merely a question of how many Wales would score. They managed two more tries, both scored by J. J. Williams to give him a hat-trick and a total of five tries in seven internationals. Gareth Edwards began the attack for his second. He put a towering kick up into the Australian 22 and Steve Fenwick charged in underneath it. Mervyn Davies was the next player to arrive and he fed Trevor Evans who was having his best game for Wales. The Swansea flanker ran right to the blind side and found J.J. outside him with a clear run to the line.

Trevor Evans also played a big part in the final try. From a ruck he ran blind and fed Ray Gravell. He moved the ball quickly to J. J. Williams and the winger showed that he was just as accurate kicking ahead on the right as on the left, chipping it over the line to chase and score. Allan Martin this time added the conversion points and Wales had won 28–3, McLean having kicked a penalty for Australia.

Mervyn Davies had again been an inspiring captain, leading his team by example and almost literally carrying them to greater efforts. The game was also a triumph for J. J. Williams. He was under considerable pressure at the beginning of it, but by the end had totally silenced his critics. He could have had no greater compliment than John Dawes' joking remark to the injured Gerald Davies after the game, 'I'll see you next Easter!'

The end result of the final trial before the 1976 Home International Championship was to tell the selectors little that they did not know already about the players, but it did cause a major rift between the Big Five and the Welsh public. As usual the original trial line-up was decimated by injury and one of those missing was Phil Bennett. His place was taken by Dai Richards, the Swansea outside half and when the squad was announced after the trial Phil Bennett was not included. Bewildered reporters checked their lists and wondered whether there had been a mistake. The Chairman of the Selectors confirmed that the names were correct. How could the brilliant Benny not find a place in the squad when half the nation thought he should be in the team in front of John D. Bevan? Some people felt that he was being made an example of because he had dropped out of the trial with an ankle injury and then played for Llanelli the following Monday night. The player insisted that he had not been fit. The selectors insisted that his omission was not because of disciplinary action and that Richards had been chosen on merit. Eventually Bennett played as both Bevan and Richards were unfit. Max Boyce called it 'divine intervention'. One half of the nation were suddenly smiling where they had been miserable and the selectors privately admitted that had it just been Bevan who had withdrawn, they would have played Bennett and left Richards on the substitutes' bench.

John Dawes maintained that Bevan and Bennett were very much on a par as players but that Bevan's style suited the Welsh team better at that time. His judgement was borne out by the control that the team showed in their victories over France and England the previous season and against Australia. Moreover, Bennett had played an uncharacteristically poor game when he took the field as substitute against Scotland and it was felt that he could not suddenly switch on concentration and tune into the pace of international rugby without the normal mental build-up on the morning of the match. It was difficult to disagree with the logic of the argument. Early in his international career the Llanelli fly half, who mesmerised defences and controlled the game with his kicking at Stradey Park, had found it difficult to do the same at the National Stadium not because he was in a higher division but because he lacked confidence. He had overcome this by 1976 and had played some wonderfully fluent attacking games for his country but he had never been able to turn it on when he took the field as a replacement.

The Bennett saga was not the only problem in the Welsh camp. Until the final practice session on the Thursday before the match there were doubts about Ray Gravell, Graham Price and Charlie

Faulkner, while Gerald Davies and Bobby Windsor had only proved their fitness at the session on the previous Sunday. Eventually, the team took the field as selected, apart from John Bevan. He was never to play for Wales again but never can a player who won only four caps have been the subject of so much controversy not of his own making.

Wales travelled to Twickenham with bitter memories of 1974, but this time there was a French referee, Georges Domercq. The game belonged to J. P. R. Williams. He seemed to be every-where and scored two tries while the rest of the team struggled to find their rhythm. However, it was Edwards who opened the scoring and almost inevitably it was from the base of a scrum. England had heeled the ball but, under good pressure from the Welsh pack, lost control of it as the scrum wheeled and the ball squirted out the side. Edwards was on to it like a flash and over the line before most of the England forwards realised that the ball was gone. Fenwick converted and Wales gradually took control with Edwards and Bennett dominating play with their tactical kicking.

Allan Martin and Alastair Hignell swapped penalties before Wales scored again. From a scrum on the 22 the ball was moved left and Gravell was missed, the ball going direct to J. J. Williams on the wing. As he was being forced towards touch he found his namesake J.P.R. beside him and veering out again the Welsh full back crashed through the remaining would-be tacklers to score in the corner. Fenwick converted casually from the touchline. Another Hignell penalty kept England just in touch but at 15–6 Wales were comfortably ahead. Late in the second half Hignell managed another penalty but J. P. R. Williams's second try put the result beyond doubt.

As the other countries became increasingly aware of J.P.R. as an attacker, he found it more difficult to find space as the extra man, and Wales continued to vary his point of entry into the line. They also used him as the crash ball receiver at times. It could be a marvellously effective move. He was fearless, fast and heavy for a back at over fourteen stones. Full back was also an ideal place to run from, the deep positioning was natural and did not alert the opposition and allowed the runner to take the ball at full tilt. J.P.R. did exactly that as he took the ball from his fly half and crashed through attempted tackles from Hignell and Duckham. As he scored he almost hit the post and most

Above: Mike Knill and Charlie Faulkner help Bobby Windsor to free the ball as the rest of the Welsh pack protect Gareth Edwards, against France, 1976. Below: Mervyn Davies, the Welsh captain, at the height of his powers in 1976. Nobody could believe he would not be around to lead Wales the following season.

Above: Allan Martin is not as balletic as Bastiat, but he's that vital four inches higher and Wales are on the attack, 1977. Below: Gerald Davies and Steve Fenwick show their delight as J.P.R. dives triumphantly over the line, leaving the English in his wake yet again.

people thought the post was lucky that he missed it.

Fenwick had no trouble in converting and Wales had won 21–9. It sounded convincing but neither captain nor coach was satisfied. Mervyn Davies said simply, 'I don't think it was a very good win.' Dawes elaborated further. 'We must buck up,' he commented. 'The players know they are capable of much better and the atmosphere in the dressing room was as if we had lost. We measure our victories not merely by the number of points but by the quality of the performance.' The main worry was about the performance of the forwards, who had been held, but it was pointed out that the English pack with Burton, Wheeler, and Cotton, Beaumont, Ripley and Neary in its ranks was very strong itself.

One player totally above reproach was J. P. R. Williams. Not only had he scored two tries from full back, the only Welshman ever to do so, but he had had a terrific game in defence with one memorable shoulder charge tackle on Hignell saving a try at a time when England were exerting great pressure. It is not often that a captain singles out one of his senior players for praise at the after-match banquet but Mervyn Davies, realising how the full back had carried the side, gave him a special mention. 'To J.P.R. I say thank you for your contribution to the victory.'

The next match was against Scotland and although it was memorable because Gareth Edwards equalled the Welsh try-scoring record and Phil Bennett created a new Welsh points-scoring record it had an element of farce about it because Dr André Cuny, the referee, insisted on continuing to referee when he was almost unable to run because of a bruised calf muscle caused by an accidental collision with one of the players. Dr Cuny was forty-eight years old, grey haired and reminded one more of a dapper French lawyer than a rugby referee. It was his first international and he was determined to see the whole occasion through. He had two international referees as touch judges and Meirion Joseph several times tried to persuade him to allow him to take over but Dr Cuny still maintained that he could see everything that was going on. Neither the crowd nor the players agreed but Dr Cuny finished the game and effectively ruined it as a contest because it is impossible to determine what goes on in the ruck and maul from twenty-five yards away. All the talk in Cardiff that evening was of the loneliness of the long distance rugby referee. Meanwhile Dr Cuny was still explaining that his eyesight was very good and therefore he was able to continue.

J. J. Williams opened the scoring while Dr Cuny was still fully fit when Phil Bennett chipped to the corner flag and Irvine and Steele collided to allow the winger to nip in and touch down. Phil Bennett was given the kick from his favourite left touchline and converted beautifully, the ball curling in from his right foot. Although Scotland equalised through a try from Irvine, which Morgan converted, two Bennett penalties gave Wales a 12–6 lead at half time. Most of the players felt that Irvine had been brought down short of the line and had crossed it in a separate movement but Dr Cuny was too far away to tell.

With the crowd chanting 'Cuny must go,' Wales extended their lead with another Bennett penalty which equalled Barry John's record of 90 points for Wales and Steve Fenwick, not to be denied a score of some sort, dropped a goal after Bobby Windsor had fed the ball from a ruck set up by J. P. R. Williams, once again on a crash ball. Then from a line out the ball was moved right and when Gerald Davies was tackled the ball ran loose and Trevor Evans used his tremendous speed to outstrip the other forwards and pick up the ball to score.

It was now 22–6 to Wales and whenever they scored over twenty points it was unusual not to see G. O. Edwards' name among the tries. There was also a record to equal so he was not to be denied. After a ruck on the Scottish 22 he was not to be seen at the base of the scrum, having stood off deliberately on the left. Bobby Windsor, who had now made the feed from the base of the maul his speciality, was forced to give the ball directly to Phil Bennett. Edwards found himself some space and Phil gave it on to him. For a change he was already at full pace when he received the ball. In a flash he dummied the Scottish scrum half Dougie Morgan and wing Billy Steele and was gone. When he was asked maliciously by a member of the press why he had not been there to feed from the maul, his answer came through surely and quickly: 'It's what you call perception.' At least he had pipped his great friend Gerald Davies to equalling the record of seventeen tries for Wales. Phil Bennett's conversion made him the all time highest points scorer with a total of 92 points.

This time both John Dawes and Mervyn Davies were more pleased with the result but Dublin had proved almost as difficult a place to win as Murrayfield in recent years. Not since 1964 had

Wales won at Lansdowne Road and none of the current players had been present at that time. There was one change forced upon the selectors. Terry Cobner was ill and Tommy David (who had returned to Pontypridd now that his home town club had moved to a new ground with a stand and club house) was recalled to the side. The game was given added significance because, for the first time since 1969, the first three games were against the home countries and therefore the Triple Crown was the reward for winning. Wales had not won the coveted, mythical trophy by beating Ireland in Dublin for twenty-four years.

At half time Wales led 10–9 and were a little fortunate to do so. The Irish pack had been as fiery as ever and completely disruptive whenever possible. Usually they reckoned on deeds speaking louder than words, but this time Phil O' Callaghan was playing and he loved to chat with the opposition. He picked on Geoff Wheel as the Welshman renowned for losing his 'cool' most easily and began to try to make him angry. He almost succeeded when he snarled in a scrum, 'Geoff, boy, behave yourself or you'll be leaving Ireland as Meals on Wheels!' Fortunately, Bobby Windsor was able to calm things down. He had met O'Callaghan the year before when he had played for the President's XV against Ireland in their centenary celebrations. The Irish prop had come on to the field as a replacement in that game and when the two packs went down for the next scrum a packet of cigarettes and a box of matches fell out of O'Callaghan's shorts' pocket. In a flash he broke up the scrum, picked up the cigarettes and took them across to the referee, Norman Sanson. 'Hold these until half time,' he said. 'I'm not too keen on oranges.' If anyone believes rugby is no longer an amateur game that should tell them something.

Ireland had opened up a 9-point lead through three Barry McGann penalty goals and it looked as if they were on the way to retaining their impressive record against Wales at Lansdowne Road. Things began to look better for Wales when Allan Martin kicked a huge penalty goal from almost fifty yards and Phil Bennett made it 9–6 by kicking another much more simple chance. The try that gave the visitors a 10–9 lead at the interval owed more to good fortune, poor Irish defence and tenacious following up than to creativity. After twenty minutes, Wales were awarded a penalty near half way and after his earlier success Martin was called up for a shot at goal. This time he sliced the ball and it sailed wide to the right of the posts where it was collected by Willie Duggan. He fed scrum half Canniffe and his attempted clearance kick was charged down by Gerald Davies. The Welsh wing was then able to tap the ball over the line and score – Phil Bennett hit the bar with the conversion attempt.

In the second half Bennett added two more penalties to make it 16–9 but Wales then hit a purple patch the like of which is seldom seen in international rugby. As the clock registered that twenty-seven minutes of the second half had gone they led 16–9 but as it came up to thirty-two minutes the score was 34–9.

Phil Bennett hoisted a high kick and was tackled as he caught it. Wales won the maul and Geoff Wheel ripped it free. Edwards, this time in the right place, spun the ball to his right and Bennett and J. P. R. Williams moved it quickly to Gerald Davies to give him a clear run to the corner. Now he too had equalled the record of seventeen tries for Wales and was back on level scoring terms with Gareth Edwards. Phil Bennett converted from the right touchline, his most difficult position.

Ken Jones, Johnny Williams, Gareth Edwards and Gerald Davies jointly held the try-scoring record for Wales for almost exactly two minutes and then Edwards, determined to keep his nose in front of Gerald Davies, who had scored twice already in the match, scored his eighteenth try to set a new mark. From a ruck about thirty yards out he went blind, kicked ahead and charged through to regather the ball and score. Incredibly it was the fifth successive game in which he had scored a try, which must be a record in itself. Bennett this time converted from the left touchline.

Three minutes later Phil Bennett, who had had such a traumatic season, set his personal seal on the game by scoring his first try for Wales. He took the ball going right from a line out and passed to Gravell, then looped around the back of him to take the return pass. McMaster, the Irish wing, elected to stay with Gerald Davies in the hope that the cover would reach Phil but the little Llanelli player pinned his ears back and made the corner himself. For the third time in five minutes he converted from the touchline and Wales had scored their most points ever against Ireland. It was left for Charlie Faulkner to go close to scoring before the end but he was just bundled into touch to the relief of his front row colleagues and the final score remained 34–9. A remarkable turn around from having been 0–9 down.

Above all it was a personal triumph for Benny. He had finally put his full vocabulary of skills together in an international match. In this sort of form it was hard to believe that he could have been second or even third choice at the beginning of the season. His running and kicking from hand had been superbly controlled and his place-kicking machine-like in its accuracy and effortless, yet full of length. His third penalty made him the first player to score 100 points for Wales and his total of 19 points in the game took him to 111 at the end. As Steve Fenwick, who was becoming famous for his dry humour, said in the dressing room, 'What's the matter, Benny? – You fed up with us having a kick?'

Nevertheless it is a reflection on the inhibitions that affected his game at international level when one realises that such a gifted attacking player and prolific try-scorer for his club did not score his first try for his country until he had already notched 100 points with his boot.

With a home match to finish the 1976 campaign, all thoughts were obviously on a Grand Slam. The prospect was made even more exciting because France were also unbeaten and with a reconstructed side that looked capable of upsetting Welsh hopes. They had thrashed England and Ireland in Paris by 30–9 and 26–3 respectively and had travelled to Murrayfield to beat Scotland 13–6.

The added thrill of the match against France is that the players are unknown. Through club rugby and television the players from the home countries become familiar to the point where you know their style of play. With France you rely much more on newspaper reports. This time there was much talk of an exciting new flank forward, Rives, who with Skréla and the giant Bastiat, made up a back row 'très formidable'. Little Fouroux, the captain, known in France as 'Napoleon', had apparently disci-plined the side so that the massive forwards put all their energies into rugby instead of private battles.

On the day of the match, Mervyn Davies turned to me as I wished him luck and said, 'Bas, it's another one of those days.' I knew exactly what he meant. International days are always tense but sometimes there is just that little extra atmosphere that makes them very special. It was 1971 in Paris all over again, winner takes all and no quarter asked or given.

When the French took the field, the power in their pack was obvious: the massive Bastiat, perhaps the only man in the world who could give Mervyn Davies trouble; Palmié, swathed in bandages but with a fearsome reputation for strength; and an impressive looking front row of Paparemborde, Paco, and Cholley, a former amateur heavy-weight boxing champion. Bill McLaren, with whom I was commentating on the match for the B.B.C. summed them up beautifully as the camera caught them in close-up. 'You'll find it hard to pick three more sturdy French citizens than these chaps.'

With so much at stake, the game was fiercely contested and sometimes boiled over. When it did, it was usually the French who were the instigators. Monsieur Palmié was often at the centre of things and Graham Price's eyes and ears took a hammering from his boots. Mervyn Davies was also in the wars. He had a badly bruised calf muscle and it gradually seized up, so that towards the end he could not run. Although Price was eventually forced to leave the field to be replaced by Mike Knill, the Cardiff prop, Merv hauled himself around the field somehow while he exhorted his men to greater efforts.

The game began disastrously for Wales with Gerald Davies, normally the last player to do such a thing, giving Steve Fenwick a 'hospital' pass in his own 22. He was tackled as he received it and Romeu quickly fed Gourdon who scored. Romeu converted and France held a 6–0 lead. Wales clawed three points back through a Phil Bennett penalty and then Allan Martin again gave his side a boost by equalising from fifty yards. Then Wales went ahead with a good try. The ball was moved right where the move was checked and it came back to the left. Phil Bennett threw a high pass to Steve Fenwick and he drew the final defender before passing to J. J. Williams who scored in the corner. Another Bennett penalty made it 13–6 and although Romeu kicked one in reply it was 13–9 at the interval and you could almost feel the crowd relax. Wales were expected to turn on the normal second half power display and move away.

As they piled on the pressure it looked as if the expectations would be fulfilled but the exchanges were becoming heated and it was obvious that this French side was not about to blow up in the same way as some of their predecessors. Bastiat became the villain when he late-tackled Phil Bennett and the funniest sight of the afternoon was little Fouroux at 5′ 5″ castigating Bastiat at 6′ 6″ like a little boy for giving away the penalty.

Bennett's leg was too bruised to allow him to place kick but

Steve Fenwick took over and landed two shots to make Wales apparently safe at 19–9. But still the French came back and Averous scored after Aguirre had kicked over the Welsh line. J. P. R. Williams protested that he had beaten Averous to the touch down but the referee gave the try. The National Stadium crowd howled their disapproval as they realised the significance of the decision. The referee was John West.

For the last fifteen minutes it was all France. They pounded away at the Welsh line and Aguirre looked to have given them a chance of levelling the scores but knocked on as he was actually going over the line. Finally, Gourdon was bundled into touch a few yards from the line by J.P.R.'s shoulder charge as he was in full flight for the corner. It was a close run thing and Wales had scored only one try against two from France but they had shown tremendous reserve of defensive strength to hold on to their lead as France threw everything into attack.

The attacking flair of the side was not in doubt after the earlier victories and the total of 102 points in one championship season, including eleven tries, remains a record.

Afterwards, Mervyn Davies, with his calf muscle now completely seized up, admitted to being grateful when he heard the final whistle. He summed up just how close it had been when he said, 'Playing on the Arms Park means six points for Wales and that's how it worked out.'

It was a typically practical comment from a man who had just achieved the highest honour – to captain his country to a Grand Slam. He had turned out to be an inspiring leader, setting an example by his own play and encouraging others to match his work rate and under him Wales had won eight out of nine matches. It gave him particular pleasure he told me afterwards because I had once said that if ever I had the misfortune to be picked to play in a side that he was to captain, I would immediately retire. My comment was a joke because at London Welsh he had always been the donkey of all donkeys as far as John Dawes was concerned. But the remark had stuck and he had proved it wrong.

Although he never believed in looking too far into the future Merv could have been forgiven for thinking that the rugby world was his oyster and that the captaincy of the 1977 Lions was his for the taking if he wanted it. But exactly a month later, surgeons were operating on him to save his life. During a Welsh Cup semi-final between his club, Swansea, and Pontypool he suddenly pitched to the ground unconscious. He had suffered a haemorrhage inside the brain. Fortunately the game was at Cardiff Arms Park and the medical facilities were good. At one stage he stopped breathing on the massage table in the medical room but a mechanical resuscitator revived him and he was taken to hospital unconscious.

From the hospital there were three terse bulletins to say that he was fighting for his life and that a major operation would be necessary if the patient survived. A week passed before Mervyn was strong enough to allow the surgeon, Dr Robert Weeks, to risk the operation. Thanks to his skill and Merv's own strength the Welsh captain survived and after some early paralysis made a complete recovery. But he had played his last game of rugby, having won thirty-eight consecutive caps for his country and every honour in the game. His contribution to Welsh rugby ranks with the greatest. Without his ball winning in the line out and rucks and mauls Gareth Edwards and Gerald Davies would never have had the opportunity to score a record number of tries. I too have good reason to be grateful to him, not only for the laughs we have had in all parts of the world as close friends, but because without his 6' 5" frame and incredible reach, 'wee' John Taylor might well have been a luxury the Welsh team could not afford.

13

J.P.R., SCOURGE OF THE ENGLISH
1976/77

Wales began the 1976/77 season with a visit from the Pumas, the national side of Argentina. The game has been played in the Argentine for many years and a British touring team visited the country in 1910. Wales had had something of a shock on their visit in 1968, losing one of the international matches and drawing the other. Those matches had not been against a full Welsh XV as those players who had just returned from the 1968 Lions tour to South Africa were not considered but the match in October 1976 was against the strongest Welsh team possible.

Phil Bennett, having in the space of two seasons moved from being under tremendous pressure for his place to being a key member of the side and now holding the Welsh scoring record, was given the captaincy. It showed the transformation that had taken place in the player. At one time his lack of confidence in himself was inhibiting his own game to such an extent that it caused the selectors to drop him. Now his control on the game was such that he also had the time and ability to lead his team mates.

The Argentinians immediately showed that they were no new-comers to the game. The forward play and the handling of the backs made it clear straightaway that they were certainly not cannon fodder presented at the National Stadium to help demonstrate the growth of the game around the world. In Hugo Porta, their outside half, they had a player who would have graced most national teams in the International Board member countries. The first scores were an exchange of penalties between Porta and Bennett and then Varela and Bennett to make the score 6–6. It remained at that until the interval and then Wales moved smoothly away and the crowd waited for the slaughter as one of the great traditional rugby giants would put the upstarts in their place. Phil Bennett kicked a third penalty and then came the first try. Gerald Davies screamed over on the right after Terry Cobner had fed the ball from a maul. Then from a ruck Edwards received the sort of ball that by now almost automatically ended in a try from a swerving, jinking, barging run. He did not disappoint his vast army of supporters and Wales were ahead 17–6.

But suddenly the script went wrong. After some adept handling by the forwards and backs Gauweloose scored for Porta to convert and the Welsh calm was disturbed. When Varela scored another try to make it 17–16 it was definitely ruffled and when the same player kicked a penalty in the closing stages to give Argentina a 17–19 lead the team and the crowd were thrown into confusion.

Fortunately the gods intervened to preserve Wales's rugby dignity. The one aspect of the Pumas' play that had been undisciplined was their tackling and Travaglini, who had already been penalised for high tackling, transgressed again. J. P. R. Williams was making a last ditch counter-attack to try and save the match. The attack did not look particularly dangerous but Travaglini stormed in with a desperate head-high tackle and was penalised by Mr Sanson, the referee, who was highly praised for his control on the day. The kick was from forty yards and half way between posts and touchline. It was also the last chance for Wales, a similar situation to the 1972 match against the All Blacks. This time, Phil Bennett was equal to the task, kicked a beautiful goal, and the whole of Wales breathed again. 20–19 was not exactly convincing but it was a win.

Because of the anachronistic agreement between the International Board countries the Welsh side were not awarded caps for this game nor are they for other matches against countries who are not International Board members, except France. Surely Argentina had proved by this display and their previous record against 'Board' countries that they are worthy international opponents? I must confess that I find the attitude of our international governing body, or indeed our national governing body, towards the rugby-playing countries who are not part of the inner sanctum somewhat insulting and very patronising. As we move into the egalitarian 'eighties they will hopefully drop this unnecessary discrimination.

The start of the Five Nations Championship saw changes in the Welsh team. Jeff Squire was chosen to fulfill the No. 8 position in front of Derek Quinnell who many had thought would be the replacement for Mervyn Davies. Once again 'Super sub', as Derek was becoming known, was relegated to the replacements bench. Derek's career undoubtedly suffered because he played so well in so many forward positions, but Squire was also something of a utility back-row man, having played much of his rugby as a wing forward.

Glyn Shaw also returned to the side, splitting up the Pontypool front row for the first time since they came together. However, there was no truth in the rumour that it was because Charlie Faulkner had to collect his old age pension on a Thursday and therefore could no longer make the final pre-match practice session. His Pontypool team mate, Terry Cobner, was unfit through illness and was replaced by Clive Burgess from Ebbw Vale, the first cap from the club since Arthur Lewis. He was very much in the same mould, what the players call a 'dog', hounding everything and always at the heart of the rucks and mauls. Finally, David Burcher, the Newport centre, won his first cap in place of the injured Ray Gravell.

The opening game of the Championship campaign was against Ireland at Cardiff and it turned out to be a very controversial one with Geoff Wheel and Willie Duggan being ordered from the field for fighting after thirty-seven minutes of the first half. The referee was again Norman Sanson who was criticised for not having taken firmer control of the game at an earlier stage. 'It was not a violent match but it lacked control from the referee downwards,' said Keith Rowlands the former Cardiff, Wales and Lions forward who was Chairman of the Selectors. Sanson received little support from any quarter, which was a pity because, in a game where the standard of refereeing is generally not up to the standard of play, he was an excellent official who was always firm and fair and understood the game far better than most of his colleagues. He never really forgave the game for not supporting his proper application of the laws and, although still a youngster in refereeing terms, he retired from the game three years later.

No player had ever been sent off in the history of the International Championship and only three players had been sent off in international matches anywhere in the world. The All Black Cyril Brownlie had been dismissed at Twickenham in 1925, Colin Meads was ordered off at Murrayfield in 1967 and Mike Burton received his marching orders in Australia during the England tour of 1975.

At the time Ireland were leading 6–0 from two Mike Gibson penalties and many people felt the incident benefited Wales because Duggan had been the outstanding forward in the match until that time, totally dominating the back of the line out in the absence of Mervyn Davies. After the game much that was hysterical was written but one of the Irish papers took the cake with a story that the sendings off had all been part of a tactical plan ordered by coach John Dawes to take Duggan out of the game.

With the back row having difficulties and Gareth Edwards struggling because of their inability to control the ball when they gave it back to him, Ireland held the lead until half time. Early in the second half Phil Bennett kicked two penalties to level the score but then Gibson put Ireland in front with another penalty.

At last, three quarters of the way through the game the first try was scored. Wales had gradually started to exert some control in the forward battle and Ireland were suffering, particularly in the line out where they certainly missed Duggan more than Wales missed Wheel. From a set piece Bennett switched the ball from left to right as Fenwick moved across behind him. The blond centre linked with Burcher and although his pass to Gerald Davies was a poor one (because he had to throw it underneath the interception attempt of his opposite number) the winger picked it up off his toes, as if he always received passes at that height, and scored in the corner to go level again on tries with Gareth Edwards. Immediately after that score Trevor Evans had to leave the field injured and 'Super sub' Quinnell yet again came on as a replacement to devastating effect.

With just over ten minutes left the score was 10–9 and the match could have gone either way, but then Wales turned on a burst of scoring power that they seem to save for Ireland. J. P. R. Williams came storming into the line and powered his way over next to the posts to start the spree and Phil Bennett had no problem in converting the try. Derek Quinnell then powered away and set up a perfect ruck for Fenwick to drop a goal that hit the cross bar and then bounced over. J. J. Williams went close to extending the lead but was stopped just short before Phil Bennett broke devastatingly to find Gerald Davies clear on the right. The winger ran just as incisively, cutting inside towards the posts. He looked as if he could score himself but with one man left to beat, found Clive Burgess on his inside. Typically, he never even thought about grabbing the try for himself even though it would have taken him ahead of Gareth Edwards in the tries stakes and gave perfectly to the new cap who stormed over to ground between the posts. Phil Bennett had obviously been told by the referee that the conversion was the last kick of the match because he chipped it over and then sprinted after the ball, grabbing it as a souvenir of his first match as captain of Wales.

He deserved it. In a match full of incident he had proved himself an able captain and stuck to the attacking plan even when it appeared that Wales were going to struggle to break through the Irish defence. His own contribution of two penalties and two conversions took his total number of points for Wales to 127.

The controversy was still not over. While the Welsh Rugby Union gave Wheel a four-week suspension for his misdemeanours, the Irish R.F.U. almost made it appear that Duggan had been wrongly dismissed by sentencing him to just two weeks' suspension which meant that he did not even miss the next international match for his country. It was a blatant case of a judgement to suit the interests of the national team and he was duly selected for the rest of the matches that season.

Wales had now won eight Championship matches in a row and faced the biggest test of the season with the match against France in Paris coming up. France had been close to upsetting the Grand Slam celebrations the year before and now had the home advantage. In addition to this the French team had grown in confidence and were fast, strong and exciting. Therefore, even as Champions, Wales began the game as underdogs. There were two forced changes in the Welsh team. Derek Quinnell moved into the second row to replace the suspended Wheel and Terry Cobner was recalled to take the place of the injured Trevor Evans who never regained his place in the side. In his two full seasons in the Welsh jersey he had been an important factor in the success of the national team. His speed in support of the ball and to the point of breakdown was vital in setting up the ruck and maul before the wrestlers arrived to wrench it free.

The match turned out to be a great disappointment for Wales. The team played as if they expected to lose and nothing the huge band of Welsh followers could do made them raise their game. It was one of those strange days when everyone felt lethargic at the same time. No player can tell you exactly what happens on these rare days but the atmosphere is not right and the game never takes off as a contest.

France with the Dax town band in full flow once again, had no such depression and set off in their best free-flowing style with the backs passing the ball steep and fast in their very individual way. The forwards meanwhile were showing off their own brand of dexterity, flipping the ball up blindly but always with so much support that there was a player on hand to continue the movement. Surprisingly it was Wales who drew first blood when Fenwick kicked a penalty from almost fifty yards after half an hour, but the Welsh line had already had some narrow squeaks and after thirty-seven minutes Romeu levelled the score at 3–3 with a penalty given away for handling in the ruck. Without appearing at all in control of the game Wales went ahead once more in the second half when Palmié was penalised for kicking one of the Welsh players. Fenwick landed the goal.

Rough play was the one blemish on the French performance. There had been comment after their previous match that certain of the big forwards were over-vigorous in the rucks and mauls and the worst was feared when the French Federation of Rugby refused to accept Norman Sanson as the referee for the match. The fears were confirmed when Gerald Davies had to leave the field with concussion after a clumsy head-high tackle from Bastiat. He was replaced by Gareth Evans of Newport who won his first cap and almost wished he hadn't, as Bastiat also had a go at him.

France then managed to score two tries in four minutes, having been the dominant side for most of the game. The pack was giving the Welsh forwards a hard time and they almost managed a push-over try in the left corner. When Wales dug in to prevent that indignity they wheeled the scrum and Skréla was able to pick up and dive over. Romeu converted with a splendid kick.

Almost straight from the kick-off they produced a beautiful, typically French handling movement involving the forwards and backs over half the length of the field. Eventually the ball was worked out to the right wing, Harize, who had a clear run to the corner. The game was won from that moment, although Wales did see a ray of hope when Fenwick kicked a third penalty to make it 13–9. But Romeu quickly closed the door with a final penalty for France. The match left a slightly bad taste in the mouth but the Welsh team knew it had not played well enough to win, so there were no complaints. To make a bad weekend disastrous half the team lost themselves at the airport, missed the plane and had to take a much later flight on the one occasion when they wanted to leave Paris as soon as possible.

When Bastiat was not trying to decapitate the Welsh backs he had a tremendously effective game for France and emphasised just how important Mervyn Davies had been to the Welsh team. Hard as he tried Jeff Squire had neither the physique nor the experience to handle a man as big and rough as the Frenchman. The selectors now decided that they needed a bigger man and so for the match against England, Geoff Wheel returned to the second row (something that is no longer possible as a player who is suspended in an international is now automatically out for the rest of the season in Wales) and Derek Quinnell was moved back to the No. 8 position. Gerald Davies, none the worse after his headache, was able to return to the right wing. There was another change forced upon the selectors. Glyn Shaw, the Neath prop who had pushed his way back into the team after a three-year gap, turned professional and took the lone trip north. Nobody was surprised. There are some players made for the League code because of their style of play and Glyn was just such a player. Clive Williams of Aberavon replaced him. The side was transformed and turned in a superb effort. France had only beaten England by one point (4–3) at Twickenham and the English forwards had held the French forwards who had been so impressive against Wales. So all the fire and vigour that had been missing in France was let loose on the English pack. Allan Martin was the star of the show, dominating the line outs and, as so often happens when a player feels that it is his day, contributing more to the loose play than he had done at any other time for Wales. He often spent too much time 'seagulling' at the rucks and mauls, looking over the top for the loose pickings instead of using his weight and considerable strength to force his way into the centre of the action. In this game he proved what a good all round forward he could be and made light of the unkind nickname 'Palm Tree' (as against Colin Meads' 'Pine Tree') given to him by those who believed he was a non-contributor outside the line out. Derek Quinnell also lived down his nickname of 'Sloppy', performing all his tasks with the maximum efficiency and Clive Williams demonstrated that he was a fine scrummager.

For all that England went into a 6–0 lead through two Alastair

Hignell penalties after five and eleven minutes. Then Welsh forward pressure began to tell and, as the Arms Park crowd roared them on, Wales scored a try. They almost made it from a maul following a high kick into the English 22 but as the referee was unsighted he gave a five-metre scrum. The Welsh eight stayed down and exerted all the pressure they could so that the English forwards were also tied in, also having to stay down to prevent a pushover try. Gareth Edwards was always difficult to stop from that range but now it was impossible. He drove to the blind side and straight through the English wing, Mike Slemen, to score. Allan Martin missed the conversion.

Right on half time Steve Fenwick added a penalty and Wales had again won the psychological advantage of going into the second half with a lead, having been behind for most of the game. In the first minutes of the second half Hignell and Fenwick kicked good penalties to keep both sides in the game and then as the Welsh forwards regained their control of both tight and loose phases of play, Wales scored a decisive try. Edwards hoisted a high kick, Wales got underneath it and won the maul. Edwards was back in position and threw a reverse pass to Phil Bennett. The captain fed Fenwick who put Burcher through the gap. As the cover closed in England seemed to have Gerald Davies covered but J. P. R. Williams appeared in the line, took the pass, and stormed over for the try. His knack of producing the goods against England was quite uncanny and the scores usually came when the game was in the balance. It was his sixth in international rugby, a record that far outstripped any other Welsh full back and five of them had been against England. It had been a tight match but once again Wales had triumphed. The score was 14–9 and England still had to go back to 1963 for a win in Cardiff. The performance of the rejuvenated pack had been decisive and Martin and Williams had been quite outstanding.

Although France looked like winning the Championship and the Grand Slam, Wales suddenly found themselves in with a chance of a second successive Triple Crown. Amazingly, Wales had not achieved successive Crowns since 1908 and 1909 which was the only time they had managed it. England had achieved the feat twice, in 1913/14 and 1923/24. Ireland had been the last country to achieve it in 1948 and 1949 and Scotland had never succeeded since the Home International Championship began.

Scotland had managed only one win in 1977 before they met

David Burcher and J. J. Williams can only watch and wonder as Phil Bennett side-steps a full two yards to leave Bill Gammell and Ian McLauchlan groping at thin air in 1977.

One of Steve Fenwick's greatest strengths is his determination and, as the look on his face shows, nothing is going to stop him this close to the line.

He didn't make the line this time, but Graham Price looks determined to repeat his debut try against France, here in front of his home crowd, 1978.

Wales, just beating Ireland in a high scoring game, and Wales should have started favourites but there had been too many unexpected reverses at Murrayfield to allow the Welshmen to feel any real confidence. It was a sign of the times and of rugby's increased popularity that Gareth Edwards had to fly back from the United States, where he had been competing in the 'World Superstars' event, to play in the game. He missed the practice on the Sunday before the match but joined the team in time to take part in the Thursday session. Apart from the worries about professionalism which were to come later when it was learned that he had won thousands of dollars, the old sages shook their heads and worried about jet lag and the effect it would have on his play. They need not have been concerned. Gareth was as ebullient as ever and contributed fully to another splendid Welsh performance.

One of the problems that Scotland have failed to come to grips with as yet is the difference in philosophy between their backs and their forwards. No Scottish coach has yet managed to create a style of play that produces a cohesive effort and from the time I began to play international rugby Scottish forwards have constantly killed the ball. They have been very brave but not at all constructive, particularly in the back row which is the vital link area between forwards and backs. That would be understandable and even acceptable within the parameters of the Home International Championship if the pack was powerful and the backs weak but by 1977 the backs were beginning to emerge as the possible match-winners and there was little chance of the forwards dominating the game up front to such an extent that they could win matches through pressure. Players such as Irvine, Renwick and McGeechan had proved themselves as attacking players of the highest class and Scotland's philosophy had to be to give them the ball at every opportunity and hope that they could weave some magic. In 1977 the forwards played much more constructively than in previous years. Scotland still lost because the pack was too weak, but at least they caused Wales problems before Welsh extra power won the day.

Scotland led after only a minute through McGeechan's smartly taken dropped goal but after ten minutes Wales were back on terms when Phil Bennett effortlessly stroked over a penalty from forty-five yards to prove yet again that kicking is all about timing and not brute force and ignorance. As each side probed and counter-attacked without making a decisive opening, the score remained level until half time. Scotland were always struggling in the forward exchanges, but because they were attacking and not spoiling they were always a threat. At the beginning of the second half they were rewarded when Scotland went ahead. Morgan ran across the field from the back of a scrum and fed Renwick running straight. The centre sliced through the first line of defence and, as he was confronted by J. P. R. Williams, found Irvine on his outside. The flying full back, the first to cause any sort of threat to J.P.R.'s supremacy in that position since the Welshman had burst upon the scene in 1969, streaked through to score. He was still streets behind Doctor John as an all round full back but he was becoming a very exciting attacking runner. Irvine converted his own try and the home side must have felt that they might be able to snatch victory against the run of play.

Three minutes later a moment of superb skill and audacious rugby thinking dashed those hopes. Gareth Edwards sprinted off to the right of a scrum with plenty of support but finding the general prospect unpromising he changed his mind and rifled a torpedo pass thirty yards across the back of the scrum. Phil Bennett took it going left and the ball travelled via Steve Fenwick and J. P. R. Williams to J. J. Williams who whistled in for a superb try that had been created when Gareth had wrong-footed the defence by changing the direction of the attack. Benny rubbed salt into the wound with a beautiful conversion and Wales never looked back.

After nineteen minutes of the second half they were in the lead. Irvine was caught with the ball and Phil Bennett kicked the penalty after he failed to release it. Just four minutes later from a superb counter-attack the same player delivered the killer blow. J. P. R. Williams fell on the ball in the Welsh 22 and regained his feet magnificently to shake off his tacklers just long enough to allow him to feed Steve Fenwick who had run back in support. Fenwick ran to the open, having checked that Gerald Davies had also raced back to make himself available, and gave the Cardiff captain the ball. With room to get himself into his stride Gerald was at full pace within ten yards and slashed open the Scottish cover before passing to Phil Bennett. The ball then went to Burcher who lobbed a high pass to Fenwick. It was almost a hospital pass but the Bridgend centre, rapidly touched it on to Phil Bennett who had followed his pass and stayed with the ball.

A characteristic lean that signalled a side-step which was unstoppable, even though the defender knew what was coming, and Benny was over under the posts. His conversion took his own points total for Wales to 141 and made the final score 9–18.

The final try had come from a superb demonstration of the skills that make rugby at its best one of the most exciting games in the world but the joy of the Welsh side at the final whistle was short-lived, as the news came over the public address system that France had beaten Ireland 15–6. Nevertheless, Wales had dominated the domestic scene yet again and had won a second successive Triple Crown for the first time for sixty-eight years. Even though it was his first season as captain of his national side, there could be no other choice as captain of the Lions to tour New Zealand than Phil Bennett. No doubt with his wry sense of humour he took a few moments off when the appointment was announced to reflect on how quickly fortunes can change. It was the last thing he could ever have expected in January 1976 when it looked as if he had been relegated to third choice outside half for his country.

14

TOURISTS AT BAY
the Lions in New Zealand, 1977

If Phil Bennett's appointment was not challenged the number of Welshmen in the party to tour New Zealand was a surprise to most people. There were sixteen and it would have been seventeen had not Geoff Wheel been advised to withdraw because of what was diagnosed as a heart complaint! Even the most diehard Welsh supporters could not believe the representation when they learned that J. P. R. Williams, Gerald Davies and Gareth Edwards were not included in the sixteen. They were unavailable for a mixture of personal and business reasons. Only Clive Burgess of the players available from the team that played against Scotland in the last match of the Home International Championship had not been selected and six players who had not represented Wales in that match were also picked. Wales had certainly dominated the Home Championship for the previous two years but the selectors were perhaps putting too much faith in the potential of players inexperienced at international level when they put so many young Welshmen together.

There were two uncapped players on the tour, Elgan Rees of Neath and Brynmor Williams of Newport who had been understudying Gareth Edwards for the previous two seasons. In addition there was Gareth Evans who had won only one cap as a replacement against France during the 1977 Home International Championship. David Burcher had just completed his first season at international level, Jeff Squire had only two caps against Ireland and France behind him, after which he had been dropped, and Clive Williams had also experience of just two internationals. Later in the tour two more Welshmen joined the party. Charlie Faulkner replaced Clive Williams, who had scrummaged magnificently until injured, and Alun Lewis, the third choice scrum half in Wales, flew out for the last two weeks when the scrum half injury situation became intolerable. However complimentary the representation might be to Welsh rugby it is hard to believe that twenty-three (the nineteen who actually toured plus Wheel who was selected and J. P. R. Williams, Gerald Davies and Gareth Edwards) of the top thirty-five players in Britain came from Wales. Apart from anything else it shows a lack of understanding of the role experience has to play in touring. The youngsters would no doubt have acquitted themselves well in a balanced framework but touring is not all fun. The pressures off the field do begin to weigh on the minds of players and three months can be a very long time away from home.

The 1977 tourists were under enormous pressure before they started just because their illustrious predecessors on the tours of 1971 and 1974 had done so well. When they arrived in the country much was expected of them but for a variety of reasons things began to go wrong and sadly there was not the experience within the party to hold things together at the vital moments.

One of the great joys of a long tour is that it gives the players a chance to have a long look at a country that they would almost certainly not otherwise have visited. New Zealand is a very beautiful place with many unique natural features all worth seeing. It also offers plenty of scope for relaxation with magnificent golf courses, plenty of swimming and a host of other entertainments. Unfortunately one can participate in none of them if the weather is dreadful. In 1971 we experienced a very mild New Zealand winter which meant that our playing conditions were invariably good, especially important as the backs were the strongest part of the team, and our recreation was unhindered. The 1977 Lions found themselves in the middle of the worst winter for many years. It was cold and wet continuously and this prevented the backs from developing their skills, sapped morale and promoted homesickness as the tourists found themselves lounging around hotels. As Derek Quinnell put it when he returned home, 'In 1971 we played golf and in 1977 we played snooker – which would you prefer?' Apart from Phil Bennett, who fancied himself as a budding Terry Griffiths, the answer would almost certainly have been golf. Only the New Zealand green-keepers were grateful for the weather.

The opening matches went well enough with the Welsh boys getting off to a flying start. In the very first match J. J. Williams scored three tries, with Cobner and Burcher bagging two apiece. At Taumaruni J.J. scored another two, while Squire, Derek

Quinnell, Brynmor Williams and Phil Bennett scored one each. Benny also kicked eight conversions in the 60–9 victory over King Country-Wanganui. The real star of that match was Andy Irvine who scored five tries from full back. Eight matches were won but then in the match before the First Test the Lions were beaten by New Zealand Universities. It was the only time that they lost outside the Test matches but it happened at a vital moment.

Wales supplied nine members of the team for the First Test, Steve Fenwick and J. J. Williams in the backs, Phil Bennett and Brynmor Williams at half back and Graham Price, Bobby Windsor, Allan Martin, Trevor Evans and Terry Cobner in the pack. The match was quite remarkable. All the scoring took place in the first half and the lead changed hands five times, the winning score coming from Grant Batty, the abrasive little winger from Wellington. He had had knee trouble and did not look fit to play but still had just enough pace to race sixty yards after intercepting, when Trevor Evans tried to lob a pass inside as he was thumped to the ground by Bruce Robertson. So bad was his knee that he gave up the battle for fitness after the game and announced his retirement but his contribution probably won New Zealand the series. The All Blacks scored three tries and all of them should have been prevented. Sid Going had time to look for a pass to the right, change his mind and look to the left and then, finding both sides covered, run on his own and break through two tackles to score. The Lions' defence had remained static, seemingly mesmerised, while he made up his mind. Phil Bennett bruised his chest as he tried to stop him but stayed on the field, although it clearly troubled him for the rest of the game.

The other try was scored by Brad Johnstone, the prop. He followed up a penalty kick by Bryan Williams which hung in the wind and, as the Lions made a mess of catching and clearing it, nipped in to score. Williams converted that try as well as Batty's to make the All Blacks' total 16 against the Lions' 12. All the Lions' points came from penalties, a huge one from Andy Irvine and three from Phil Bennett. In Test matches it is usually the side that makes the least mistakes which wins and the Lions had made far too many on this occasion.

In a much cleaner match than in 1971 Canterbury almost achieved the aim of every province, a win against a touring side, but finally went down 14–13. Apart from that there were no shocks before the Second Test. Lancaster Park, Christchurch, did not have happy memories for Welshmen. It had been the scene of one of the 1969 thrashings at the hands of the All Blacks and it was the venue for the Second Test, the only one lost, of the 1971 Lions tour. In 1977 the luck changed and the Lions hauled themselves back into the series with a victory by 13–9.

It was a slightly fortuitous win because Bryan Williams missed two very kickable penalties but the game will be remembered for two things. The outbreaks of violence caused primarily by a late tackle by Ken Eveleigh on Phil Bennett which looked as if it was a deliberate attempt to nobble the Lions' captain and place-kicker. The only worthwhile rugby memory was a fine try from J. J. Williams. Phil Bennett broke from inside his own half and then chipped ahead. It was a heavy, muddy day and the ball squirted free when Farrell tried to fall on it, so the Lions kept going. Eventually the ball was picked up and moved to J.J. who dummied the remaining cover and cut through to score. All the other points came from penalty goals.

It had certainly not been a great match but the Lions were back in the hunt and many people expected them to find their confidence and begin to dominate to a much greater extent than previously. Form had been so erratic that John Dawes appeared to be finding it difficult to settle on his best side, although the reconstituted pack, with Beaumont and Brown in the second row, Wheeler at hooker and Derek Quinnell playing at blind-side wing forward, looked a powerful combination. Generally the forwards had done well. The scrummaging had been particularly impressive and even in the Test matches the Lions' forwards had been able to push their opposite numbers around the park at will. Only in the line outs were there continuous problems because New Zealand appeared to have ignored the new laws completely and were continuing to block and barge as they had always done.

The backs were the real problem. Mike Gibson who had played some of his greatest rugby in 1971 was now thirty-four and could no longer produce the magic. Without him there was no experience to support Phil Bennett and this became a vital weakness as the young players, all picked for their potential rather than on their track record, failed to measure up to expectations because the conditions constantly caused them frustration and did not allow them to develop confidence.

As he tried to compensate for this Phil Bennett's own game suffered. His tactical kicking lacked accuracy and his captaincy was indecisive. Normally with a powerful pack in front of him he would have controlled the game totally but the Lions persisted in trying to play 'overlap' rugby. In bad conditions the outside backs made mistakes and confidence was undermined. Everything really went wrong when letters from wives and girlfriends at home told of heavy criticism from the British press and from that point the 1977 Lions began to feel bitter. They were having a miserable time because of the weather, they had to face a hostile press in New Zealand, which was the norm, but now they felt betrayed on all sides.

John Dawes rushed to the defence of his players and did it in such a forthright manner that it became almost open war between him and some members of the British press and this resulted in further criticism. As a result the whole party became insular and Dawes and the manager of the party, George Burrell, became a buffer between the players and the media. A tour party has to be happy to survive. If they feel constantly at bay it must affect their play and, although the spirit within the party was strong, as the players tried to prove the critics wrong, the strain was too great when it came to the Test matches, although they remained unbeaten in provincial games.

New Zealand duly won the Third Test 19–7, having been soundly beaten up front where Terry Cobner led his pack magnificently by example. He had become the natural leader of the forwards and furthered his reputation as a leader of men enormously as he instilled a sort of Dunkirk spirit into them. The problem once again was that the backs wasted the excellent possession they received.

The game began disastrously for the tourists. After only forty-seven seconds Ian Kirkpatrick scored after Bruce Robertson chipped ahead. Bev Wilson, the new full back, converted and almost without having touched the ball the Lions were 6–0 down. Willie Duggan, the big Irish No. 8, plunged over from the back of a scrum to reduce the leeway, but after ten minutes Andy Haden scored in similar fashion to keep the points difference at 6. The score remained at 10–4 until half time and the Lions missed a good chance to draw level in the first quarter of an hour of the second half when two very kickable penalties were missed. A total of six fairly straightforward kicks went begging in what was a very poor Lions performance. Irvine at last succeeded with a penalty but it was cancelled out by one from Bev Wilson and the All Blacks had survived any attempt at a Lions comeback. To make victory even more decisive Bruce Robertson dropped a goal in the last minute.

Although it was now impossible to emulate the 1971 Lions and win the series the 1977 Lions could still tie it by winning the Final Test. This would have made them the second most successful British team to visit New Zealand and would have salvaged something from what had become an unhappy tour. But even that was not to be, despite another tremendous display by the Lions forwards. As if the fates had ordained it Phil Bennett made a fatal blunder in the second minute of injury time to give New Zealand the match and the series. At that time the Lions were leading 9–6. It should have been more but that did not seem to matter as Benny shaped up for what might well have been the final kick to touch. He missed it and the New Zealand centre, Osborne, caught the ball and hoisted a high kick. He chased after it to put his forwards on side and nailed Steve Fenwick as he caught it. Although Fenwick managed to get the ball away to Wheeler, the hooker was also tackled by Mourie. The ball rolled loose to the No. 8, Knight, who seized on it and sprinted twenty yards to score. Phil Bennett tried to catch him but could only bury his head in his hands as the enormity of the calamity dawned upon him. It was a tragedy of Shakespearean proportions. All hopes of salvaging something for himself and the tour had gone with that one missed kick.

Earlier Dougie Morgan, who had come into the side to replace the injured Brynmor Williams, had put the Lions in the lead. He scored a try after the forwards had set up a good attacking position and converted it himself. He then added a penalty to give the Lions a 9–3 interval lead. Wilson had made it 9–6 when he kicked his second penalty but it seemed unimportant until that injury time error. Even then the Lions had had enough kickable penalty chances in the second half to have made the game safe.

It was a disillusioned and disappointed party that left New Zealand. The last thing they needed was another game but the itinerary included a stop in Fiji on the way back with a match to help raise funds for the local Rugby Union. Beautiful as Fiji is the players were in no mood to appreciate it. They wanted to get home and the last thing they wanted to see was a rugby ball. The

Lions had been very upset by the standard of refereeing in New Zealand but that was nothing to their disenchantment with the local Fijian official. They were battered and weary, with an injury list so long that Moss Keane was nominated as a replacement back, and now found themselves up against a referee who gave only four penalties in their favour and twenty-four against them. Not surprisingly they lost 25–21 but joined in the celebrations afterwards. The islanders thought it was the best game they had ever seen and Bosco Tikoisuva proclaimed that it was the greatest day in the history of Fijian rugby. The Lions did not agree but had the good grace not to say so.

There was no avoiding the fact that the tour had been a huge disappointment. The Lions' backs had never fulfilled their potential and had been unable to capitalise on the superiority of the forwards. Even then the team could have won the series. Without the Batty interception they would have won the First Test without deserving to do so, and they should have won the Third and Fourth on penalty chances alone. However, there were some pluses for the Welsh contingent. Phil Bennett, although not at his best and criticised by the press to such an extent that it affected his confidence, had scored over 100 points for the second successive tour, to equal Bob Hiller's achievement. Terry Cobner and Derek Quinnell both had fine tours as leaders as well as players. Elgan Rees played a Test match for the Lions before he had been capped for Wales. Graham Price returned home recognised as a world-class prop. He, Phil Bennett and Steve Fenwick, who had kept up his own high standard of play whatever was going wrong around him, shared the distinction of being the only players to appear in all four Tests with Andy Irvine, Ian McGeechan and Willie Duggan.

Remarkably the 1977 Lions scored more points than any other British Isles team to tour New Zealand. Unfortunately, they also conceded more than any other side. Their final record in New Zealand was twenty-one wins and four defeats, a better record than the tourists of 1966, 1959, 1950, 1930 and 1908. However, they could have done better and they had been preceded by two winning tours. They had been expected to win and when they did not live up to expectations they were branded as failures.

15

A TRIPLE TRIPLE
1978

To lose a Lions Test series is always disappointing, especially when you feel you could have won. It can even be demoralising, if you know that the chance to achieve the feat will never arise again. For John Dawes and Phil Bennett, both coming towards the end of long and distinguished careers, the tour had been a disaster and, feeling deserted and let down by certain sections of the rugby fraternity, both could have been forgiven for calling it a day. Perhaps fortunately there was no visiting touring team in the autumn of 1977 and both John and Benny had a chance to allow their anger to die away and their enthusiasm for the game to re-emerge. After a long rest they began to prepare for the Home International Championship, determined that they would prove the critics wrong.

The first encounter was against England at Twickenham and it was expected to be a hard match with the English forwards giving the Welsh pack a thorough testing. Nobody doubted that Wales would be superior behind, it was just a matter of whether they would get the ball. There were no new faces in the Welsh side but four old ones returned. Ray Gravell, having missed the whole of the 1977 season, returned to partner Steve Fenwick in the centre. Everyone wants to play for his country but Ray's delight at being selected knew no bounds. He looks a craggy individual with his beard and bulky frame but he is probably the most emotional of all the Welshmen to play international rugby recently and will often, as on learning of his re-selection, shed a few tears while what it means to be playing for his country sinks in. He also has a highly individual way of preparing for the game. He will get changed early and retire to the loo where in wonderful solitude he can sing 'Myfanwy' or 'Ar lan y mor', the more melancholy the better to get himself into the right frame of mind for the game. Unbelievably, Charlie Faulkner also returned to make the

Pontypool front row complete once more. People began to believe that he must be the age he claimed or he would have found it impossible. It was proof that motivation can overcome most things and Charlie might have started his career late but he was going to make it last long enough to enjoy a few tours and the other perks that make all the hours of practice and training worthwhile. The Lions tour had given him an appetite for more.

Jeff Squire also won back a place in the team but this time as a flanker. It was a significant move because it showed just how much Wales were missing Mervyn Davies. His presence at the back of the line out had left the selectors totally free to choose whichever player they wished on the flanks but without him they had to go for two big men out of the three. Thus, Squire, Quinnell and Cobner were selected. It was a formidable back row and would do a tremendous job in foraging and in defence. However, as in the previous season, it lacked a creative player. Since the departure of Trevor Evans the fast creative flanker was just not being produced in Wales. Phil Bennett was again made captain of the side and Gareth Edwards set yet another record as he became the first ever Welshman to win fifty caps.

The game itself was a disappointment. The pitch was water-logged and there was flooding in the car parks. Nobody could remember such bad conditions at Twickenham. There was also a blustery wind blowing down the pitch and England, led by Billy Beaumont, took first use of it. It was obvious from the start that the backs were going to find moving the ball very difficult and so it proved. Every time they did try anything it faltered to a slithering halt and in these conditions the half backs are the crucial players if possession is equal. Although Young, the English scrum half, was used to pushing the ball forward behind the Gosforth pack, his partner, Horton, was basically a running outside half and looked ill-suited for the occasion. Edwards and Bennett had summed up the situation immediately and slipped into a well-oiled routine, gaining precious ground with kicks down the touchline and into the spaces behind the English forwards. Even then Wales struggled in the early stages because the English pack won more of the possession with the wind at their backs but each time England made fifty yards from one kick downwind, Edwards and Bennett would claw it back with several, each making an invaluable fifteen or twenty yards. It might not have been spectacular stuff but it was the masters at work.

England led 6–3 at half time – two Alastair Hignell penalties against one Phil Bennett penalty. Hignell's first kick came after only eight minutes when the Welsh front row offended and Bennett equalised two minutes later after Malcolm Young tried to pick the ball out of the scrum from between Derek Quinnell's legs, but Hignell kicked his second goal after twenty-five minutes. Wales could have gone into the interval on level terms, as they had another reasonably easy penalty chance after Phil Bennett had been late-tackled by John Scott, the English No. 8. Although he still appeared shaken, he elected to take the kick himself and missed. It was his only failure of the match. The only other notable moment of the first half came when J. P. R. Williams joined the backs and almost made it to the line to score his customary try against England. This time they held him short of the line – just.

A 3-point lead, with the whole of the second half to go against the wind, always seemed too slender and when Phil Bennett levelled the scores after only three minutes even the English spectators expected Wales to move smoothly away. It appeared more certain as the Welsh pack, now enjoying the wind and the psychological advantage of being shunted forward huge distances by the half backs, began to win the battle in the set pieces. Allan Martin was having another fine game in the line out and Wales were able to indulge themselves and try to move the ball back to the three-quarters. J. P. R. Williams again went close and Edwards went through all but the last tackler after powering away from a ruck, but the scores just would not come.

Eventually, after Edwards had made sixty-five yards with a perfectly judged clearance to put England under pressure, they made the vital breakthrough. Bob Mordell, winning his first cap at wing forward, suicidally burrowed to the bottom of a ruck with his hands to stop the ball emerging on the Welsh side, and was penalised on his own 22. He later made a great fuss about the decision being wrong but he was the only person in Twickenham who thought so. Most had clearly seen him drive in on the wrong side after Cobner had set up the ball for Wales.

That winning penalty was only eight minutes from the end and Welsh supporters had been getting worried. They still had a few more moments of agony to endure as Hignell was given a reasonable chance to put England back on level terms with a penalty at the other end. He hit the ball well but just outside the posts and the final chance had gone. It had been a close run thing as Hignell had had six attempts at goal, against Bennett's three, and two of his four misses were very close to going over. It was the first time for sixteen years that Wales had not scored a try at Twickenham but Phil Bennett's 9 points brought his total for Wales to 150.

From a Welsh point of view it was not the convincing performance for which they had hoped to start the season, but it was a victory and conditions had been so bad that it had been impossible to play to the strength of the side. Gerald Davies and J. J. Williams left the field looking as if they needed to be run through a spin dryer, but they were also clean enough to have just left a washing machine because they had seen so little of the ball.

The first match of the season at Cardiff was against Scotland and once more the weather was inclement. This time it was not rain but cold that caused the problems and the players not constantly involved in the action found it difficult to handle the ball as their fingers froze. Even the pitch was hard, if not frozen, and had the match been scheduled twenty-four hours later it would not have been played. Wales eventually won 22–14. Scotland's 14 points was their highest score ever at the Arms Park, and the most in Wales since the game at Swansea in 1925.

The game had three distinct phases. At the end of the first half Wales led by the slimmest of margins, 8–7, and then in the first fourteen minutes of the second half, they added the same number of points. Having effectively won the game, they then eased off badly and allowed Scotland to come back at them. It was almost as if the deluge of points after the interval came too easily.

Scotland took the lead through a penalty from their captain, Dougie Morgan, after ten minutes but then Wales went ahead with a try. Gerald Davies made a superb run down the right but when he was tackled Wales could not win the ruck and had to settle for a set scrum. It made no difference. They controlled the heel and that man Gareth Edwards took off to the blind side of the scrum. He dummied to give the ball back to Gerald and yet again convinced Scotland that this time he was really going to pass. Instead, of course, he sliced through to score his twentieth and, as it turned out, his last try for Wales.

Scotland took the lead again after Cranston and McGeechan put away Renwick who side-stepped his way over for a beautiful try. Wales retaliated with an equally good if slightly less delicate touch down in reply. Wales always have a number of options available from a short penalty and this time Phil Bennett chose one of the simplest – the crash move. Gareth Edwards tapped the ball to himself and ran flat across the field. After dummying to give the ball to his captain, who scissored across him, he gave the ball out to Ray Gravell on the burst. He hurtled through the gap and then weaved around the full back before charging through the last desperate cover to score. It was his first try for Wales and he did not smile. Playing for Wales was a great honour and to put them into the lead at a vital moment in the game was all that he had ever dreamt of, a dreadfully serious moment and one to be treated with reverence. All the other players did his laughing for him. Every single one of them went up to tap his shoulder or ruffle his hair. They all knew how desperate he had been to put his name on the score sheet. It was the only way that he could reassure himself that he was really good enough to be in the side.

An 8–7 lead at half time, having twice fallen behind, was no preparation for what was about to happen. In the first minute of the second half Phil Bennett dropped a beautiful goal after Gareth Edwards had fed him from a line out. From the kick-off Wales moved down to the Scottish 22 and again won a line out on the right. For once the chilled fingers worked perfectly and the ball was spun quickly along the line to J. J. Williams. Even though J. P. R. Williams had come into the line to make the extra man, J.J. was tackled short of the line and as he hit the ground the ball bounced forward and further out to the left wing where Steve Fenwick snapped it up and dived over. All the Scots supporters yelled 'Knock-on!' and were astounded when the referee awarded the try, but in fact he was right. The International Board Laws Committee in their wisdom had changed the law relating to the tackle the previous summer and, for some reason best known to themselves, had ruled that if the ball went forward as a consequence of the tackle it would no longer constitute a knock on. It seemed a stupid revision of the law at first reading and the unnatural look of the try confirmed suspicions that it was not a law change which would improve the game. However, it was not quite as stupid as the suggestion in one quarter of the press that this was a planned move which John Dawes had been coaching from the time the change came into being.

Wales now led 15–7 and continued to pile on the pressure. It became so intense that Scotland was forced to collapse a scrum and Phil Bennett at last kicked a goal from thirty-five yards. To end the scoring spree Edwards passed to J. J. Williams on the short side from a scrum and the winger found Derek Quinnell on his inside as he was tackled. The big Llanelli man took the ball at full pace and a combination of dropping his shoulder and a strong right arm cleared three Scots from his path in a storming run that took him twenty-five yards for his first try for his country. Llanelli was certainly a happy town as two of its favourite sons broke their ducks. Both were prolific scorers in club rugby but had had to wait a long time for that elusive first try in an international.

Wales now obviously decided that they had the game in the bag and unconsciously eased off, allowing Scotland to regain the initiative. Morgan kicked an easy penalty goal and then from a tapped penalty set up a try for the big second-row forward, Tomes. Scotland were back in the game at 22–14 but Wales realised the danger and tightened up once again to show that when it mattered they were always in control and at the final whistle they were on the attack. The game had produced six tries and not one of them converted.

Wales were now once again on the Triple Crown trail. If we could beat Ireland in Dublin it would be the third in a row – a feat which no country had previously achieved. Ireland had already beaten Scotland in Dublin and had lost to France in Paris by just one point and they were looking for a first victory against Wales since the famous 14–0 hiding they had handed out in 1970. Wales fielded an unchanged team and Ireland's Mike Gibson made his sixty-fourth appearance for his country, a new world record. It was a match, therefore, with a tremendous build-up and everything at stake. Sometimes this proves too much and the game does not live up to the occasion but in this case the players staged a fitting drama.

Ireland showed their determination right from the start and there was no room for cowards up front but, as the Irish forwards were penalised, Steve Fenwick in superb kicking form punished them with penalties from fifty-five and forty-five yards in the first twelve minutes. Tony Ward, Ireland's great new discovery at outside half, kicked a penalty in reply but Fenwick added his third half way through the first period to make it 9–3. Fenwick also added a try before half time. Derek Quinnell and Ray

Gravell drove deep into the Irish 22 before setting up a ruck. Wales won it and Price fed Fenwick directly and the centre dived over in the corner with his would-be tacklers still clinging on to him but unable to prevent the try. Ward kicked a penalty before half time but Wales still led 13–6.

Wales seldom scored fewer points in the second half than in the first during the period covered by this book and had built a reputation for being a team who gradually asserted forward supremacy and then capitalised on it. But after the interval it was Ireland who raised their forward game. With Keane, McKinney and Slattery leading the charge, they hounded the Welsh forwards and backs alike and foraged for the ball to such good effect that they soon managed to get back on to level terms. An indirect free kick gave Ward the chance to tap the ball to himself and drop a goal (a move that was made illegal after the first season's operation of the indirect penalty) and then forward pressure gave them a try. Wales were forced to pass the ball back to J. P. R. Williams behind his own line but he was harassed so successfully that he almost missed the ball when he tried to put in a clearance kick and sliced it so badly that it did not even go into touch in goal. Scrum half John Moloney won the race to the ball to score.

It was now absolutely even and for fifteen minutes the game could have gone either way until Gareth Edwards produced an overhead pass that found Steve Fenwick. The centre followed suit and his high floated pass reached J. J. Williams who raced over to score wide out. It was the winning score and came just seven minutes from the end. There was still time for Fenwick and Ward to kick another penalty each but everyone knew that second try for Wales had decided the match.

Wales were obviously elated but Phil Bennett was full of praise for Ireland's performance and obviously felt how disappointed they must be. Moss Keane in particular, taking over the role occupied for so long and with such distinction by Willie John McBride, played the game of his life. He obviously saves his best performances for Wales because he turned in another great game in 1980 when Ireland eventually emulated their feat of 1970 and gave Wales a sound beating. So good was his performance that day that an exhausted Steve Fenwick exclaimed as he got back to the dressing room, 'I'm not accepting the result until I find out whether Moss Keane has passed his dope test.'

For Wales Fenwick with 16 points, including those very difficult early penalties to his credit, and Terry Cobner who kept the
pack together when they were really under siege from the Irish
eight were the heroes of the day. They had shown that this Welsh
team could absorb the pressure as well as running riot when they
were on top.

A record hat trick of Triple Crowns was now in the bag and this
gave Wales a total of fifteen, again a record, taking them one
ahead of England. An eighth Grand Slam was now in the offing.
This would also be a record but to win it Wales had to face France
who had won the Grand Slam the year before. Wales in fact had
to repeat their feat of 1976 when they met France in Cardiff in the
last match of the international season to clinch the Championship and Grand Slam just as they had lost both titles by being
defeated in Paris in 1977.

Although France had an impressive looking pack they had
found the 1978 Championship season hard going. England were
beaten comfortably enough in Paris but then Scotland and
Ireland had run them very close, the scores being 16–19 and 9–10
respectively. Wales had not been beaten in a Five Nations
Championship home match since 1968 but France hoped to
emulate that feat ten years on to celebrate their acceptance as a
member of the International Board. Wales had been forced to
make one change. Gerald Davies yet again had hamstring
trouble and so the selectors repeated their earlier experiment of
moving J. J. Williams to the right wing and brought in Gareth
Evans of Newport who had won his first cap as a replacement in
1977 and had subsequently toured with the Lions.

It was a classic encounter with a tremendous battle for forward
supremacy. France began by winning most of the ball but were
gradually forced to surrender the initiative so that Wales had
wrested control from them by the end of the game. Capitalising
on the early forward drive France took a 7-point lead half way
through the first half. Skréla dived through a maul to score a try
and then Viviès tapped an indirect penalty to himself and
dropped a goal. At this point things looked bleak for Wales but
their answer was swift and decisive. They were at last beginning
to come to terms with the French forwards and wheeled one of
their set scrums so that Allan Martin was able to pick up. He fed
Phil Bennett who had seen the position evolving and took the
ball at full pace, going on the blind side of the scrum on the

left-hand side of the field. There are not many better players at beating a man than Benny when he is in full flow and he side-stepped two Frenchmen absolutely cleanly, leaving himself a clear run in for a try. To set the seal on things he also converted it. Five minutes later Gareth Edwards stood back and dropped a goal after Graham Price had fed him, having first driven on from a line out peel. Wales were now in the lead and two minutes later increased it with another beautiful try.

Gareth Edwards made a huge touch kick and from the subsequent line out Wales won the ball and Gravell made a storming run through the middle. When he was checked, Steve Fenwick was on hand to pick up and switched the direction of the attack with a pass to Edwards. At the end of a diagonal run he passed as he was collared and, although the pass went to the floor, J. J. Williams scooped it up and made a couple of yards before giving Phil Bennett a perfect inside overhead pass that left his captain just enough room to nip in for his second try.

France must have been demoralised, having seen a 7–0 lead become a 7–13 deficit in just ten minutes, that vital ten minutes before half time. However, in the second half they stormed back and might have had a chance had they had a reliable place-kicker, but they had chosen Viviès instead of Romeu at fly half and Aguirre, the full back, now entrusted with the kicking duties, missed several kickable penalties. As the game wore on they looked less likely to score and the Welsh pack gradually tied up most of the possession. Allan Martin who had had his best season for his country was again a force in the line out and Geoff Wheel was in great form winning ball after ball from the mauls. When France did win the ball the back row snuffed out the threat of the dangerous Gallion. It was an impressive all round performance.

Nevertheless France would not capitulate and it seemed as if the second half would be scoreless. Then in injury time Gareth Edwards threw a pass to Phil Bennett but missed him. Fenwick swooped on it to clear the mistake but found himself in space, as the pass had fooled the opposition as well as Phil, so he turned and dropped a goal. Geoff Wheel was heard to mutter something about Edwards having something golden about his anatomy because even when he did something wrong it came out right and then the game was over. Wales had won the Grand Slam for the second time in three years. To mark the occasion the Prime

Minister, James Callaghan, honoured the team with a reception
at 10 Downing Street. He did after all represent a Cardiff
constituency. It was a great team that had fought magnificently,
especially when behind, and John Dawes commented, 'I think
this team deserves to be recognised as one of the greatest of all
time.'

Although he did not announce his retirement until well into
the summer, Gareth Edwards had played his last game of rugby.
He decided to make a clean break with the game and finished at
all levels, having played fifty-three consecutive games for his
country. In all the years from 1967 to 1978 he allowed Chico
Hopkins and Clive Shell about twenty-five minutes of international rugby between them and hogged the rest for himself. It
was a mighty achievement but he was a mighty player, one to
whom the word 'great' can be truly applied.

The problem with great players is that people tend to remember them as perfect and that sometimes hides the qualities that
made them great. By the end of his career Gareth was as complete a player as one could hope for. His running, passing,
kicking and judgement were all superb, but this was not so when
he began playing for Wales. At that time and for some seasons he
had to wind up his pass and some of the basic scrum half skills,
like putting a ball into a scrum, were not very consistent. He also
sometimes misjudged the time to run himself instead of giving
the ball to someone else, but the thing even at that stage that
made him a remarkable player was his explosive strength. I rarely
had to play against him, thank goodness, but on one of the few
occasions we did oppose each other I took the full force of one of
his charges and it was quite different to tackling any other player.
At the moment of impact he drove doubly hard, taking me by
surprise and breaking the tackle. I learned that the only way to
combat him was to hit him just as hard and he never got away
again, but once is too many times in an international match.
Nearly all his twenty tries were scored without anyone else being
involved which is again testament to his ability. Most people
score a few where they are put clear, but in most cases Gareth
made his own. The only other thing to say about him is that he
never missed the chance to play a practical joke or join a party
with the lads. But the way he used to hog that massage table did
annoy me.

It was also Phil Bennett's last international, although he is still playing so well for Llanelli that he might be persuaded to return if Wales hit a crisis. He decided that captaining Wales to a Grand Slam would take some beating as a way to finish and who can blame him, especially when you have scored two tries in the final match of the season to clinch it. His career had its ups and downs more than most but at the end of it he emerged as the all-time record points-scorer for Wales with 166. If you add the 44 points he scored for the Lions in Test matches to that he was also the world record-holder for points scored in international rugby.

A totally different character to Gareth, Phil took time to settle into the international rugby arena and his tendency towards introversion meant that sometimes he had not enough confidence to play his natural attacking game. When he shook off his worries everyone marvelled at his ability to wrong-foot opponents. Unlike Gerald Davies, who would not show his intention to side-step, Benny had a very individual 'lean' that told the tackler he was about to jink. The problem was that there was still nothing that could be done about it! He was also a superb line kicker, turning the skill into an art form as only Barry John had done before him. Off the field he had a very determined outlook on what he wanted to do. For example, no amount of disapproval from Committee or whoever would dissuade him from having a couple of pints on a Friday when we returned from the pictures. As he put it, 'How else would I go to sleep, Bas?'

He remained his own man throughout. Criticism hurt him but he always retained a dignified silence and disproved his critics in the only place that counts – on the field. He and John Dawes must have been very happy men at the end of the 1978 season.

16

A SIZZLING BURST FROM SIX INCHES
1979

In some ways the achievement of winning the 1979 Triple Crown was one of the greatest of the decade. The squad system had made team changes far easier than ever before, with players thoroughly familiar with the style and emphasis of the team waiting in the wings to take over. But the loss of four players with a total of 144 caps between them, all of whom had captained Wales, entitled even the most diehard supporter to view the season's prospects with some trepidation. At the end of the day the much changed Welsh XV had won the Five Nations Championship for the fourth year out of five and in so doing had collected a record-breaking fourth consecutive Triple Crown.

The groundwork for that triumph was laid down during a very unsuccessful tour of Australia during the summer of 1978. Phil Bennett and Gareth Edwards both refused the invitation to tour because of work and family commitments, despite a last minute wooing by the very persuasive Clive Rowlands, this time the manager of the touring party. In their absence the captaincy went to Terry Cobner, the experienced Pontypool skipper. This was Wales' first tour to Australia alone and with nine matches on the itinerary was seen as the prototype for future trips now that more people than ever before were finding it impossible to make a full length Lions tour. It turned out to be a harrowing experience which most of the players wanted to forget, but the criticism of the way the team played helped to strengthen their determination and resulted in the Home International Championship.

There were twenty-five players in the party and they included eleven who were uncapped, including all four half backs. Nevertheless Wales was still optimistic. Australia had been going through a bad time on the international scene and Wales had won very comfortably in 1975 when the Wallabies toured the British

Isles. However, the reports had filtered back from emigre Welshmen that there was a new determination in Australian rugby and that they were sick of being the poor relations on the circuit. They had set themselves the target of beating Wales in 1978. The reports also mentioned that they were not too bothered about how they did it. Australian rugby had been undisciplined in 1975 and at home it was apparently becoming more and more gladiatorial.

The strength of rugby in Australia is patchy and the first two games were against Western Australia and Victoria, two of the weakest areas. Both sides were beaten handsomely but then the tourists suffered a shock defeat at the hands of Sydney. New South Wales and Queensland are the two strongest areas for the game but this was a team selected only from the city. There were no arguments about the victory as the home side outscored Wales by three tries to one. New South Wales Country and the full New South Wales team were then comfortably beaten, even though the latter team was comprised mainly of Sydney players, but it was when the touring party moved up to Brisbane that things began to go sour.

There is great rivalry between Queensland and New South Wales for rugby supremacy and recently Queensland had had the better of their internal encounters. Therefore they were honour-bound to emulate the Sydney victory over the Welsh team. Unfortunately their officials feel equally chauvinistic about the whole thing and although the Welsh XV eventually won the game 31–24 they were most unhappy about the Queensland referee, Mr Burnett. He awarded penalties in the ratio of two to one against them, often for infringements that they could not understand and the Queensland outside half, Paul McLean, a fine place-kicker, had a field day with five penalty goals, a dropped goal and a conversion, all but four of his side's points.

When the Australian R.F.U. proposed Burnett as referee for the First Test match Wales objected and this became open bickering when their request for him to be replaced was refused. The tour agreement had set down that referees were to be appointed after consultation for the international matches – a clause no doubt insisted upon after the experiences in 1969 and 1971 – and it was now apparent that the Australians had no intention of paying more than lip service to that agreement. Of all the countries represented on the International Board, they alone have remained adamant that the introduction of neutral referees is unnecessary. Even if the visiting country accepts this, it is surely too much to expect them to accept also the arbitrary appointment of one official, instead of having the choice of several nominated to a panel by the home union. The game therefore began surrounded by acrimony and Wales's worst fears were upheld as they were again penalised incessantly. It is bad enough to be refereed by a 'home' official, but to have to take the field with one who knows that he is there despite protests from the visiting team cannot help him to remain unbiased.

McLean was again on target and Wales, fielding their Grand Slam team from the previous year, but with Brynmor Williams and Gareth Davies replacing Edwards and Bennett, were behind 9–4 at half time, three penalty goals to Australia against a Gerald Davies try. He had collected a beautifully placed diagonal kick from Gareth Davies and sprinted over in the corner. Fifteen minutes into the second half Wales scored another try. This time Brynmor Williams supported a three-quarter movement, having initiated it, and took an inside pass from Ray Gravell to race over. Once more the conversion failed but they were now within one point of the Wallabies.

However, controversy about Mr Burnett apart, Wales had to admit that Australia were playing well and they proved their point by scoring a try that won them the match. Their rucking had been particularly effective throughout the game and, having won a beautiful ball yet again, they released Crowe, on the left wing. He made a tremendous run through a Welsh defence that was in disarray and, having cut inside several times, scored under the posts. McLean converted and Australia had won 15–8, a result that was as much a shock as their first ever win over Wales in Cardiff in 1966.

For Wales worse was to follow. Capital Territory, regarded as an easy fixture between the two Test matches, beat them 21–20, in a game where Wales scored four tries against one. By now the players were very unhappy and it showed in their play. Decisions were questioned and accepted with bad grace. They felt that the games were a travesty of justice because of the refereeing and as they showed their discontent they alienated more of the local support. Don Wilkey, an Australian journalist, wrote in his summation of the tour, 'Their attitudes were not helped by on- and off-the-field bickering with referees, who were often made

Above: Geoff Wheel rips the ball free and Bobby Windsor moves in to secure it and make the feed, a classic combination from two of the strongest men of the decade at Murrayfield in 1979. Below: Paul Ringer salutes the crowd as Wales go on a scoring orgy against the old enemy.

A storming try for Derek Quinnell. Biggar and McHarg can do nothing as he plunges over from twenty-five yards, facing page above.

Below: Swansea's fly half, Dai Richards, shows why he was picked at centre as he scores a quicksilver debut try after a loop move with Fenwick.

Welsh hopes for the 'eighties depend a great deal on the two young half backs: Terry Holmes, all strength and bustle, but already a beautiful passer of the ball and, below, Gareth Davies, full of style and poise, with never a hair out of place.

scapegoats for the players' own shortcomings.'

To the team this was just not true. Experienced players were suddenly being caught offside with unbelievable frequency and some laws were being applied in a totally different way to that accepted by the rest of the world. As Steve Fenwick said on his return home, 'I'd heard of Australian Rules Football but I thought it was a totally different game.'

Wales were also having problems in getting fifteen players on the field by the time of the Second Test to be played in Sydney. The captain, Terry Cobner, was unavailable through illness and Squire and Quinnell, also back-row forwards, were injured. The selectors therefore had to press J. P. R. Williams into service as a wing forward. Many people who had seen him play thought he was more suited to the back row than full back and he had often expressed a wish to play there himself, now was the moment of truth. The line-up was very strange. Alan Donovan, normally a centre for Swansea, at full back, Gerald Davies, Ray Gravell, Steve Fenwick and J. J. Williams in the backs, Gareth Davies and Terry Holmes at half back (Holmes had an outstanding tour and replaced Brynmor Williams on merit). In the forwards the Pontypool front row with Geoff Wheel and Allan Martin behind them made up the front five with Stuart Lane of Cardiff and J. P. R. Williams on the flank and Clive Davis, the Newbridge second row, at No. 8.

With such a makeshift combination Wales were going to have problems containing the Wallabies, who were growing more confident, and by the time the day of the Second Test arrived the Welsh team were up against the Australian public as well as the team. The game was played at the Sydney Cricket Ground and the hostility towards the visitors resembled that usually reserved for an Australia v England cricket match. Australian sports fans love to hate their opponents and a crowd of 41,000, absolutely enormous for a rugby union game over there, turned up to watch the confrontation. They were not disappointed but rugby was done a great disservice. Just three minutes into the game the two packs of forwards erupted and in the great slugging match that followed Graham Price, that hardest of hard men, had his jaw broken by a punch from Steve Finnane, his opposite number. The next fifteen minutes were torrid but once the game settled down Wales suffered further injury problems.

Just before the end of the first half Donovan was injured and was replaced by Gareth Evans, the Newport centre, who had toured New Zealand as a wing with the British Lions in 1977. He was tackled high the first time he got the ball and suffered a depressed fracture of the cheekbone, but because John Richardson of Aberavon had already replaced Graham Price no more substitutes were allowed. Evans remained on the field, as did J. J. Williams after he had twisted his ankle so badly that he would also normally have been replaced and Wales ended up with an unusual formation. J. P. R. Williams reverted to full back, seven forwards tried to hold the Australian eight and J. J. Williams and Gareth Evans tried to cover the left wing between them. Presumably Gareth manoeuvred the opposite wing into position because he could run but not make contact with J.J. who could not run but was able to tackle, hobbling up to complete the task.

In between all these mishaps Wales played their best rugby of the tour. In the first half Gareth Davies kicked a penalty and then dropped a goal but Wales still turned round three points down as McLean was again on target with two penalties and full back Monaghan dropped a superb forty-yard goal. Early in the second half Holmes gave notice that he was not the traditional sort of scrum half by barging his way over from a five-metre scrum to give Wales the lead but a bad mistake by the inexperienced, and by now depleted, back row allowed Loane, the Australian No. 8, to score direct from the line out.

The Welsh side might well have felt like trooping off the field when McLean was awarded a drop goal which they were certain passed under the bar, but instead came back to 19–17 when Gerald Davies, captaining the side for the first time in a full international, darted over for a try. It was his twentieth for Wales and again brought him level with Gareth Edwards to share the Welsh record. Gareth Davies could have given Wales a draw had he kicked the conversions but failed from wide out and Wales had lost the series 2–0.

Paul McLean had been the hero of the Australian team, scoring 26 of their 37 points in internationals. Wales had scored thirty-four tries on the tour against their opponents' seven and yet almost unbelievably they had lost four of the nine matches.

Had Wales been luckier on the injury front, they would probably have salvaged the Second Test but, although it was an important moment for Australia to win a series against Wales, and it has certainly stimulated interest in the game in that country, rugby was the loser. The Welsh side were no angels, believing that they had to look after themselves, as the referee would take no action. They were right in my experience. Clive Rowlands made the point bitterly in his final after-match speech: 'One of my players is in a hospital bed tonight with a double fracture of the jaw. If we are rugby people and endorse thuggery, then I don't want any part of it.'

However, out of all bad things something usually emerges which is good and the most heartening aspect of this tour had been the play of the new half backs. Brynmor Williams, Dai Richards, Gareth Davies and Terry Holmes had all emerged with credit which became vitally important when Gareth Edwards announced his retirement before the start of the season and Phil Bennett announced that he was no longer available for international rugby. Although they had not decided it at the time, the two men who had captained Wales in the Tests on tour had also played their last games of international rugby.

Gerald Davies delayed his return to the game because he felt he had no enthusiasm for it – perhaps after what he had seen in Australia – and eventually decided that it was time to call it a day. He had been elected captain of Cardiff for the season and many club members felt bitter that he had not made his intentions clear before allowing his name to go forward. They obviously failed to understand the dilemma he was in. He had never given less than his all but had been on the international scene for twelve years and suddenly the zest for the game had gone. That's how it happens. As always with Gerald, it was an honest decision. In many ways it would have been easier to play out the season just going through the motions. Doing that Gerald would still have been better than most. His acceleration, his swerve and side-step, his acute sense of awareness and his unselfishness certainly make him the best wing I have ever seen. Others who can go back much further hold the same view. His contribution to the decade is equalled only by that of Gareth Edwards and J. P. R. Williams.

Terry Cobner also decided to retire from international rugby even though he continued to play for his beloved Pontypool. He had suffered various problems with injury and illness over the previous couple of years and found it hard to maintain the level of fitness he demanded of himself. Having arrived on the scene late (he played his first international on his twenty-eighth birthday) he made a tremendous impact in his first five years with the national team. His leadership qualities were legendary at Pontypool and soon had their effect on Wales as he first became pack leader and finally captain. The Australian tour was not the happiest way to finish but, as always, it was not through any lack of effort on Cob's part.

Before the Home International Championship there was the little matter of another visit from New Zealand. The whole of Wales remembered the last dramatic encounter between the two sides in 1972. They were also aware that Wales had not beaten the all Blacks since 1953 – twenty-five years previously. Many of the New Zealand team were familiar names because they had played against the 1977 Lions, even though only three of the 1972 party, Robertson and Williams in the backs and Haden of the forwards, were included.

The Welsh team was also considerably changed from the one which had finished the 1978 season. Gerald Davies had missed the last match but now Clive Rees from London Welsh, who had won his two caps in 1974 and 1975, was preferred to Gareth Evans. Holmes and Davies, after their tremendous perform-ances in Australia, took over from Edwards and Bennett and Paul Ringer from Ebbw Vale replaced Terry Cobner. J. P. R. Williams became the new captain. Few people expected the team to beat the All Blacks without the key players of 1978 but the match turned out to be far closer and more sensational than anyone could have imagined.

Contrary to their usual style, the Welsh took the game to the All Blacks right from the whistle with the whole pack out to prove that the Australian results were not a true reflection of the strength of the Welsh team. Quinnell, Wheel and new cap, Ringer, all made charges that rocked the All Blacks back on their heels. Several times New Zealand were forced to resort to desperate measures to stop the Welsh attacks and uncharacter-istically gave away penalties in their panic. Their defence became over-physical on several occasions and Frank Oliver received a stern warning from referee Roger Quittenton when he struck Paul Ringer while the Welshman was on the ground.

Wales were awarded four penalty kicks at goal in the opening twenty minutes. They kicked three of them and were deservedly, and to the crowd's delighted amazement, 9–0 in the lead. Steve Fenwick kicked a long one, while Gareth Davies landed two from easier positions. Wales were still beating New Zealand in the forward exchanges and it seemed that the tourists, who had looked an efficient but never a really powerful side, might be struggling. Then Wales gave away a soft try.

There appeared little danger when the All Blacks won the ball on the left-hand side around the Welsh 22 and when they moved the ball to Osborne the Welsh centres looked set to chase him down. He obviously thought so too and chipped to the right corner. Suddenly there was danger. The wing had come up on his man as well, thinking they were going to move the ball and J. P. R. Williams had also committed himself to come forward. There was only Gareth Davies covering back and Stuart Wilson, the speedy New Zealand right wing, sprinted past Clive Rees and won the race for the touch down. The conversion attempt was taken by Brian McKechnie who had replaced Clive Currie, the first choice full back having broken his jaw in stopping one of the early Welsh raids. He missed that kick, but vitally for New Zealand he was a much more reliable kicker than the man who had left the field. He was successful with his next kick in injury time in the first half, but that still left Wales with a 5-point advantage as Gareth Davies had added a fourth penalty goal for Wales just before.

12–7 at half time was better than anyone had dared hope for, but it was not as clear a lead as Wales should have had after the period of total domination by the forwards in the first twenty minutes. Hopes were high, but the one real misgiving had been the play of the three-quarters. Even though they received plenty of ball, they had never looked dangerous and the New Zealand defence had found them easy to handle. The two players who could not be blamed for this were the young half backs, Holmes and Davies. They had both won caps in Australia but this was their first match on home territory and, following on Gareth Edwards and Phil Bennett, many people thought they would be found lacking in skill and experience. They surprised the whole of the rugby world with their poise and determination.

After Wales had missed a penalty goal thirteen minutes into the second half, McKechnie kicked his second one to make the score 12–10. It was now far too close for comfort, but the Welsh pack was still going well and matched the New Zealanders in every department, even if they were not dominating as at the beginning of the game. It even seemed as if Wales would score that elusive try when Terry Holmes made a strong break down the middle which took play fifty yards. Unfortunately his pass needed to be a long one and J. J. Williams had to wait for an awkward bounce which gave the All Blacks' cover time to cut him off.

Still Wales were holding on and, as the game went into the eightieth minute, it seemed that they must hold on to win, but a controversial penalty awarded at a line out on the Welsh 22 was to rob them of victory. It says volumes for McKechnie's goal-kicking ability and his nerve that he managed to convert the penalty, but to most Welshmen, and many other people who hold the concept of fair play dear to their hearts, it should never have been given. Having seen filmed replays of the incident more than enough times to make a judgement, I am sure that both Haden and Oliver dived out of the line out. It can only have been a deliberately planned move between the two of them because they moved so theatrically that it was not even credible – as the ball was thrown they threw themselves backwards in unison. Unfortunately it is also obvious from the film that Geoff Wheel did attempt to win the ball with his outside arm and 'leaned on' with the other one.

I was sitting with Terry Cobner watching the game and he echoed my thoughts when he said as they lined up, 'Just stand still boys with your hands by your sides and let them win it, make them score a try.' I think I replied by saying, 'Fall over, do anything, but don't contest it.' Unfortunately, the captain obviously did not give the same instructions and Geoff Wheel must take the blame for losing Wales the match.

Roger Quittenton, the referee, was obviously looking for a line out infringement more than anything else. He certainly was not watching for the antics of Haden and Oliver. The fact that he found one does not absolve him from a miscarriage of justice. He had allowed jumping with the outside arm to go on throughout the match without penalising it, except in the first four minutes, and suddenly to make it his prime concern at that stage of the game still seems odd. More importantly, the Oliver and Haden trick should have been penalised just as much, and some international status referees have declared that they would have reversed the penalty, even if they had penalised Wheel first.

It was a sick end to the game and although the Welsh complaints afterwards once again prompted New Zealanders to quote Sid Going who said, 'You never win in Wales, just score more points', on this occasion those who were not completely one-eyed had to admit that we had a case. However, the referee is the sole judge of fact, so the law book tells us, and therefore the result stood and Wales still have not beaten New Zealand since 1953.

The arguments about the match were still raging on January 25th when the Home International Championship campaign began with a visit to Murrayfield. The team had shown plenty of fire against New Zealand but had lost, and there was still a big question mark over the two new half backs. Nobody could believe that Wales would have lost had Edwards and Bennett been playing. The only new cap was Elgan Rees. He had played in one Test for the British Lions in New Zealand in 1977 but had to wait until the master, Gerald Davies, retired before being capped by his country.

At half time it seemed as if Murrayfield was going to be an unlucky bogy ground yet again for Wales. Scotland led by 13–6, all their points having been scored by Andy Irvine and they could well have had more points on the board. For Wales Fenwick kicked two penalties, one in the very first minute. However the telling factor was the wind and in the second half Wales had it helping them.

The Welsh pack immediately became a different outfit with it at their backs and with Quinnell and Squire in particular in devastating form they began to pursue the Scots. Fenwick kicked his third penalty to put Wales within reach of Scotland and then Elgan Rees scored a debut try to bring them level. The captain, J. P. R. Williams, joined a straightforward Welsh three-quarter movement and chipped a perfectly weighted kick to the right-hand corner where the Neath winger took the ball going flat out and dived over. Only eight minutes of the second half had gone and it seemed certain that Wales would pull away. The forwards were now dominating every phase of play, but the Scots held out until eight minutes from time.

Wales forced a scrum almost on the Scottish line and once they had heeled it they held it in the back row, drove forward, and wheeled at the same time to allow Terry Holmes to dive into the melee to touch down. Fenwick kicked the conversion and Wales had scored 13 points in the second half to turn a 6–13 deficit into a 19–13 victory.

Again there was cautious optimism in the Welsh camp. The youngsters had acquitted themselves well and the only problem seemed to be in the three-quarters where there was a lack of penetration from Fenwick and Gravell, despite a good service from Holmes and Davies. Nevertheless the selectors picked the same team for Ireland's visit to the Arms Park.

At the end of the day Ireland had scored more points than ever before against Wales, but they still lost, although they had the home side very worried about its ground record which had lasted in the Five Nations Championship since 1968. With only fifteen minutes to go Wales were leading 21–9 but needed a Steve Fenwick penalty sandwiched between two converted Irish tries to stay in front. Ireland had really thrown the game away earlier. They began well enough with two penalty goals from Ward, but then gave away an easy try. Fenwick hoisted a high kick to the Irish line and Spring, the defending full back, never looked like catching it cleanly. He only succeeded in deflecting it to Allan Martin who gratefully accepted the gift and plunged over for a try. Fenwick converted to cancel out the Irish lead and then kicked two penalty goals before half time, against Ward's one, to give Wales the lead by 12–9.

Even though Wheel retired early in the second half, causing a major reshuffle of the pack with Lane going to wing forward, Squire to No. 8 and Quinnell into the second row, Wales still kept up the forward pressure. Wales took play right up to the Irish line where the defending side were given the put-in at a scrum. Whelan heeled it cleanly but the Welsh pack put on the pressure strongly enough to make it difficult for Patterson to clear the ball. As he went to pass to Ward, Holmes grabbed his leg and he was forced to try a one-handed flip. He only succeeded in moving the ball a yard back over the line and Paul Ringer dived on it for a simple try. Fenwick converted and then kicked a penalty goal before Ireland came back with tries through McLennan and Patterson, both of which were converted by Ward. At the end the difference between the sides was just one kick. Ward totalled 13 points again Fenwick's 16 and the blond Bridgend centre became only the second Welshman to pass 100 points for his country.

The Welsh team had allowed Ireland back into the game when they should have shut the door, but nevertheless they had won and, despite misgivings, they were in line for another Triple

Crown and perhaps for a Grand Slam if they could conquer France in Paris. Holmes was proving to be a totally different scrum half from Gareth Edwards, but was mightily effective. His kicking was limited and he sometimes wound up for his pass, but his strength was already apparent as being extraordinary for a scrum half. Unlike Gareth, who relied upon explosive power to go through the opposition, Terry Holmes had shown that he was as strong in the upper body as most forwards. He could take them on standing still, and still emerge from a maul with the ball! Coming from the tough side of Cardiff and working manually running his own factory clearance company had certainly helped develop this extraordinary power. Unlike most scrum halves he had also shown a relish for cover tackling. No wonder Cardiff supporters called him a ninth forward. His partnership with Gareth Davies was already impressing many people. They were an unlikely duo, Holmes working with scrap metal and Davies just having come down from Oxford. Where Holmes was rough, Davies was smooth, never a hair out of place and full of grace, stroking the ball like Barry John rather than kicking it. The only thing that was important was that it worked and Welsh rugby has thrived on such combinations over the years. Holmes in particular was adding a new dimension to scrum half play as, from being much criticised at the start of the season, he went on to win most people's Player of the Year Award.

For the game against France Wales capped two new players, both from Swansea. Barry Clegg replaced Geoff Wheel as the latter's shoulder had not recovered since he injured it against Ireland, and Dai Richards replaced Ray Gravell in the centre.

It was a brave move by the selectors and particularly coach, John Dawes. Gravell and Fenwick were excellent players but very similar. They were both battering rams rather than rapiers and the midfield had been impotent as an attacking force because of it. The final crunch had come in the Irish match where they had several times tried to take on their opposite numbers only to be shunted sideways with embarrassing ease and a loss of ground. Fenwick had the advantage of also being a kicker so Ray had to go. Even then playing Richards was a gamble because he was a fly half. Dawes was relying on his exceptional pace and exciting footwork to cover his inexperience in the centre position.

It was impossible to decide whether Richards' selection had worked after the French game. Wales had turned in another strangely lacklustre performance in Paris, just as in 1977, and although they only lost by one point and the match sounded close, France could well have won more easily by taking their chances. Only Holmes furthered his reputation, although Fenwick had a tremendous game in defence and kicked three penalty goals. It was Holmes who scored the Welsh try, seizing upon a loose ball after France had tapped back from a line out to crash through a heap of bodies to score. That made three tries in five games, a feat not even the young Gareth Edwards could match when he burst upon the international scene in 1967.

Aguirre kicked two penalty goals for France and Gourdon became the first player for twelve years to score two tries against Wales in a Championship match. His first came after Aguirre joined the line on the blind side, giving him room to cut inside J. J. Williams, and the second came after some superb rugby from France. They began an attack in their own half and then won two successive rucks before Gallion moved the ball right and Wales ran out of defenders. Gourdon raced unopposed to the corner. The score was only 14–13 but it did not reflect France's superiority which merited a wider margin.

Once again it looked as if the Championship would follow the pattern of the previous three years. Wales or France to win, depending on which country had the home matches against the other, but the pattern was upset when England beat France unexpectedly 7–6 at Twickenham. This immediately changed the whole prospect for the final weekend of the international season. If France lost to Scotland and England beat Wales, England could be Champions, and if Wales won they would be Champions and would win a fourth consecutive Triple Crown. France beat Scotland and Wales beat England decisively in the end to take the title and the crown.

Wales had been forced into changes that did not seem to strengthen their team. Charlie Faulkner was injured and had played his last game for his country, but had nineteen caps to look back on, a marvellous tally for a man who began his career so late and a lesson to all would-be internationals never to give up hope. His team mate, Bobby Windsor, also had to drop out. He had played in a club match and the lines had been marked out with lime by a council groundsman. The lime had burned Bobby's back so badly that he had to withdraw. He had also played his last game because he developed a back injury that prevented him challenging for his place the following season. His career for Wales had been a string of successes. Coming into the side when it was at its lowest point in the decade, he was a key figure in rebuilding and rejuvenating the pack. Hard and uncompromising on the field, he could not have been more different off it, always joking and the life and soul of the party – a great man.

John Richardson of Aberavon and Alan Phillips of Cardiff replaced the two Pontypool men and at lock the veteran Mike Roberts was recalled to add power to the engine-room of the scrum, as Barry Clegg had not been an adequate replacement for Geoff Wheel in Paris. Robbo was now thirty-two and had not even been playing continuously for London Welsh. There were doubts about his ability to play flat out for eighty minutes, but the selectors opted for his unquestioned strength in the mauls – if he got to them.

The final score was 27–3 to Wales, their biggest margin of victory since 1905 when they had won 25–0, but it did not seem possible twenty minutes from the end. At that time Wales were leading 7–3. Gareth Davies had dropped a neat goal and Dai Richards had scored a quicksilver try after a loop move with Fenwick which showed the critical Welsh crowd exactly why he had been brought into the side as a centre. They were not so pleased when he knocked on with the line at his mercy later in the half after Terry Holmes had made a storming run from the back of the scrum, handing off Rafter before he set off, as if he were the wing forward instead of the Englishman. The signal for the match to explode into action was when the Welsh captain, J. P. R. Williams, left the field with a badly gashed calf. Immediately after this the English pack camped on the Welsh line and it needed all the support of the crowd as well as stout Welsh defence to keep them out. Three times they won scrums and launched assaults at the try line, but on each occasion they were stopped just short. Then suddenly Wales broke out of the stranglehold and, as if they had staked everything on breaking through at that point, England crumbled.

Unbelievably, it was Mike Roberts who in his own words 'made a sizzling burst from six inches' to score his first international try, having been brought back into the side after a gap of four years. Then Ringer was the lucky Welsh player (any one of three were on hand) to finish off a back movement and score, wide out on the left again, and only eight minutes after Roberts' score J. J. Williams tore away on the outside to score again. Allan Martin converted with a fine kick. Wales were still not finished. Clive Griffiths of Llanelli, who had come on as a replacement for J. P. R. Williams, launched a counter-attack with a dazzling burst of speed and when he punted ahead he allowed Elgan Rees to score, even though he might well have been able to reach the ball first himself. Twenty points in twenty minutes was deserving of a fourth Triple Crown and no wonder the crowd thronged onto the pitch and would not leave until J. P. R. Williams limped to the front of the grandstand to be given a rapturous reception.

It had not been the way he would have wanted to finish, in the dressing room while his players ran riot on the pitch, but he had announced before the game, amid some controversy over the impending publication of his autobiography, that this was to be his last international. Nobody quite believed him and although he stayed out of rugby for much of the 1979/80 season, the temptation is obviously still there for him to make a comeback. He was the only player to span the whole period and when the time comes to carve his gravestone it will surely read: 'He taught the world how to play the running full back game.' He would have been a mighty figure in world rugby in any era, but in the modern game, he ruled supreme for the whole of his career with nobody challenging his position as world number one. He had become only the second player to win over fifty caps for Wales.

His namesake, J. J. Williams also decided it was time to bow out gracefully. He won thirty caps between 1973 and 1979 and had developed out of all recognition as a player. When he began most people believed he would never be more than an athlete turned rugby player and thought he had nothing more in his attacking armoury than the kick ahead and chase. He proved them wrong on the hard grounds of South Africa in 1974 and from there went from strength to strength. Even in his last game he had to prove the critics wrong by scoring a sizzling try when they said that the sparkle had gone.

As if to emphasise that Wales was at a watershed John Dawes also retired before the start of the next campaign. He too spanned the decade as player and coach. In his five seasons as coach Wales won the Championship four times, the Triple Crown four times and the Grand Slam twice. There is nothing more to say, the record speaks for itself. He had left a largely reconstituted side still with room to improve but with the

confidence and bonus of an unexpected Five Nations Championship and Triple Crown behind them. They could afford to
look ahead to the next decade with hopes of emulating their
predecessors of the 'seventies.

17

A VERY SERIOUS NONSENSE

Much has been written at various times throughout the golden decade about the reasons for the Welsh success. Some critics put it down to Wales having had three or four world-class players who carried the others through, but this gross over-simplification had finally been disproved with the Triple Crown and Championship win in 1979. Only J. P. R. Williams of the players the pundits cared to call 'world class' was left and yet the new team had immediately shown that it could rise to the occasion, even when he had left the field.

Certainly Welsh rugby has been lucky to have players good enough to cover some weaknesses at various times but the brilliant backs would be the first to recognise the tremendous contribution made by the tight forwards, even though they might denigrate 'the donkeys' in fun. Nevertheless players such as Gareth Edwards, Barry John, Phil Bennett, J. P. R. Williams, Gerald Davies and Mervyn Davies do not appear often. One has only to look at the number of records for appearances and points scoring between them to realise that these were players who would stand out as great in any era. It has been the greatest era for British rugby as well as Welsh rugby and just as it is said that English cricket is never strong unless Yorkshire are strong the same can be said about British and Welsh rugby.

This book has been devoted to chronicling, praising and enjoying the years 1969–1979 with the Welsh team but, having done that, let the Decade of the Dragon take its place in history. Rugby is a live game and its future lies with the players who are in the game today. For Wales that should make the future bright. Because the top clubs are few in number and players filter through to them from the junior clubs very efficiently, even though there is no organised system of promotion, the standard of club rugby is much higher than anywhere else in the U.K. The top players soon lose their rough edges and overcome weaknesses or they are replaced. They do not have a chance to develop bad habits by playing against poor opposition and therefore learn to reproduce their skills under pressure. Although there is no official league in South Wales, the clubs are in fact playing in one and if there were to be three or four divisions of a league including clubs from all over Britain most of the Welsh clubs would be in Division One.

The coaching organisation pioneered by Ray Williams, and now in the capable hands of John Dawes, should ensure that the clubs can capitalise on the enthusiasm for the game generated by the success of the past ten years and push forward players better prepared than ever before for the national team.

In 1980 Wales could not maintain the high standards of the past ten years and there are certain positions in the team for which it is difficult to see cover as the present incumbents approach retirement, but then many people believed it would be a national disaster when Gareth Edwards and Phil Bennett retired. Terry Holmes and Gareth Davies have already proved themselves worthy successors. After all, who had heard of J. P. R. Williams and Mervyn Davies before the start of the 1969 international season?

It was not only a momentous decade for Welsh rugby, it was also a period when the game changed its face a great deal. During the late 'fifties and the early 'sixties the Home International Championship had produced a large number of games which were very boring. As the Championship is the criterion by which the public judge the game it was suffering, especially as Rugby League was by then being shown regularly on television. The professional code is not as good as the original game because the man who is tackled is allowed to hold on to the ball while the defence realigns itself. However, because the players are not allowed to kick directly to touch and there are no line outs, it does re-start more quickly and the emphasis is on running and passing the ball. Therefore Rugby League was often more exciting than safety-first Rugby Union.

However the adoption of the Australian dispensation, as it was at first known, which prohibited kicking to touch directly from outside the 22 made the game much more fluent, especially to the non-aficionado. At virtually the same time replacements were allowed in international football so that games were no longer decided by an unfortunate or, worse still, deliberate injury to a key player.

In 1972 the try was upgraded to four points making it the most rewarded score, even if the International Board were too conservative to go the whole way and make all place kicks worth two points at the same time. It seems ludicrous that two kicks from the same position can be given different values, even though they are both place-kicks. The drop-kick as a method of scoring is part of continuous play and therefore the kicker is under considerably more pressure and deserves greater reward. Try – 4 points, dropped goal – 3 points, and all place-kicks – 2 points would seem to be an ideal distribution.

The law relating to the knock on was also changed, from clean catch, to allowing a readjustment, to allowing the ball to be juggled as long as it does not touch the ground. Although there is an argument that says it is a bad thing because it encourages sloppy handling, it does at least keep the game going and ensure a uniform interpretation from referees.

More recently the introduction of the indirect free kick also seems sensible. It has always seemed inconsistent to me that the man who throws the ball in towards his own forwards in a line out can only cost his side a scrum while the scrum half who feeds his own man sacrifices a penalty. They are both technical offences and should be treated in the same way. Perhaps an indirect penalty for not straight at the line out would improve the present appalling standard of throwing in. Generally technical offences should not be penalised as harshly as deliberate fouls and therefore the new law is a good innovation.

Some of the other changes have not been so beneficial. In 1974 the International Board decided that we must go metric. We now have to refer to the 22 instead of the 25 and referees take such giant strides to make up the three inches (sorry – eight centimetres) difference that a side which had to retreat ten yards now has to go back twenty.

There has also been a change in the tackle law which has actively undermined the development of rucking and mauling, particularly in the northern hemisphere where players were only just learning to ruck instinctively. Instead we now have an unproductive heap called the Pile-up. Hopefully, someone on the Laws Committee will have the guts to admit it has been a disaster and will press for a revision that will allow the readoption of the old law if nothing better can be drafted.

Improvements to the laws must always be considered, but if they cause the game to progress backwards they must be speedily discarded before they cause permanent damage. Most of the changes have been to the good, spreading the appeal of the game throughout the world as well as the fame of its leading players. In Britain a top rugby player is as well known as his counterpart in any other sport.

At the moment, perhaps the biggest crisis the game is facing relates to dirty play and yet paradoxically it is generally a much cleaner game at club level than it was between 1960 and 1970. Because the spotlight is now firmly on the game as a major spectator sport the pressures on national sides to win are far greater. Indeed, in Australia where the game was losing out badly to Rugby League in the popularity stakes, success became imperative if the game was to survive as a major winter sport. Thus international games have become almost gladiatorial, most recently resulting in the unpleasant incidents in the 1980 Five Nations Championship. Ringer was certainly not innocent but he was as much a victim of the direction in which the game was going as he was of his own misconduct. Hopefully, although it is sad that it took such an incident to make the point, players and administrators have now realised the dangers of putting too much importance on winning.

Players have always had their own code relating to rough play. The occasional flare up in the heat of the moment is accepted as inevitable in a contact game where knocking a man down and wrestling the ball free are all part of the skills. A marginally late tackle is also something that can be excused because the decision as to whether to go through with the action is made in a split second. Even though it is still foul play, it is in a totally different category to punching or, more particularly, kicking with no excuse other than to gain advantage. Most players accept that the game is dangerous without deliberate foul play and generally any player who endangers the health of another player is ostracised by his own team mates.

At its best rugby is magnificent, with all the elements of a great game, contact, speed, continuity, running and kicking – one man's combination of strength, power and pace pitted against his opponent within a team situation. Rugby has been, and will continue to be, a major influence on my life, but as John Dawes

was fond of saying at the end of a bad day, 'It's only a game.'
Hugh McIlvanney, a sports nut, captured what he meant when
he said, 'At the end of the day we must remember that sport is a
load of nonsense – a very serious nonsense, but still a nonsense.'

STATISTICS

The Five Nations Championship 1969–1979
Players in the decade
Full International point-scorers 1969–1979
Club representation in the National XV 1969–1979
Welsh players on Lions tours 1969–1979
Welsh internationals in Lions Test teams 1969–1979
Welsh point-scoring records
Welsh cap-winning records
Welsh XV matches v Non-International Board countries
1969–1979
Point-scorers against Non-International Board countries
Other representative matches
Point-scorers in other representative matches
Some scoring records in representative matches

The Five Nations Championship 1969–1979

WALES v ENGLAND
(*Home matches in odd years*)

	Winner	*Score*
1969	Wales	30–9
1970	Wales	17–13
1971	Wales	22–6
1972	Wales	12–3
1973	Wales	25–9
1974	England	16–12
1975	Wales	20–4
1976	Wales	21–9
1977	Wales	14–9
1978	Wales	9–6
1979	Wales	27–3

	P	W	D	L	F	A
(H)	6	6	0	0	138	40
(A)	5	4	0	1	71	47
TOTAL:	11	10	0	1	209	87

WALES v SCOTLAND
(*Home matches in even years*)

	Winner	*Score*
1969	Wales	17–3
1970	Wales	18–9
1971	Wales	19–18
1972	Wales	35–12
1973	Scotland	10–9
1974	Wales	6–0
1975	Scotland	12–10
1976	Wales	28–6
1977	Wales	18–9
1978	Wales	22–14
1979	Wales	19–13

	P	W	D	L	F	A
(H)	5	5	0	0	109	41
(A)	6	4	0	2	92	65
TOTAL:	11	9	0	2	201	106

WALES v IRELAND
(*Home matches in odd years*)

		Winner	*Score*
	1969	Wales	24–11
	1970	Ireland	14–0
	1971	Wales	23–9
	1972	–	
	1973	Wales	16–12
	1974	Draw	9–9
	1975	Wales	32–4
	1976	Wales	34–9
	1977	Wales	25–9
	1978	Wales	20–16
	1979	Wales	24–21

	P	W	D	L	F	A
(H)	6	6	0	0	144	66
(A)	4	2	1	1	63	48
TOTAL:	10	8	1	1	207	114

WALES v FRANCE
(Home matches in even years)

		Winner	*Score*
	1969	Draw	8–8
	1970	Wales	11–6
	1971	Wales	9–5
	1972	Wales	20–6
	1973	France	12–3
	1974	Draw	16–16
	1975	Wales	25–10
	1976	Wales	19–13
	1977	France	16–9
	1978	Wales	16–7
	1979	France	14–13

	P	W	D	L	F	A
(H)	5	4	1	0	82	50
(A)	6	2	1	3	67	65
TOTAL:	11	6	2	3	149	115

FIVE NATIONS TOTALS

	P	W	D	L	F	A
(H)	22	21	1	0	473	197
(A)	21	12	2	7	293	225
GRAND TOTAL:	43	33	3	7	766	422

Wales v Tourists 1969–1979

WALES v NEW ZEALAND

	P	W	D	L	F	A
(H)	2	0	0	2	28	32
(A)	2	0	0	2	12	52
TOTAL:	4	0	0	4	40	84

WALES v SOUTH AFRICA

	P	W	D	L	F	A
(H)	1	0	1	0	6	6

WALES v AUSTRALIA

	P	W	D	L	F	A
(H)	2	2	0	0	52	3
(A)	3	1	0	2	44	53
TOTAL:	5	3	0	2	96	56

WALES v TOURISTS (TOTALS)

	P	W	D	L	F	A
(H)	5	2	1	2	86	41
(A)	5	1	0	4	56	105
GRAND TOTAL:	10	3	1	6	142	146

Five Nations and Tourist results 1969–1979

	HOME						AWAY					
	P	W	D	L	F	A	P	W	D	L	F	A
Eng	6	6	0	0	138	40	5	4	0	1	71	47
Scot	5	5	0	0	109	41	6	4	0	2	92	65
Ire	6	6	0	0	144	66	4	2	1	1	63	48
Fra	5	4	1	0	82	50	6	2	1	3	67	65
N.Z.	2	0	0	2	28	32	2	0	0	2	12	52
S.A.	1	0	1	0	6	6						
Aust	2	2	0	0	52	3	3	1	0	2	44	53

	P	W	D	L	F	A
(H)	27	23	2	2	559	238
(A)	26	13	2	11	349	330
GRAND TOTAL:	53	36	4	13	908	568

Five Nations score analysis of games at Cardiff

	FOR				AGAINST			
v England								
	G	T	DG	PG	G	T	DG	PG
1969	3	2	1	2				3
1971	2	1	2	1		1		1
1973	1	4		1			1	2
1975	1	2		2		1		
1977		2		2				3
1979	2	3	1					1
	9	14	4	8		2	1	10
v Scotland								
	G	T	DG	PG	G	T	DG	PG
1970	3	1				1	1	1
1972	3	2		3	1			2
1974	1							
1976	2	1	1	3	1			
1978		4	1	1		2		2
	9	8	2	7	2	3	1	5
v Ireland								
	G	T	DG	PG	G	T	DG	PG
1969	3	1	1	1	1			2
1971	1	3	1	2				2
1973	1	1		2	1			2
1975	3	2		2		1		
1977	2	1	1	2				3
1979	2			4	2			3
	12	8	3	13	4	1		13
v France								
	G	T	DG	PG	G	T	DG	PG
1970	1			2		2		
1972		2		4				2
1974		1	1	3		1	1	3
1976		1		5	1	1		1
1978	1	1	2			1	1	
	2	5	3	14	1	5	2	6
Five Nations Home Totals:	32	35	12	42	7	11	4	34

Score analysis of Tourist games at Cardiff

	FOR				AGAINST			
v New Zealand	G	T	DG	PG	G	T	DG	PG
1972		1		4		1		5
1978				4		1		3
		1		8		2		8

	FOR				AGAINST			
v South Africa	G	T	DG	PG	G	T	DG	PG
1970		1		1		1		1

	FOR				AGAINST			
v Australia	G	T	DG	PG	G	T	DG	PG
1973		3		4				
1975	3	1	1	5				1
	3	4	1	9				1

	FOR				AGAINST			
Tourist Totals at Cardiff:	3	6	1	18		3		10
Totals for all Home Internationals:	35	41	13	60	7	14	4	44

Five Nations score analysis of away games

v England

	FOR				AGAINST			
	G	T	DG	PG	G	T	DG	PG
1970	1	3	1		2			1
1972	1			2				1
1974	1			2	1	1		2
1976	3			1				3
1978				3				2
	6	3	1	8	3	1		9

v Scotland

	FOR				AGAINST			
	G	T	DG	PG	G	T	DG	PG
1969	1	2		2				1
1971	2	2		1		2		4
1973				3	1	1		
1975		1		2			1	3
1977	2			2	1		1	
1979	1	1		3		1		3
	6	6		13	2	4	2	11

v Ireland

	FOR				AGAINST			
	G	T	DG	PG	G	T	DG	PG
1970					1	1	1	1
1972		–				–		
1974	1			1				3
1976	3	1		4				3
1978		2		4		1	1	3
	4	3		9	1	2	2	10

v France

	FOR				AGAINST			
	G	T	DG	PG	G	T	DG	PG
1969	1	1			1			1
1971		2		2	1			
1973			1				1	3
1975	1	4		1		1		2
1977				3	1	1	2	
1979		1		3		2		2
	2	8	1	9	3	4	3	8

| Five Nations Away Totals: | 18 | 20 | 2 | 39 | 9 | 11 | 7 | 38 |

Score analysis in New Zealand and Australia

	FOR				AGAINST			
v New Zealand	G	T	DG	PG	G	T	DG	PG
1969					2	2		1
1969		2		2	3		1	5
		2		2	5	2	1	6

	FOR				AGAINST			
v Australia	G	T	DG	PG	G	T	DG	PG
1969	2	1		2	2			2
1978		2			1			4
1978		2	1	2		1	2	3
	2	5	1	4	3	1	2	9

	G	T	DG	PG	G	T	DG	PG
Touring Totals:	2	7	1	6	8	3	3	15
Totals for all Away Internationals:	20	27	3	45	17	14	10	53
Totals for all Internationals Home and Away:	55	68	16	105	24	28	14	97

Home International Championship 1969–1979

1969

	P	W	D	L	Pts
Wales	4	3	1	0	7
Ireland	4	3	0	1	6
England	4	2	0	2	4
Scotland	4	1	0	3	2
France	4	0	1	3	1

1970

	P	W	D	L	Pts
Wales	4	3	0	1	6
France	4	3	0	1	6
Ireland	4	2	0	2	4
Scotland	4	1	0	3	2
England	4	1	0	3	2

1971

	P	W	D	L	Pts
Wales	4	4	0	0	8
France	4	1	2	1	4
England	4	1	1	2	3
Ireland	4	1	1	2	3
Scotland	4	1	0	3	2

1972

	P	W	D	L	Pts
Wales	3	3	0	0	6.
Ireland	2	2	0	0	4
Scotland	3	2	0	1	4
France	4	1	0	3	2
England	4	0	0	4	0

1973

	P	W	D	L	Pts
Wales	4	2	0	2	4
France	4	2	0	2	4
Ireland	4	2	0	2	4
Scotland	4	2	0	2	4
England	4	2	0	2	4

1974

	P	W	D	L	Pts
Ireland	4	2	1	1	5
Wales	4	1	2	1	4
France	4	1	2	1	4
Scotland	4	2	0	2	4
England	4	1	1	2	3

1975

	P	W	D	L	Pts
Wales	4	3	0	1	6
Ireland	4	2	0	2	4
France	4	2	0	2	4
Scotland	4	2	0	2	4
England	4	1	0	3	2

1976

	P	W	D	L	Pts
Wales	4	4	0	0	8
France	4	3	0	1	6
Scotland	4	2	0	2	4
Ireland	4	1	0	3	2
England	4	0	0	4	0

1977

	P	W	D	L	Pts
France	4	4	0	0	8
Wales	4	3	0	1	6
England	4	2	0	2	4
Scotland	4	1	0	3	2
Ireland	4	0	0	4	0

1978

	P	W	D	L	Pts
Wales	4	4	0	0	8
France	4	3	0	1	6
England	4	2	0	2	4
Ireland	4	1	0	3	2
Scotland	4	0	0	4	0

1979

	P	W	D	L	Pts
Wales	4	3	0	1	6
France	4	2	1	1	5
Ireland	4	1	2	1	4
England	4	1	1	2	3
Scotland	4	0	2	2	2

Players in the Decade

		CAPS IN DECADE (*total number of caps to March 1980 in brackets*)
PHIL BENNETT	Llanelli	29
ROY BERGIERS	Cardiff College, Llanelli	10
JOHN BEVAN	Cardiff College, Cardiff	10
JOHN D. BEVAN	Aberavon	4
ROGER BLYTH	Swansea	2 (6)
DAVID BURCHER	Newport	4
CLIVE BURGESS	Ebbw Vale	4
BARRY CLEGG	Swansea	1
TERRY COBNER	Pontypool	19
LAURIE DANIEL	Newport	1
TOMMY DAVID	Llanelli, Pontypridd	4
GARETH DAVIES	Cardiff	7 (10)
GERALD DAVIES	London Welsh, Cardiff	39 (46)
MERVYN DAVIES	London Welsh, Swansea	38
CLIVE DAVIS	Newbridge	1
JOHN DAWES	London Welsh	12 (22)
ALAN DONOVAN	Swansea	1
GARETH EDWARDS	Cardiff	46 (53)
GARETH EVANS	Newport	3
GEOFF EVANS	London Welsh	7
TREVOR EVANS	Swansea	10
CHARLIE FAULKNER	Pontypool	19
STEVE FENWICK	Bridgend	23 (27)
ALEX FINLAYSON	Cardiff	3
NORMAN GALE	Llanelli	3 (25)
STUART GALLACHER	Llanelli	1
RAY GRAVELL	Llanelli	18
CLIVE GRIFFITHS	Llanelli	1
IAN HALL	Aberavon	7 (8)
TERRY HOLMES	Cardiff	6 (10)
CHICO HOPKINS	Maesteg	1
DENNIS HUGHES	Newbridge	5 (6)
KEITH HUGHES	Cambridge U., London Welsh	3
KEITH JARRETT	Newport	7 (10)
BARRY JOHN	Cardiff	18 (25)

MIKE KNILL	Cardiff	1
STUART LANE	Cardiff	3 (5)
ARTHUR LEWIS	Ebbw Vale	11
PHIL LLEWELLYN	Swansea	5
BARRY LLEWELYN	Newport,	
	Llanelli	13
JOHN LLOYD	Bridgend	12 (24)
ALLAN MARTIN	Aberavon	27 (31)
ROY MATHIAS	Llanelli	1
DAI MORRIS	Neath	28 (34)
VIC PERRINS	Newport	2
ALAN PHILLIPS	Cardiff	1 (5)
BRIAN PRICE	Newport	6 (32)
GRAHAM PRICE	Pontypool	24 (28)
DEREK QUINNELL	Llanelli	22
BILLY RAYBOULD	London Welsh,	
	Newport	7 (11)
CLIVE REES	London Welsh	3
ELGAN REES	Neath	4 (8)
DAI RICHARDS	Swansea	2 (6)
MAURICE RICHARDS	Cardiff	7 (9)
JOHN RICHARDSON	Aberavon	3
PAUL RINGER	Ebbw Vale,	
	Llanelli	5 (7)
MIKE ROBERTS	London Welsh	8
IAN ROBINSON	Cardiff	2
JIM SHANKLIN	London Welsh	4
GLYN SHAW	Neath	12
CLIVE SHELL	Aberavon	1
JEFF SQUIRE	Newport,	
	Pontypool	12 (16)
JOHN TAYLOR	London Welsh	19 (26)
BRIAN THOMAS	Neath	6 (21)
DELME THOMAS	Llanelli	21 (25)
STUART WATKINS	Newport,	
	Cardiff	7 (26)
GEOFF WHEEL	Swansea	21 (25)
BRYNMOR WILLIAMS	Newport	1
CLIVE WILLIAMS	Aberavon	
	(Swansea)	2 (6)
DENZIL WILLIAMS	Ebbw Vale	15 (36)
J. J. WILLIAMS	Llanelli	30
J. P. R. WILLIAMS	London Welsh,	
	Bridgend	52
WALTER WILLIAMS	Neath	2
BOBBY WINDSOR	Pontypool	28
JEFF YOUNG	Harrogate,	
	RAF,	
	London Welsh	20 (23)

Most appearances in the decade
J. P. R. WILLIAMS   52
GARETH EDWARDS   46
GERALD DAVIES   39

Most consecutive appearances
GARETH EDWARDS   46
MERVYN DAVIES   38

Captains in the decade

	number of matches		*number of matches*
GARETH EDWARDS	12	ARTHUR LEWIS	3
MERVYN DAVIES	9	JOHN LLOYD	3
PHIL BENNETT	8	TERRY COBNER	1
JOHN DAWES	5	GERALD DAVIES	1
BRIAN PRICE	5	DELME THOMAS	1
J. P. R. WILLIAMS	5		

One-cap appearances 1969–1979

BARRY CLEGG (Swansea)	v France	1979
LAURIE DANIEL (Newport)	v Scotland	1970
CLIVE DAVIS (Newbridge)	v Australia	1978
ALAN DONOVAN (Swansea)	v Australia	1978
STUART GALLACHER (Llanelli)	v France	1970
CLIVE GRIFFITHS (Llanelli)	v England	1979 (sub)
CHICO HOPKINS (Maesteg)	v England	1970 (sub)
MIKE KNILL (Cardiff)	v France	1976 (sub)
CLIVE SHELL (Aberavon)	v Australia	1973 (sub)
BRYNMOR WILLIAMS (Newport)	v Australia	1978

Full International point-scorers 1969–1979

	T		DG		PG		C		PTS	
PHIL BENNETT	4		2		36		18		166	
STEVE FENWICK	3		3		28		11		127	
GARETH EDWARDS	19	(20)	2	(3)	1		2		85	(91)
BARRY JOHN	5		6	(8)	13		6		84	(90)
GERALD DAVIES	18	(20)	–		–		–		66	(72)
KEITH JARRETT	1	(2)	–		9	(11)	10	(17)	50	(73)
J. J. WILLIAMS	12		–		–		–		48	
J. P. R. WILLIAMS	6		–		3		1		31	
JOHN TAYLOR	4		–		2		3		23	
GARETH DAVIES	–		2		5		–		21	
MAURICE RICHARDS	7		–		–		–		21	
JOHN BEVAN	5		–		–		–		19	
ALLAN MARTIN	1		–		4		1		18	
DAI MORRIS	5	(6)	–		–		–		16	(19)
TERRY HOLMES	3		–		–		–		12	
ROY BERGIERS	2		–		–		–		8	
ELGAN REES	2		–		–		–		8	
TERRY COBNER	2		–		–		–		8	
TREVOR EVANS	2		–		–		–		8	
PAUL RINGER	2		–		–		–		8	
MERVYN DAVIES	2		–		–		–		7	
LAURIE DANIEL	1		–		–		1		5	
BOBBY WINDSOR	1		–		–		–		4	
CLIVE BURGESS	1		–		–		–		4	
CHARLIE FAULKNER	1		–		–		–		4	
RAY GRAVELL	1		–		–		–		4	
DEREK QUINNELL	1		–		–		–		4	
JIM SHANKLIN	1		–		–		–		4	
GRAHAM PRICE	1		–		–		–		4	
ARTHUR LEWIS	1		–		–		–		4	
DAVID RICHARDS	1		–		–		–		4	
MIKE ROBERTS	1		–		–		–		4	
JOHN D. BEVAN	–		1		–		–		3	
CHICO HOPKINS	1		–		–		–		3	
BARRY LLEWELYN	1		–		–		–		3	
JOHN DAWES	1	(4)	–		–		–		3	(12)
DENZIL WILLIAMS	1		–		–		–		3	
STUART WATKINS	1	(9)	–		–		–		3	(27)

897

1980 games not included.
Brian Thomas, who played in 1969, scored one try against Scotland in 1964.
N.B. – 4 points for a try since 1972

Club representation in the National XV 1969–1979

	number of players		number of players
CARDIFF	13	BRIDGEND	3
LLANELLI	13	CARDIFF COLLEGE OF	
LONDON WELSH	12	EDUCATION	2
NEWPORT	11	NEWBRIDGE	2
SWANSEA	8	CAMBRIDGE UNIVERSITY	1
ABERAVON	6	HARROGATE	1
NEATH	5	MAESTEG	1
PONTYPOOL	5	PONTYPRIDD	1
EBBW VALE	4	R.A.F.	1

Most players from one club in an International

6 from London Welsh

J. P. R. Williams, Gerald Davies, John Dawes, Mike Roberts, Mervyn Davies and John Taylor in all four Championship matches in 1971.

J. P. R. Williams, Gerald Davies, Jim Shanklin, Jeff Young, Mike Roberts and John Taylor v France in 1973.

Players for Wales while with an English club

Jeff Young (Harrogate)

Players against Wales while with a Welsh club

Neil Bennett (London Welsh and England)
Mark Keyworth (Swansea and England)
Wilson Lauder (Neath and Scotland)
Barry Nelmes (Cardiff and England)
John Scott (Cardiff and England)
Colin Smart (Newport and England)
Lewis Dick played for Scotland while he was at Swansea, but not in a game against Wales.

Welsh players on Lions tours 1969–1979

1971   To Australia and New Zealand

J. P. R. WILLIAMS, GERALD DAVIES, JOHN BEVAN, ARTHUR LEWIS, JOHN DAWES (capt.), BARRY JOHN, GARETH EDWARDS, CHICO HOPKINS, MERVYN DAVIES, JOHN TAYLOR, DEREK QUINNELL, DELME THOMAS, MIKE ROBERTS, GEOFF EVANS

1974 To South Africa
J. P. R. WILLIAMS, CLIVE REES, J. J. WILLIAMS, ROY BERGIERS, PHIL BENNETT, GARETH EDWARDS, MERVYN DAVIES, TOMMY DAVID, BOBBY WINDSOR

1977 To New Zealand
ELGAN REES, J. J. WILLIAMS, GARETH EVANS, STEVE FENWICK, DAVID BURCHER, PHIL BENNETT, JOHN BEVAN, DENZIL WILLIAMS, ALUN LEWIS, JEFF SQUIRE, TERRY COBNER, DEREK QUINNELL, ALLAN MARTIN, GRAHAM PRICE, CLIVE WILLIAMS, CHARLIE FAULKNER, BOBBY WINDSOR, TREVOR EVANS

The only player not to play for Wales in a full international during this period was Alun Lewis (London Welsh).

Welsh Internationals in Lions Test teams 1969–1979

	Number of appearances	
PHIL BENNETT	8	v South Africa 1974 (4); v New Zealand 1977 (4)
JOHN BEVAN	1	v New Zealand 1971
DAVID BURCHER	1	v New Zealand 1977
TERRY COBNER	3	v New Zealand 1977
GERALD DAVIES	4 of 5	v New Zealand 1971
MERVYN DAVIES	8	v New Zealand 1971 (4); v South Africa 1974 (4)
JOHN DAWES	4	v New Zealand 1971
GARETH EDWARDS	8 of 10	v South Africa 1974 (4); v New Zealand 1971 (4)
GARETH EVANS	3	v New Zealand 1977
TREVOR EVANS	1	v New Zealand 1977
STEVE FENWICK	4	v New Zealand 1977
CHICO HOPKINS	1	v New Zealand 1971
BARRY JOHN	4 of 5	v New Zealand 1971
ALLAN MARTIN	1	v New Zealand 1977
GRAHAM PRICE	4	v New Zealand 1977
DEREK QUINNELL	3	v New Zealand 1971 (1); 1977 (2)
ELGAN REES	1	v New Zealand 1977
JEFF SQUIRE	1	v New Zealand 1977
JOHN TAYLOR	4	v New Zealand 1971
DELME THOMAS	2 of 6	v New Zealand 1971
BRYNMOR WILLIAMS	3	v New Zealand 1977
J. J. WILLIAMS	7	v South Africa 1974 (4); v New Zealand 1977 (3)
J. P. R. WILLIAMS	8	v New Zealand 1971 (4); v South Africa 1974 (4)
BOBBY WINDSOR	5	v South Africa 1974 (4); v New Zealand 1977 (1)

GERALD DAVIES played once v South Africa in 1968; GARETH EDWARDS twice v South Africa in 1968; BARRY JOHN once v South Africa in 1968; and DELME THOMAS twice v New Zealand in 1966 and twice v South Africa in 1968.

The following played in Tests for the Lions before 1969, as well as for Wales in the 1969–1979 decade.

BRIAN PRICE 4 – v Australia 1966 (2); v New Zealand 1966 (2)

MAURICE RICHARDS 3 – v South Africa 1968 (3)

STUART WATKINS 3 – v Australia 1966 (2); v New Zealand 1966

DENZIL WILLIAMS 5 – v Australia 1966 (2); New Zealand 1966 (3)

JEFF YOUNG 1 – v South Africa 1968

All time point-scorers for Wales

*PHIL BENNETT	166
*STEVE FENWICK	127
*GARETH EDWARDS	91
*BARRY JOHN	90
JACK BANCROFT	88
*KEITH JARRETT	73
*GERALD DAVIES	72
W. J. BANCROFT	60
REGGIE GIBBS	57
KEN JONES	51
JOHNNIE WILLIAMS	51
TERRY DAVIES	50
BERT WHINFIELD	50

All time try-scorers

*GERALD DAVIES	20
*GARETH EDWARDS	20
REGGIE GIBBS	17
KEN JONES	17
JOHNNIE WILLIAMS	17
WILLIE LLEWELLYN	16
TERRY MORGAN	14
*J. J. WILLIAMS	12

*Played for Wales 1969–1979

All time conversion kickers

JACK BANCROFT	38
W. J. BANCROFT	20
*PHIL BENNETT	18
*KEITH JARRETT	17
BERT WINFIELD	14
*STEVE FENWICK	11
JACK BASSETT	10
VIVIAN JENKINS	10

All time drop goal kickers

*BARRY JOHN	8
PERCY BUSH	3
*GARETH EDWARDS	3
*STEVE FENWICK	3
ALBERT JENKINS	3

All time penalty goal kickers

*PHIL BENNETT	36
*STEVE FENWICK	28
*BARRY JOHN	13
TERRY DAVIES	12
*KEITH JARRETT	11

Some scoring records

During the decade Wales gained new highest scores against

Scotland 35–12 in 1972
Ireland 34–9 in 1976
Australia 28–3 in 1975
New Zealand 16–19 in 1972
South Africa 6–6 in 1970

However, the 12–33 loss to New Zealand in 1969 and 8–18 to Australia in 1978 were new losing points margin records for Wales against those countries.

Wales failed to score in two matches in the decade, losing to 19 points against New Zealand in 1969 and to 14 points against Ireland in 1970.

Wales's 102 points in the 1975/76 season is a record for the Five Nations Championship.

Phil Bennett's total of 166 points for Wales, and 44 for the British Isles (210 in all) is a world record.

Maurice Richards's six tries in 1969 equalled the Welsh record, first set in 1908 by Reggie Gibbs.

Keith Jarrett's 19 points v England in 1967, and Jack Bancroft's 19 points v France in 1910 were equalled by Phil Bennett in 1976 against Ireland.

Most points scored in an international championship season

Phil Bennett 38 points in 1976
Steve Fenwick 38 points in 1979
Barry John 35 points in 1972

Some cap-winning records

The all time top ten are

53	*Gareth Edwards	36	*Denzil Williams
52	*John P. R. Williams	35	R. M. Owen
46	*Gerald Davies	34	Bryn Meredith
44	Ken Jones	34	Dewi Bebb
38	*Mervyn Davies	34	*Dai Morris

*Played for Wales 1969–1979

Gareth Edwards's 53 caps in succession is a world record.

Gareth Edwards's 53 caps is a world record for a scrum half.

J. P. R. Williams's 52 caps is a world record for a full back, though he started one match at wing forward.

J. P. R. Williams (52 caps at full back), Steve Fenwick (23 caps at centre), Gareth Edwards (53 caps at scrum half), Denzil Williams (36 caps as prop), Brian Price (32 caps at lock), Mervyn Davies (38 caps at No. 8), and Dai Morris (32 of 34 caps as flanker) hold Welsh cap records in their individual positions. All played in the decade 1969–1979 in all or part of their careers.

Welsh XV matches v Non-International Board countries 1969–1979

1969	Fiji	11	Welsh XV	31
1971	Welsh XV	26	R.F.U. Presidents XV	11
1972	Welsh XV	56	Canada	10
1973	Canada	20	Welsh XV	58
1973	Welsh XV	62	Japan	14
1974	Welsh XV	26	Tonga	7
1974	Welsh XV	3	New Zealand	12
1975	Hong Kong	3	Welsh XV	57
1975	Japan	12	Welsh XV	56
1975	Japan	6	Welsh XV	82
1976	Welsh XV	20	Argentina	19
1979	Welsh XV	13	Rumania	12

	P	W	D	L	F	A
(H)	7	6	0	1	206	85
(A)	5	5	0	0	284	52
TOTAL:	12	11	0	1	490	137

Point-scorers against Non-International Board countries

	T	DG	PG	C	PTS
PHIL BENNETT	6		10	34	122
J. J. WILLIAMS	8	–	–	–	32
STEVE FENWICK	2	–	3	5	27
GERALD DAVIES	6	–	–	–	24
KEITH HUGHES	6	–	–	–	24
JOHN TAYLOR	5	–	–	1	19
J. P. R. WILLIAMS	4	1	–	–	19
GARETH EVANS	4	–	–	–	16
TOMMY DAVID	4	–	–	–	16
ROBIN WILLIAMS	–	1	1	5	16
GRAHAM PRICE	3	–	–	–	12
RAY GRAVELL	3	–	–	–	12
JOHN D. BEVAN	3	–	–	–	12
ROY MATHIAS	3	–	–	–	12
KEITH JARRETT	–	–	–	5	10
GARETH EDWARDS	2	1	–	–	10
DENNIS HUGHES	3	–	–	–	9
MERVYN DAVIES	2	–	–	–	8
CLIVE SHELL	2	–	–	–	8
ALEX FINLAYSON	2	–	–	–	8
BARRY LLEWELYN	2	–	–	–	7
DAI MORRIS	2	–	–	–	7
GARETH DAVIES	–	2	–	–	6
ANDY HILL	–	–	1	1	5
ROY THOMAS	1	–	–	–	4
ROGER BLYTH	1	–	–	–	4
CHARLIE FAULKNER	1	–	–	–	4
TERRY COBNER	1	–	–	–	4
PHIL LLEWELLYN	1	–	–	–	4
ROY BERGIERS	1	–	–	–	4
BOBBY WINDSOR	1	–	–	–	4
JEFF GRIFFITHS	1	–	–	–	4
ALAN TOVEY	1	–	–	–	4
MAURICE RICHARDS	1	–	–	–	3
ALLAN MARTIN	–	–	1	–	3
ARTHUR LEWIS	1	–	–	–	3
BARRY JOHN	–	1	–	–	3

490

N.B. – 4 points for a try since 1972

Record number of points scored by a Welsh XV: 82 (82–6 v Japan, 1975)

Record number of points scored against a Welsh XV: 20 (20–58 by Canada, 1973), 19 (20–19 by Argentina, 1976).

Record individual points scorer in one match: Phil Bennett scored 34 points (2T, 10C, 2PG) v Japan, 1975.

Try-scoring records: 3 by Dennis Hughes v Fiji, 1969; 3 by Roy Mathias v Canada, 1972; 3 by J. P. R. Williams v Japan, 1975.

Other representative matches

1969	Taranaki	9	Welsh XV	9
	Otago	9	Welsh XV	27
	Wellington	6	Welsh XV	14
1973	British Columbia	6	Welsh XV	31
	Alberta	6	Welsh XV	76
	Quebec-Maritimes	9	Welsh XV	44
	Ontario	0	Welsh XV	79
1975	Combined Japan Universities	3	Welsh XV	32
	Japan 'B'	7	Welsh XV	34
1978	Western Australia	3	Welsh XV	32
	Victoria	3	Welsh XV	52
	Sydney	18	Welsh XV	16
	NSW Country	0	Welsh XV	33
	NSW	0	Welsh XV	18
	Queensland	24	Welsh XV	31
	Capital Territory	21	Welsh XV	20

	P	W	D	L	F	A
TOTALS: (All games away)	16	13	1	2	548	133
Totals of all matches v Non-International Board countries:	28	24	1	3	1038	270

Point-scorers in other representative matches

	T	DG	PG	C	PTS
STEVE FENWICK	2	–	13	10	64
ALLAN MARTIN	–	–	8	15	54
PHIL BENNETT	1	–	4	12	40
J. J. WILLIAMS	8	–	–	–	32
JOHN D. BEVAN	7	–	–	–	28
GERALD DAVIES	7	–	–	–	28
JOHN TAYLOR	6	–	–	–	24
J. P. R. WILLIAMS	6	–	–	–	23
GARETH DAVIES	–	–	3	7	23
KEITH JARRETT	–	–	5	4	23
TERRY HOLMES	4	1	–	–	19
GARETH EVANS	4	–	–	–	16
GARETH EDWARDS	4	–	–	–	16
MAURICE RICHARDS	4	–	–	–	12
PHIL LLEWELLYN	3	–	–	–	12
KEITH HUGHES	3	–	–	–	12
STUART LANE	3	–	–	–	12
CLIVE REES	2	–	–	–	8
DAI RICHARDS	2	–	–	–	8
TERRY COBNER	2	–	–	–	8
LAURIE DANIEL	2	–	–	–	8
ARTHUR LEWIS	2	–	–	–	8
DELME THOMAS	1	–	–	–	4
DAI MORRIS	1	–	–	–	4
MIKE ROBERTS	1	–	–	–	4
TOMMY DAVID	1	–	–	–	4
IAN LEWIS	1	–	–	–	4
CLIVE SHELL	1	–	–	–	4
RAY GRAVELL	1	–	–	–	4
COLIN DAVIS	1	–	–	–	4
BRYNMOR WILLIAMS	1	–	–	–	4
JEFF SQUIRE	1	–	–	–	4
BOBBY WINDSOR	1	–	–	–	4
ALAN DONOVAN	–	–	–	2	4
ROY BERGIERS	1	–	–	–	4
ROGER BLYTH	1	–	–	–	4
BRIAN PRICE	1	–	–	–	3
CHICO HOPKINS	1	–	–	–	3
BARRY JOHN	–	1	–	–	3

N.B. 4 points for a try since 1972

Some scoring records in representative matches

Record number of points scored by a Welsh XV in one representative match: 79 (79–0 v Ontario, 1973)

Record number of points scored against a Welsh XV in one representative match: 24 (24–31 by Queensland, 1978)

Record number of points scored by one player in one match: 28 (4PG, 8CON) by Allan Martin v Alberta, 1973

Try-scoring records in one match:

    3 by Maurice Richards v Otago, 1969
    3 by John Taylor v Ontario, 1973
    3 by John Taylor v Quebec-Maritimes, 1973
    3 by John D. Bevan v Alberta, 1973

Top ten point scorers in all matches against Non-International Board countries

Phil Bennett	162	John Taylor	43
Steve Fenwick	91	J. P. R. Williams	42
J. J. Williams	64	John D. Bevan	40
Allan Martin	57	Keith Hughes	36
Gerald Davies	52	Keith Jarrett	32

Top try-scorers in all matches against Non-International Board countries

J. J. Williams	16	John D. Bevan	10
Gerald Davies	13	J. P. R. Williams	10
John Taylor	11		

Totals for all games in a Welsh jersey

P	W	D	L	F	A
81	60	5	16	1946	838

Players to score over a hundred points in a Welsh jersey

Phil Bennett	328	Gareth Edwards	117
Steve Fenwick	218	J. J. Williams	112
Gerald Davies	124	Keith Jarrett	106

(Barry John scored 96 points)

INDEX

Aberavon, 16, 60, 61, 121, 131, 145, 175, 202, 211; Aberavon sands, see squad training

Abertillery, 15

Aguirre, Jean-Michel, 167, 195, 210

All Blacks tours: Brian Lochore's (1967), 24, 45, 50, 60; Ian Kirkpatrick's (1972), 108–12; Andy Leslie's (1974), 144–5; Graham Mourie's (1978), 204–7

Allan, Freddie, 56

Amman United RFC, 112

Ammanford, 112

Anthony, John, 59

Argentinian tourists, 167–70

Auckland, 50–2, 91, 95; North Auckland, 93, 94, 95

Australian tourists (1973), 125–7; (1975), 157–8

Averous, Jean-Luc, 164

Badin, Christian, 119

Bancroft, Jack, 104

Barbarians v All Blacks (1973), 114–15, 153

Bastiat, Jean-Pierre, 165, 166, 174, 175

Batty, Grant, 182, 186

Beaumont, Billy, 161, 183, 188

Bebb, Dewi, 21, 23

Bedford, Tommy, 142

Beese, Roger, 59

Bennett, Phil, 18, 34; first cap as first Welsh sub, 40; on left wing, 60; in centre, 61, 62; as fly half, 68; subs as full back, 101; 106, 108–9, 110, 111, 112, 113, 114–15, 115, 116, 117, 118, 119, 122, 123, 124–5, 126, 127, 128, 129, 130, 131, 132, 133, 134, 136, 138, 139, 140, 142, 145, 147, 149, 151, 152, 153, 154, 156, 157, 158; divine intervention, and, 159; 160; creates new Welsh point-scoring record, 161, 162; 163, 164, 165, 166; first captains Wales, 169, 170; 172, 173, 176, 177, 178–9; captains 1977 Lions, 179; 180, 181, 182, 183, 184, 185, 186, 187, 188, 189, 190, 191, 192, 193, 194–5, 196; all time record points scorer for Wales, 197; retires from International rugby, 197; 198; partnership with Gareth Edwards, 117, 118, 145, 204, 205, 207, 215

Bergiers, Roy, 98, 102, 108–9, 114, 125, 127, 133, 136, 140, 146, 152, 153

Berot, Jean-Louis, 80

Bertranne, Roland, 79

Bevan, John, 70, 72, 73, 74, 75, 76, 79, 81, 86, 88, 89, 93–4, 98, 104–5, 111, 114, 116, 121, 123, 144

Bevan, John D., 131, 145, 147, 149, 150, 151, 152, 155, 157, 158, 159, 160

Biemouret, Pierre, 80, 105

Biggar, Alastair, 101

Blackie, Colin, 36

Bonal, Jean-Marie, 67

Bougarel, Roger, 79, 80

Bowcott, Harry, 26, 30

Boyce, Max, 67, 208, 134, 159

Bridgend, 16, 27, 98, 121, 127, 146, 150, 178, 208

British Lions tours, to South Africa (1962), 23; to New Zealand (1966),

21, 82, 83; to South Africa (1968),
26, 58, 121, 136; to Australasia
(1971), 85–95: Dunedin Test,
88–9; Christchurch Test, 89–90;
Wellington Test, 91–2; Auckland
Test, 94; to South Africa (1974),
136–43: Cape Town Test, 138–9;
Pretoria Test, 139; Port Elizabeth
Test, 141–2; Johannesburg Test,
142; to New Zealand (1977),
180–6: Wellington Test, 182;
Christchurch Test, 183; Dunedin
Test, 184–5; Auckland Test, 185
Brown, Gordon, 92, 139, 141–2, 183
Brown, Peter, 74, 75, 76, 77, 101
Brownlie, Cyril, 171
Burcher, David, 171, 172, 176, 178,
180, 181
Burgess, Bob, 92
Burgess, Clive, 171, 173, 180

Calmet, Robert, 64
Camberabero brothers, 40
Campaes, Andrés, 40
Canniffe, Donal, 164
Canterbury, 51, 87–8, 94, 182
Cantoni, Jacques, 67, 79, 119
Capital Territory (Australia), 200
Cardiff, 16, 21, 35, 43, 71, 114, 129,
131, 148, 166, 171, 178, 201, 203,
209, 211
Cardiff College of Education, 21, 59,
70, 98
Carmarthen, 152
Carmichael, Sandy, 75, 87–8, 89, 115,
129
Carrère, Christian, 30, 79
Cavanagh, Vic, 49
Cester, Elie, 82, 131, 132
Cholley, Gerard, 166
Christchurch, 48–9, 89–90
Clark, Bobby, 101
Clarke, Don, 111
Clegg, Barry, 209, 211
Clement, Bill, 19
coaching, see squad training
Cobner, Terry, 128, 129, 144, 146,
147, 148, 149, 150, 153, 163, 170,
171, 173, 181, 182, 184, 186, 188,
189, 194, 198, 201, 203–4, 206

Colling, Lyn, 109
Colwyn Bay, 70
Cotton, Fran, 161
Cornwall, David, 59
Cowman, Dick, 113
Cranston, Alastair, 190
Craven, Danie, 141
Crocker, Tony, 108
Cronje, Peter, 142
Cross Keys, 59, 121, 126
Crowe, Phil, 200
Cuny, Dr André, 161–2
Currie, Clive, 205
Cwmtwrch, Upper of course, 29

Daniel, Laurie, 61, 62–3
Dauga, Benoit, 79, 80, 104, 105
Davies, Gareth, 200, 201, 202, 203,
204, 205, 208, 209, 211, 215
Davies, Gerald, 22, 23, 32, 40, 41, 47;
moves from centre to wing, 50,
52–3; 60, 67, 69, 71, 72, 73, 74, 76,
78, 83, 90, 91, 92, 97, 101, 102, 104,
114, 117, 123, 124, 125, 127, 128–9,
130, 134, 136; captains Wales v
Tongans, 144; 146, 147, 148, 150,
151, 152, 155, 156, 157, 158, 160,
164, 166, 168, 170, 174, 175, 176,
178, 180, 181, 190, 194, 197, 200
201; captains Wales v Australians,
202; 203, 204, 207, 214; try-scoring
rivalry with Gareth Edwards, 78,
148, 162, 164, 172–3, 202
Davies, Mervyn, 28, 31, 32, 38, 39,
42, 56, 57, 71, 72, 77, 83, 88, 92,
100, 101, 102, 105, 114, 116, 117,
118, 124, 128, 129, 132, 133, 136,
138; bitten by crocodile, 139; 141,
142, 146; first captains Wales, 147;
150, 154, 155, 156, 158, 161, 162,
165, 166, 167–8; difficulty of replacing, 171, 172, 175, 188; 214–15
Davies, Roger, 108
Davis, Clive, 201
Dawes, John, first captains Wales,
24, 26; 27, 41, 42, 50, 53, 60, 62, 66,
67; takes over Welsh captaincy
again, 68; 72, 73, 75, 76, 77, 81; as
bilingual orator, 81–2; captains
1971 Lions, 83; 86, 90, 94, 96, 98,

114, 115; as Welsh National Coach,
26, 135, 145, 148, 149, 150, 152,
154, 155–6, 158, 159, 161, 162, 172,
183, 184, 187, 191, 196, 197, 209,
212–13; as National Coaching
Organiser, 215, 218
Dax town band, 119, 120, 174
De Villiers, H. O., 61
Dick, Malcolm, 49
dirty play, 37–8, 87–8, 174, 217
Dixon, Peter, 91, 94, 99
Doble, Sam, 114
Domercq, Georges, 160
Donovan, Alan, 201
Doyle, Micky, 24
Duckham, David, 64, 87, 93, 133,
134, 137, 160
Duggan, Alan, 66
Duggan, Willie, 154, 164, 171–3, 184,
186
Duprat, Bernard, 104

East Wales (v Australians, 1973),
125; (v Tongans, 1974), 144
Eastern Province (South Africa), 138
Ebbw Vale, 16, 38, 50, 59, 67, 97, 171,
204
Edwards, Gareth, 21, 24, 32; queue-
jumping technique, 34; 35, 39;
partnership with Barry John, 40,
65; youngest player to captain
Wales, 41; 43, 48, 53, 60, 62, 63, 64,
68, 70, 71, 72, 73, 75, 77, 78, 80, 81,
89, 92, 98, 99, 100, 101–2, 104, 112,
114; Barbarians try v 1973 All
Blacks, 114–15; 116, 117; reinstated as Welsh captain, 118, 119,
120; 121, 124, 125, 126, 127, 128,
129, 130, 132, 136, 138, 139, 141,
142, 146, 147; applies psychology to
squad training, 149; 150, 151, 152,
153, 154, 158, 160, 161, 162; beats
Welsh try-scoring record, 164; 168,
170, 172, 173, 176, 177, 178, 180,
181; first Welsh player to win fifty
caps, 188; 189; scores his twentieth
(and last) try for Wales, 190; 191,
192, 193, 195, 196, 197, 198, 203,
209, 210, 214; try-scoring rivalry
with Gerald Davies, 78, 148, 162,

164, 172–3, 202; partnership with
Phil Bennett, 117, 118, 145, 204,
205, 207, 215
Ellis, Jan, 137, 141
Ensor, Tony, 130, 153
Estève, Alain, 104, 105, 131, 132
Evans, Gareth, 174, 180, 194, 202,
204
Evans, Geoff, 60, 67–8, 83, 89, 91, 98
Evans, Geoff (English centre), 133
Evans, Trevor, 145, 149, 150, 151,
155, 158, 162, 172, 173, 182, 188
Eveleigh, Ken, 183

Fairbrother, Keith, 42
Farrell, Colin, 183
Faulkner, Charlie, 145–6, 153, 156,
160, 164, 171, 180, 187–8, 210
Fenwick, Steve, 127, 144, 146, 147,
150, 151, 152, 155, 157, 158, 160,
161, 162, 165, 166, 167, 172, 174,
176, 178, 182, 185, 186, 187, 191,
192, 193, 194, 195, 201, 204, 207;
passes 100 points for Wales, 208;
210, 211
Ferndale, 111
Fielding, Keith, 64, 99
Fiji (1969), 54–7; (1977), 185–6
Finlan, John, 43
Finlayson, Alex, 129, 144
Finnane, Steve, 201
Five Nations Championship
1967: v S, 21, 22–3; v I, 21, 25;
v F, 21; v E, 21–2, 25
1968: v S, 24; v E, 24; v I, 24; v F, 24
1969: v S, 31, 35–6; v I, 19, 36–40;
v F, 40; v E, 40–4
1970: v S, 61–2; v E, 62–5;
v I, 65–6; v F, 66–8
1971: v E, 70–3; v S, 73–7;
v I, 77–8; v F, 78–82
1972: v E, 98–9; v S, 100–2;
v I cancelled, 103, 105–6; v F,
103–5
1973: v E, 113–14; v S. 115–16;
v I, 116–17; v F, 117–20
1974: v S, 128–9; v I, 129–30;
v F, 130–2; v E, 132–4
1975: v F, 147–8; v E, 148–50;
v S, 150–1; v I, 152–4

1976: v E, 160–1; v S, 161–2;
    v I, 162–5; v F, 165–7
1977: v I, 171–3; v F, 173–5;
    v E, 175–6; v S, 176–9
1978: v E, 187–90; v S, 190–2;
    v I 192–3; v F, 194–6
1979: v S, 207; v I, 208; v F, 209–10;
    v E, 210–12
Fouroux, Jacques, 165, 166
Frame, John, 101, 102

Gale, Norman, 24, 45, 48
Gallacher, Stuart, 67, 68
Gallion, Jerome, 195, 210
Garnant, 112
Gibbs, Reggie, 43
Gibson, Mike, 24, 39, 78, 86, 90, 117,
    172, 183, 192
gin and tonic, its part in Welsh team
    preparation, 26
Going, Sid, 90, 92, 110, 182, 207;
    Going brothers, 93
Goodall, Ken, 66
Gourdon, Jean-François, 147, 166,
    167, 210
Grand Slam winning games, see: v F,
    1971; v F, 1976; v F, 1978
Gravell, Ray, 108, 146, 147, 149, 150,
    151, 152, 155, 156, 158, 159, 160,
    164, 171, 187, 191, 193, 195, 200,
    201, 208, 209
Gray, Ken, 49
Griffiths, Clive, 212
Gwaun-Cae-Gurwen, 112
Gwent (v Springboks, 1970), 59
Gwilym, Ken, 121, 122

Haden, Andy, 184, 204, 206
Hales, Duncan, 111
Hall, Ian, 60–2, 65, 73, 128, 129, 133
Hannaford, Charlie, 71
Harize, Dominique, 174
Hawkes Bay, 91
Hignell, Alastair, 160, 176, 189, 190
Hill, Andy, 108–9
Hiller, Bob, 43, 44, 63, 64, 86, 94, 95,
    98, 186
Hipwell, John, 158
Hipwell, Mick, 87, 88
Hodgson, Graeme, 21

Holmes, Terry, 201, 202, 203, 204,
    205, 206, 207, 208, 209, 210
Hopkins, Chico, 45, 47, 48, 52; beats
    England, 63–4; 83, 89, 108, 127,
    196
Horton, John, 188
Horton, Nigel, 150
Hughes, Dennis, 28, 45, 50, 56–7, 60
Hughes, Keith, 65, 68, 118, 121, 123,
    125, 127, 128, 129
Hullin, Billy, 21, 23

Internationals, see Five Nations
    Championship
International weekend rituals, 18,
    30–5
Ireland, 103, 106, see also Five
    Nations Championship
Irvine, Andy, 115, 141, 142, 162, 177,
    178, 182, 185, 186, 207

James, Carwyn, 84, 85, 88, 90, 93,
    108–9. 137, 144
James, Gareth, 28
Janion, Jeremy, 72
Japanese tourists (1973), 124–5
Jarrett, Keith, legendary debut, 21–
    2, 25; 35, 38, 39, 40, 42, 43, 44, 49,
    50, 51, 53; toads improve side-step,
    55; 60, 61, 63, 71
Jenkins, Gareth, 108
Jenkins, Hefin, 108
Jenkins, Vivian, 63
Jennings, Mark, 59
John, Barry, 21, 22, 23; views on the
    forward function, 25; 32, 36, 39;
    partnership with Gareth Edwards,
    40, 65; 42, 43, 43–4, 64, 66, 68, 70,
    71, 72, 73, 74, 75–6, 77, 78, 80, 81,
    86–7, 88, 92, 97, 98–9, 99–100, 101,
    102; beats Jack Bancroft's points-
    scoring record, 104; 106–7, 108,
    114, 126, 134, 154, 162, 197, 209,
    214; and the Divine Right of Kings,
    72, 75, 87, 90, 92, 94
Johnson, R. F. ('Johnnie'), 64, 110
Johnstone, Brad, 182
Jones, Cliff, 30
Jones, Ivor, 54

Jones, Ken, 21, 148, 164
Joseph, Meirion, 161

Karam, Joe, 109. 110–11, 112, 145
Keane, Moss, 186, 193
Kennedy, Ken, 37
Kiernan, Tom, 37, 38, 65, 66, 94
King Country – Wanganui, 186
Kirkpatrick, Ian, 49, 89, 108, 110, 112, 184
Knight, Gary, 185
Knill, Mike, 166

Laidlaw, Frank, 74
Lane, Stuart, 201, 208
laws, changes in and interpretation of, 28, 48, 63, 96, 124, 148, 191, 193, 215–17
Lewis, Alun, 21
Lewis, Alun (London Welsh), 180
Lewis, Arthur, 67, 71, 72, 73, 78, 87–8; scourge of New Zealand golf courses, 90–1; 104, 109; first captains Wales, 113, 114; 116, 117, 118, 120, 122
Lewis, Gerry, 18, 32–3, 34, 75, 79, 101, 120–1
Lewis, Ian, 121
Llanelli, 14, 16, 24, 40, 45, 65, 66, 67, 83, 84, 101; beats the All Blacks, 108–9; 114, 116, 127, 128, 142, 144, 159, 164, 192, 197, 212
Llansaint, 76
Llewellyn, Phil, 116, 123, 129, 133
Llewellyn, Willie, 43
Llewelyn, Barry, 45, 60, 61, 62, 82, 102, 108, 109, 113, 128, 129, 131
Lloyd, John, 26, 32, 33, 42, 46, 60, 67, 81; first captains Wales, 98; 109, 113, 114
Llwynpia, 43
Llynfi valley, 89
Loane, Mark, 202
Lochore, Brian, 24, 45, 49
London Welsh, 13–14, 22, 23, 27–8, 30, 60, 65, 66, 67, 71, 76, 77, 83–4, 89, 94, 98, 103, 106, 109, 114, 116, 117, 130, 148, 167, 204, 211
Lux, Jean-Pierre, 67, 79, 105, 131
Lynch, Sean, 89

McBride, Willie John, 85, 90, 93, 95, 136, 141, 152, 193
McCormick, Fergie, 49, 51
MacEwan, Nairn, 101
McGann, Barry, 66, 117, 130, 163
McGeechan, Ian, 139, 151, 177, 186, 190
McGill, Arthur, 53
McHarg, Alastair, 35, 75
McKechnie, Brian, 205, 206
McKinney, Stewart, 193
McLaren, Bill, 166
McLauchlan, Ian, 89, 115, 129, 150
McLean, Paul, 158, 199, 200, 202
McLennan, Andy, 208
McLeod, Bruce, 49
McLoughlin, Ray, 85, 87–8
McMaster, Andy, 164
Maesteg, 16, 45, 63, 64
Mainwaring, Billy, 23
Manawatu and Horowhenua, 93
Maoris, 85–6
Marais, Hannes, 141
Martin, Allan, 121, 123, 124, 131, 144, 149, 150, 151, 155–6, 158, 160, 163, 164, 175, 176, 182, 189, 194, 195, 201, 208, 212
Maso, Jo, 105
Mathias, Roy, 66
Meads, Colin, 48, 49, 171, 175
Merthyr Tydfil, 16
Millar, Syd, 136, 138
Milliken, Dick, 139, 142
Moloney, John, 152, 193
Monaghan, Laurie, 202
Monmouth School, 21
Mordell, Bob, 189
Morgan, Dougie, 115, 151, 162, 178, 185, 190, 192
Morgan, Haydn, 15, 21
Morgan, Rod, 149
Morley, Alan, 140
Morris, Dai, 22, 26, 32, 39, 43, 46, 50, 53, 62, 68, 70, 81, 82–3, 102, 117, 118, 121, 125, 126–7, 130, 133
Mourie, Graham, 185
Mulligan, Andy, 89
Murdoch, Keith, 110, 111, 112
Murphy, Noel, 37
Murphy, Pat, 48, 51

Nash, David, 23, 26, 136
Natal, 142
National Coach appointed, 23, 25; see also, David Nash, Clive Rowlands, John Dawes
Neary, Tony, 161
Neath, 14, 16, 47, 60, 109, 129, 175, 180, 207; Neath Athletic, 30
New Dock Stars, 65
New South Wales, 199
New Zealand Universities, 182
Newbridge, 16, 45, 56, 201
Newport, 16, 30, 35, 45, 48, 60, 61, 144, 148, 171, 174, 180, 194, 202
Nomis, Sid, 61
North Wales (v Tongans, 1974), 144
Northern Transvaal, 141
Novak, John, 64–5

O'Callaghan, Phil, 163
O'Driscoll, Barry, 78
Ogmore, 30
Old, Alan, 99, 133, 134, 138
Old Guildfordians, 28
Oliver, Frank, 204, 206
Orange Free State, 141
O'Reilly, Tony, 86, 89, 93
Osborne, Bill, 185, 205
Otago, 49, 87, 94–5, 110

Paco, Alain, 166
Palmerstone North, 92
Palmié, Michel, 166, 174
Paparemborde, Robert, 166
Parfitt, Vernon, 30, 66
Paries, Lucien, 68
Pask, Alun, 21, 22, 23, 83
Patterson, Colin, 208
Pattinson, Ken, 130
Pembrey, 67
Perrins, Vic, 48, 60
Phillips, Alan, 211
Plummer, Ken, 43
Pontyclun, 30
Pontypool, 16, 97, 126, 148, 149, 168, 198, 203, 204, 211; Pontypool front row, 145–6, 153, 164, 171, 188, 201
Pontypridd, 16, 114, 163
Porta, Hugo, 169, 170
Powell, David, 42

Price, Brian, 23, 31, 35, 36, 37, 38, 41, 43, 48, 50, 54–5, 57, 60, 67
Price, Graham, 97, 145–6, 148, 153, 156, 159, 166, 182, 186, 193, 195, 201, 202
Price, Terry, 21, 22
Prosser, Ray, 140, 145–6
Pullin, John, 98, 100, 115, 140
Pumas, see Argentinian tourists

Quaggas, the, 140
Queensland, 85, 199
Quinn, Mick, 130
Quinnell, Derek, 18, 83, 91, 92, 94, 105, 108, 109, 113–14, 115, 116, 118, 124, 127, 128, 129, 131, 133, 150, 151, 155, 171, 172, 173, 175, 181, 182, 183, 186, 188, 189, 192, 201, 204, 207, 208
Quittenton, Roger, 204, 206

Rafter, Mike, 211
Ralston, Chris, 99
Raybould, Billy, 23, 59, 60, 61, 62
Rea, Chris, 76, 90
Reason, John, 146
Rees, Brian, 23
Rees, Clive, 130, 136, 140, 157, 204, 205
Rees, Elgan, 180, 186, 207, 212
refereeing, standards of, 48, 51, 53–4, 92, 161–2, 171, 199–201
Renwick, Jim, 101, 177, 178, 190
Rhondda valley, 89
Richards, Dai, 159, 203, 209, 211
Richards, Glan, 28
Richards, Maurice, 35–6, 39, 40, 43–4, 47, 50, 53, 56, 60, 67, 69
Richardson, John, 202, 211
Ringer, Paul, 204, 208, 211, 217
Ripley, Andy, 134, 161
Rives, Jean-Pierre, 165
Roberts, Mike, 70, 72, 83, 89, 91, 98, 116, 117, 151, 152, 211
Robertson, Bruce, 182, 184, 185, 204
Robertson, Ian, 61, 62
Robinson, Ian, 131
Rogers, Handel, 45, 52, 54–5
Romeu, Jean-Pierre, 119, 131, 132, 166, 174, 195

Rossborough, Peter, 72
Rowlands, Clive, 23, 26; appointed National Coach, 29–30; appreciation of the passing game, 29; team talks, 33, 41–2, 110; 45, 49, 52, 66, 77, 81, 96, 122, 132, 135, 154, 198, 203
Rowlands, Keith, 171

Sanson, Norman, 163, 170, 171, 174
Scott, John, 189
Seven Sisters, 109
Shackleton, Roger, 64, 65
Shanklin, Jim, 66, 109, 116, 117, 120, 121
Shaw, Glyn, 109–10, 117, 122, 127, 171, 175
Shell, Clive, 121, 124, 125, 127, 155, 196
Sillières, Jean, 104
Skréla, Jean-Claude, 105, 165, 174, 194
Skinner, A. J., 53
Skirving, Alan, 45, 46, 50, 59
Slattery, Fergus, 87, 91, 139, 142, 193
Slemen, Mike, 176
Smith, Ian, 74, 76
Smith, P. V., 53
Snyman, Dawie, 138, 142
South Africans, see Springbok tour
South Wales Police, 149
South West Africa, 137
South Western Districts (South Africa) 137–8
Spanghero, Claude, 79
Spanghero, Walter, 79, 103, 105
Spence, Les, 154
Spencer, John. 72, 90
Spring, Dick, 208
Springbok tour (1970), 58–61: v Newport, 58–9; v Gwent, 59; v Wales, 59–61
squad training, 22–3, 23–4, 25, 29–30, 118, 146, 149
Squire, Jeff, 170–1, 175, 180, 181, 188, 201, 207, 208
Squires, Peter, 134
St Mary's Hospital, 27, 155
Stagg, Peter, 35
Steele, Billy, 101, 115, 141, 162

Stephens, Rees, 30
Sutherland, Alan, 110
Swansea, 14, 16, 28, 58, 98, 106, 116, 129, 133, 149, 158, 168, 190, 201, 209
Sydney, 52–4, 199

Taffary, Michel, 147, 148
Taranaki, 46, 47–8, 89
Taumaruni, 181
Tauranga, 94
Taylor, Bob, 65
Taylor, John, 13–14, 15, 22, 23, 24, 39, 43, 50, 59–60, 67, 70, 71, 72, 74–5; vital conversion at Murrayfield, 76–7; 82, 83, 88, 91, 93, 97, 100, 102, 114, 115, 116, 117, 118, 119, 121, 123; captains Wales v Japan, 124–5; 167, 168
Telfer, Colin, 36, 115
Telfer, Jim, 62
Tenby, 66
Thomas, Alun, 136
Thomas, Brian, 14–15, 31, 33, 35, 38–9, 41, 42; as female impersonator, 46–7; 48, 50, 57, 60, 70
Thomas, Delme, 22, 31, 33, 41, 43, 50, 60, 71, 76, 77, 92, 97, 108–9; captains Wales, 109, 110, 111, 112; 113, 116, 133
Thomas, Malcolm, 86, 87
Thomas, Roy, 108
Tikoisuva, Bosco, 186
Titcomb, Mike, 24
Tomes, Alan, 192
Tongan tourists (1974), 144
tonic, see gin
Transvaal, 139
Tredegar, 16
Triple Crown winning games, see: v E, 1969; v I, 1971; v I, 1976; v S, 1977; v I, 1978; v E. 1979

Uttley, Roger, 133, 142

Victoria, 199
Villepreux, Pierre, 40, 68, 79, 80, 104–5
Visagie, Piet, 59

Viviès, Bernard, 194, 195

Wallabies, see Australian tourists
Wallace, Gerry, 121, 122
Ward, Tony, 192, 193, 208
Watkins, David, 22, 106
Watkins, Stuart, 35, 39, 41, 43, 50,
   62, 66–7
Wellington, 49, 86, 88, 91–2, 94, 182
Welsh selectors, 21, 22, 25, 30, 61, 66,
   100, 118, 158–9, 171
Welsh Rugby Union, 15, 19, 73
Welsh tours, to Argentina (1968), 26,
   169; to Australasia (1969), 27, 45–
   60: Christchurch Test, 48–9;
   Auckland Test, 50–1; Sydney Test,
   52–4; to Canada (1973), 120–3; to
   Japan (1975), 154–6; to Australia
   (1978), 198–203: Brisbane Test,
   200; Sydney Test, 201–3
West Coast and Buller, 87, 88
West, John, 134, 167
West Wales (v Tongans, 1974), 144
Western Australia, 199
Western Transvaal, 137
Wheel, Geoff, 129–30, 131, 148, 150,
   152, 163, 164, 171–3, 175, 180, 181,
   195, 201, 204, 206, 208, 209, 211
Wheeler, Peter, 161, 183, 185
Whelan, Pat, 208
White 'Snow', 51–2
Williams, Bryan, 111, 182, 183, 204
Williams, Brynmor, 180, 182, 185,
   200, 201, 203
Williams, Clive, 175, 180
Williams, Denzil, 38, 41, 42, 50, 55,
   61, 67, 70, 72, 75, 80, 82, 96–7
Williams, Graham, 86
Williams, Johnny (Cardiff), 148, 164

Williams, J. J., 108, 120, 123, 124–5,
   130, 132, 133, 134, 136, 137, 138,
   139, 141, 142, 148, 150, 153, 155,
   156, 157, 158, 160, 162, 166, 172,
   178, 181, 182, 183, 190, 191, 192,
   193, 194, 195, 201, 202, 206, 210,
   212
Williams, J. P. R., predestination
   and, 13; 26, 27–8, 31, 32, 39, 61, 63,
   64, 65, 66, 68, 71, 72, 73–4, 76, 77,
   78, 79, 80, 81, 82, 83, 86, 93, 94, 97,
   99, 101, 102–3, 111, 114–15, 119,
   125, 126, 127, 129, 130, 133, 136,
   138, 142, 146, 148, 150, 153, 156,
   160, 161, 162, 164, 167, 170, 172;
   record sixth try, 176; 178, 180, 181,
   189, 191, 193, 201, 203; first
   captains Wales, 204, 250; 207, 211,
   212, 214, 215; as medical authority,
   46, 85, 103, 155
Williams, Ray, 29, 130, 215
Williams, Robin, 59
Williams, Walter, 129, 131, 133
Wilson, Bev, 184, 185
Wilson, Stuart, 205
Wiltshire, Max, 31
Windsor, Bobby, 121, 122, 125, 126;
   first hooker to score on international debut, 127; 128, 133, 136,
   138–9, 140, 142, 145, 148, 150, 152,
   153, 160, 162, 163, 182, 210–11
Wintle, Trevor, 43
Wright, Ian, 72
Wylie, Alex, 110

Young, Jack, 30
Young, Jeff, 30, 42, 47, 48, 49, 60, 63,
   75, 81, 82, 100, 104, 114, 121, 126
Young, Malcolm, 188, 189
Young, Roger, 66, 78